Ramya Ramanath skillfully engages an incredible range of women whose experiences vividly illustrate their struggle to make homes, access livelihoods, rebuild lives and construct new identities in the aftermath of their resettlement. These voices are a powerful mode to understand the dynamics of the brutal dislocations, disruptions, and transitions the poor experience in Mumbai.

Rahul Mehrotra, Professor of Urban Design and Planning, Harvard University

Ramanath shows us the value to be gained when women are 'listened' to. Most literature on slums and relocation/rehabilitation takes particular stances on the existence of informal settlements and state intervention in them. The author adds nuance and complexity to these conventional narratives on both fronts. Above all, these narratives also expose the falsehood of the claims of participatory processes by movements, its politics and dynamics and their vulnerability to pressures of the larger political economy. This book will be a learning tool for cities around the world.

Amita Bhide, Professoor and Dean of the School of Habitat Studies, Tata Institute of Social Sciences, India

A Place to Call Home sensitively highlights the everyday rhythms of the lives, aspirations and frustrations of a diverse group of 120 women before and after their displacement from a slum in Mumbai's famous national park to Asia's largest urban resettlement scheme. It is a must read for anybody interested in gender, place making, urban resettlement and public policy.

Lyla Mehta, Professor, Institute of Development Studies, UK

A Place to Call Home

Any city is a product of politics and economics, organizations and people. Yet, the life experiences of women uprooted from its poorest quarters seldom inform urban resettlement plans.

In this ethnographic field study, Ramya Ramanath, Associate Professor at DePaul University, examines the lives of women displaced by slum clearance and relocated to the largest slum resettlement site in Asia. Through conversations with diverse women of different ages, levels of education, types of employment, marital status, ethnicity, caste, religion, and household make-up, Ramanath recounts how women negotiate a drastic change in environment, from makeshift housing in a park slum to ownership of a high-rise apartment in a posh Mumbai suburb. Each phase of their city lives reflects how women initiate change and disseminate a vision valuable to planners intent on urban and residential transformations. Ramanath urges the concerted engagement of residents in design, development, and evaluation of place-making processes in cities and within their own neighborhoods especially.

This book will interest scholars of public policy, women and gender studies, South Asian studies, and urban planning.

Ramya Ramanath is Associate Professor and Chair of International Public Service at DePaul University. Her research, spread over three continents, draws on disciplinary perspectives in urban planning, anthropology, and urban sociology. Her research focuses on the behavior of international and domestic nongovernmental organizations (NGOs) in the context of their interactions with government agencies, other NGOs, and intended beneficiaries. Ramanath teaches courses on the management of international NGOs, sustainable international development, cross-sector interactions, and policy implementation.

A Place to Call Home
Women as Agents of Change in Mumbai

Ramya Ramanath

Routledge
Taylor & Francis Group
LONDON AND NEW YORK

First published 2019 by Routledge

2 Park Square, Milton Park, Abingdon, Oxfordshire OX14 4RN
52 Vanderbilt Avenue, New York, NY 10017

Routledge is an imprint of the Taylor & Francis Group, an informa business

First issued in paperback 2020

Library of Congress Cataloging in Publication Data
Names: Ramanath, Ramya, author.
Title: A place to call home : women as agents of change in Mumbai / Ramya Ramanath.
Description: New York, NY : Routledge, 2018.
Identifiers: LCCN 2018008987| ISBN 9781138667341 (hardback) | ISBN 9781317212461 (webpdf) | ISBN 9781317212454 (epub) | ISBN 9781317212447 (mobipocket/kindle)
Subjects: LCSH: Relocation (Housing)–India–Mumbai. | Slums–India–Mumbai. | Women–India–Mumbai–Social conditions. | City planning–India–Mumbai. | Housing policy–India–Mumbai. | Urban policy–India–Mumbai.
Classification: LCC HD7288.92.I42 M8673 2018 | DDC 363.50954/792–dc23
LC record available at https://lccn.loc.gov/2018008987

ISBN: 978-1-138-66734-1 (hbk)
ISBN: 978-0-367-66589-0 (pbk)

Typeset in Times New Roman
by Taylor & Francis Books

To my grandparents

Contents

Illustrations

Figures

Maps

Tables

Acknowledgments

A city, any city, can be understood as a product of politics and economics, organizations and people, even bricks, tarpaulin sheets, and words. In this book, my intention is to show how diverse women use storytelling to make sense of their identities as relocated residents who were granted homeownership in the largest urban slum resettlement site in Mumbai, India. I am deeply indebted to the women who permitted my scholarly gaze into their minds and everyday life and who generously gave their time to answer questions and be interviewed. I truly believe that it is through attention to their words and undertakings that a better city can be made. I thank the staff and leaders of Nivara Hakk Suraksha Samiti whose encouragement, insights, and friendship had an immeasurable influence on this work.

The research was supported by DePaul University's Research Council, the Social Science Research Center, and the School of Public Service. Over the last five years, I presented various parts of the book at the Urban Affairs Association, the International Society for Third Sector Research, the Association for Nonprofit Organizations and Voluntary Action, and the Mumbai-Harvard Urban Mellon Initiative. Feedback from colleagues and attendees at all these venues as well as comments from the book's anonymous reviewers were incredibly important in sharpening the arguments of this book.

Many more people have contributed to this project in several different ways. I have specific debts to Linda Levendusky for her friendship and consistent commitment to discussing and editing this work with an eye for detail that was inspiring and kept me on my toes; to Nandhini Gulasingham for her nimble work on the maps; Haven Barnes for doing the drawings amidst a busy school schedule; Andrew Doak for the cover design; and, graduate assistants Julia Martinez, Katie Brown, Katherine Poziemski, and Whitney Hein for their careful work. I am thankful to my many graduate students who joined me on study-abroad trips, whose questions and observations during our treks up the park hills and walks around the resettlement site unconsciously informed this work's creation. Lively debates and discussions with friends in Mumbai—Surendra Hiwarale and his family, Muthu Perumal, and Vaijayanthi Mahabale—encouraged me through several stages of this work.

Natalja Mortensen at Routledge was intrigued by the project even before it was conceived as a manuscript and steadfastly supported this book's creation. Lillian Rand and Maria Landschoot patiently responded to my many queries.

I am deeply grateful to all my near and dear ones: my late grandparents whose contributions are hard to put in words; Meera and Ramanath; Sheri and Timothy; Rajeev, Sumathi and my charming nephews Abhinav and Pranav; and my partner Andrew with whom I first explored the theme of this book and whose optimism and support were a constant inspiration.

Glossary

achaar	South Asian variety of pickle made of vegetables and/or fruits marinated in spices and edible oils
adivasi/s	indigenous people/s
autorickshaw/s	three-wheeled motorized vehicle commonly used for transportation on Indian roads; also referred to as *auto* or *rickshaw*
bajra roti	flatbread made of millet
balwadi	government- or NGO-run pre-school centers for the economically disadvantaged
basti	a neighborhood/district
bazaar	marketplace
Bihari/s	of the Indian state of Bihar, whose capital Patna is more than 1,800 kilometers (more than 1,100 miles) northeast of Mumbai
bishi/s	rotating savings and credit association/s
BJP	Bharatiya Janata Party
BMC	Brihanmumbai Municipal Corporation (another name for the Municipal Corporation of Greater Mumbai)
bombaiyya	of Bombay/Mumbai
bombaiyya Hindi	Mumbai's slang version of Hindi
BUDP	Bombay Urban Development Project
CBO	community-based organization
chaali/s	10–30 proximate households in the slum that grouped to qualify for basic infrastructure improvements, such as a municipal water connection
chawl/s	a three- to five-story structure with distinctive verandas along the façade at each story where utilities are shared and each one-room unit measures less than 20 square meters; first built to accommodate textile-mill workers during the early 1900s
chit/chit fund	a drawn lot/note/voucher; the pooled amount of savings in a group are auctioned among the members during

	their meeting, and the member who bids the highest interest for an amount is awarded the chit
chowky	police checkpoint/workstation
CHS	Cooperative Housing Society
churidar-kurta	tight pants-tunic
corporator	elected municipal official in charge of an administrative division in Mumbai called ward
Dalit/s	term coined by Bhimrao Ramji Ambedkar to characterize the experiences of deprivation, marginalization and stigmatization suffered by India's outcasts; over time, it has come to refer to a non-Hindu, a political minority and member of the country's most marginalized socioeconomic group
Dawoodi bohra	a sect within the Ismaili branch of Shia Islam
dhobi ghaat	open-air laundromat
Diwali	Hindu festival of lights celebrated in the fall
dongar	Marathi for hill
FAR	Floor Area Ration
haldi-kumkum	turmeric-vermillion, a ritual that celebrates the role of Hindu women as wives
INR	Indian Rupees and written also as Rupees and abbreviated Rs; as of January 19, 2018, the exchange rate was USD $1 = INR 63.83
itr	oil extracted from botanical sources and used as perfume
Jai Bhim	followers of the late political thinker and activist Bhimrao Ramji Ambedkar; also a greeting and translates as "victory to Bhim" used by his followers
kabariwalla	waste collector
kuchcha	unfinished
lathi-charge	a lead-weighted bamboo stick carried by police
lungi	sarong worn around the waist
mahasangh	grand association, collective
mahila mandal	women's group
mandal	group
Maratha/ Maratha-Kunbi	The term Maratha is used by participating women to refer to their caste affiliation. It refers to the precolonial warrior king Shivaji who resisted Mughal expansion into the Deccan region of India during 17th and 18th century India. In the 20th century, the term Maratha began to be used to refer to a specific social group who are politically dominant in Maharashtra and are often referred to as Maratha-Kunbi. They are recognized in the Indian constitution as the other backward caste (OBC)

	but many within the community, including the women, identified themselves as an upper-caste group.
Marathi	Language spoken in the state of Maharashtra; also used to refer to the ethnic group that speaks the language of Marathi
masala	mix of spices
matkals or handaals	Clay/metal or plastic pot/s to carry water
MCGM	Municipal Corporation of Greater Mumbai
MHADA	Maharashtra Housing and Area Development Authority
MLA	Member of the Legislative Assembly
MMR	Mumbai Metropolitan Region
MNS	Maharashtra Navnirman Sena, the army for the reconstruction of Maharashtra, is a regional political party
morcha	protest march/demonstration
nagar	neighborhood/city/town
NGO	nongovernmental organization
Nivara Hakk Suraksha Samiti	Committee for the Protection of Housing Rights
OBC	Other Backward Caste representing a more recent administrative listing of the Indian Constitution and comprise those that are neither upper caste nor listed in the schedules (scheduled caste and scheduled tribe) of the Indian Constitution
OHCHR	Office of the High Commissioner for Human Rights
pada	tribal hamlet
pandal	tent
papad/s	dried flat bread made of lentils/rice
pucca	finished, solid
R&R	Resettlement and Rehabilitation
salwar-kameez	tunic-loose pants
sangharsh	struggle
SC	Scheduled Caste representing a category of people included in the schedule of the Indian Constitution for provision of employment, education, and a variety of other welfare assistance
seth	boss
shaana	Mumbai-style-Hindi word for street-smart, cunning
shanki	someone prone to be suspicious
Shiv Sena	Army of Shiva; a Hindu fundamentalist regional political party founded in 1966
SRD	Slum Redevelopment Scheme
SRA	Slum Rehabilitation Authority
SRS	Slum Rehabilitation Scheme

surya namaskar	salutation to the sun
tapori/s	Mumbai term for *rowdy/rowdies*
TDR	transferable development rights
Teli	traditionally the caste of oil-pressers, part of a more recent administrative listing of the Indian Constitution called the Other Backward Caste (OBC)
tempo	a four-wheeler/light truck used to carry goods and commonly seen on Indian roads
UNCHS	United Nations Centre for Human Settlements
U.P.	Uttar Pradesh, a northern Indian state whose capital Lucknow is situated more than 1,400 kilometers (870 miles) northeast of Mumbai
yuva mandal	youth group
zopadpatti/s	slum settlement/s comprising shacks made of a variety of materials including bits of wood, rag, tin, sheets, mud, brick, and anything at hand; usually lacking in such physical amenities, as common toilet blocks, municipal water connections, or garbage disposal systems
Zopadpatti Bachao Parishad	Save the Slums Assembly

1 Introduction

JAMUNA DEVI: We are not educated, but we can work. We will work a lot. We will do any work that is handed to us. We will fall sick if we just stay idle.

SUMITRA: If only ten of us come together, then we can ask the government. But if the other person is not ready to come, then what can we do? The ones who need a pipeline [for cooking gas connection] must fill out a form. And then we can be comfortable. In some buildings there is unity, and in others there isn't.

ANUPAMA: What happened is that they [the boys] have changed. Meaning, meaning a lot of them seem to have the understanding that we have now started living in buildings, [but] how should we stay? We should live here like professionals. Some people are just like rowdies. They live like it is their birthright [to be a rowdy]. [They believe] they are born this way and should die this way. That is how these people continue to behave.

For most people life is chock-full of daily hassles and stressful events. Many of these are relatively minor (e.g. a leaking bathroom tap, loud music, noisy neighbors), but others can be labelled major stresses that test one's skills to problem-solve and effectively cope (e.g. events like death, divorce, sexual harassment, job loss). All three of the women who lead off this chapter—Jamuna Devi, 60, Sumitra, 39, and Anupama, 20—had migrated to Mumbai from different areas across India and settled in adjoining slums, the first two as young brides in their 20s and the other as an infant. In 2012 when they made their comments, it had been five years since each had witnessed a series of massive state-led demolitions that had levelled large portions of the densely populated slum settlements where they had lived. These experiences could well qualify as major life stresses. The demolitions were the result of a 1995 High Court ruling that declared their slum settlements an intrusion on the city's reserved forest cover that formed part of Sanjay Gandhi National Park in northern Mumbai (see Map 1.1). Added to the stress of losing an entire community of fellow residents and most of its physical infrastructure of toilets, shops, and roadways were the dozen-plus years they'd spent scarcely believing that the state would honor its promise to settle them in adequate, legal housing. Starting in 2007, they became the legal occupants and owners of a 225-square-foot apartment unit in the largest urban resettlement program in Mumbai, an outcome promoted as among the "few torturous struggles that actually ended with success" ("The Long Road", 2013).

Yet hardly any of the 120 women whose pre- and post-resettlement experiences are the subject of this work spontaneously recollected the demolitions as a noteworthy event in their personal stories, least of all a "tortuous struggle". Was it because they accepted the state's resettlement and rehabilitation (R&R) policy to destroy the slums and resettle the inhabitants? Had new hassles and stresses following involuntary displacement overshadowed memories of evictions and demolitions? Perhaps. But each place-making experience the women recalled was a story overlaid with practical suggestions on how they can and should be understood and what the content of "city strategies" to accommodate them could be (Healey, 2002, p. 1778). This book takes up each phase in the place-making stories of the women, from pre- to post-relocation, to demonstrate the assorted strategies and tactics women used to initiate change and disseminate a vision that planners can comprehend, accept, and act upon to institute desired transformations. Urban scholars

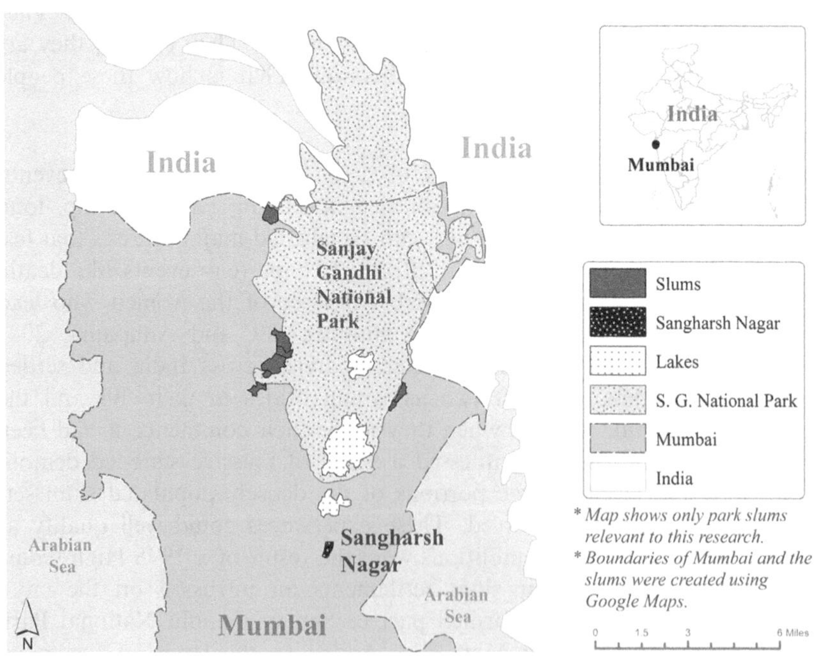

Map 1.1 Sanjay Gandhi National Park, Mumbai, India

acknowledge locally anchored individual and collective stories as an important planning tool for communicating not just *what was* or *is* but also *what ought to be* (Rein & Schön, 1977; Forester, 1999; Sandercock, 2003; Throgmorton, 2003). Even though women like Jamuna Devi and numerous others in developing countries across the world have come to be universally recognized as the most vulnerable faces of displacement (OUNHCHR, 2013; Menon-Sen, 2006; Mehta, 2009; Desmond, 2012), their lived experiences and visions are seldom utilized to inform and benefit the design and development of resettlement and rehabilitation (R&R)[1] activities (Gilbert, 2000).

To give credit where it is due, this book avails itself of the important but underutilized method of stories and storytelling by assorted women to highlight how an affected population experiences their residential lives over time. The narratives—rife with metaphors, metonyms, ironies, and analogies—begin with the women's recollection of their years as new migrants (or as native-born) in Mumbai's ubiquitous slums. They then move to descriptions of how they weathered eviction and acted upon their post-displacement uncertainties. Their narratives culminate with the adjustments and adaptations made (and desired) as they restart their new lives under legal housing tenure and negotiate their new surroundings. The book goes beyond the considerations of leaders and staff of external entities that have a stake in the lives of the urban poor to understand how those at its heart, the women, actively engage in sense-giving with one another and others, to help make sense of what is going on with their built environment. How these women give sense to events, threats, and opportunities in their rebuilt environment and develop strategies to reconstruct their lives and livelihoods has not been, but, the book argues, must be, incorporated into framing national and international policies in planning practice.

The Setting

The book draws attention to the experiences of women who recently gained legal home ownership after at least two decades of life lived in the slums of Mumbai (formerly Bombay). I became familiar with their one-time homes in the slums, though not necessarily these specific women and their respective homes, in 2002, while I was doing fieldwork for my doctoral dissertation. When I first set foot in the slums of Sanjay Gandhi National Park (henceforth, "the park"), the area was emerging from the throes of a series of demolition exercises that had commenced in 1997. By 2002, these demolitions had destroyed nearly 48,000 slum homes and rendered homeless 300,000 slum dwellers of the park. A satellite survey published in 1995 had reported that the slums occupied over 1,909 acres, a majority of which were in the park's buffer zone, an area preserved to mitigate and contain conflicts between human activity and the park's natural flora and fauna (*Bombay Environmental Action Group & Others v. A.R.*

Bharati Deputy Conservator of Forests & Others, 2003). Amidst the piles of rubble left by the demolitions, some 22,000 households that met the criteria for eligibility for alternate housing continued to cling to their dwellings in the park's buffer zone. Per state policy, their homes in the park's periphery were to remain unharmed until the state approved their resettlement elsewhere. These eligible households lived in eight slums (see Map 1.2), many of them in the park's southwestern parts and a few others in its northwestern and southeastern border areas. Each of the eight slums had a distinctive history, for they were settled at different times and had come to host a different assortment of amenities. The most well-consolidated slums–those with piped water connections, electricity, roadways, and common toilets were settled earliest and were located in the lower elevations of the park's peripheral areas (i.e. its buffer zone). Other slums on higher elevations stood precariously atop rocky hillside slopes and sheltered the city's more recent migrants. Pockets of homogeneity had developed within the various slums wherein those who had migrated at the same time or who shared the same religion, caste, language, and/or geographical origins settled down alongside each other in homes of various sizes that they built, leased, or subleased. Overall, each slum was home to an assorted mix of migrants from different parts of India, both from Maharashtra, the state in which Mumbai is the capital city, and out-of-state migrants. Many came from other slums and neighborhoods within Mumbai.

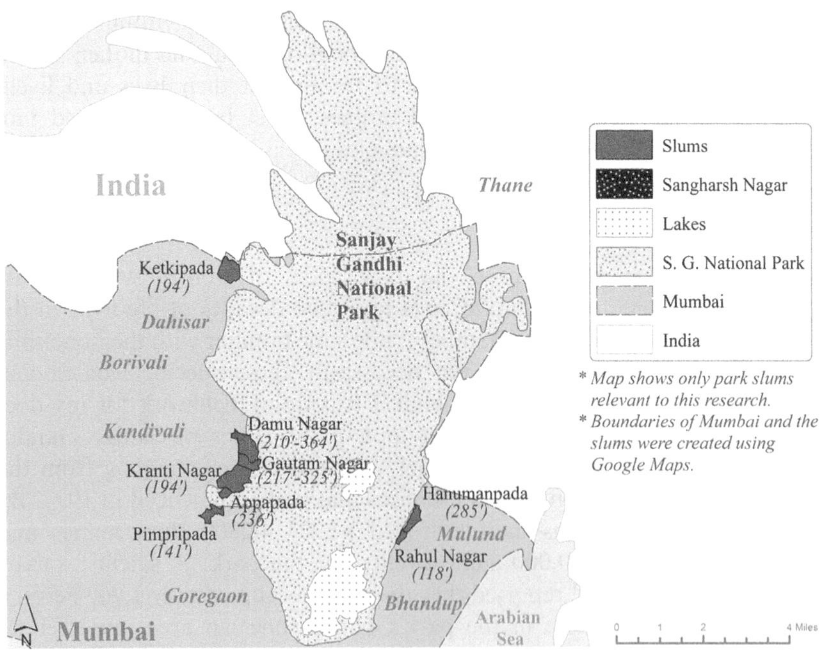

Map 1.2 Sanjay Gandhi National Park and slums on its buffer zone

What took me up the hills in early December 2002 on my first orientation to the park's landscape and slums was a day trip organized by a Mumbai-based nongovernmental organization (NGO) named Nivara Hakk Suraksha Samiti (translated as the Committee for the Protection of Housing Rights, henceforth "Nivara"). Nivara's leaders wanted me to experience the expanse of the slums in the park's buffer zone and witness the enormity of the challenge to find alternate accommodation, a task that was putting all the NGO's existing resources to the test. My objective at the time was to gather data on how the city's housing NGOs had managed their relations with government agencies to address the housing concerns of the city's slum and squatter residents. Two of Nivara's male volunteers, one who lived in a park slum and another from a different slum in the city, escorted me on the walking tour that started around 9:30 a.m. and ended well after nightfall at around 10:00 p.m. The volunteers had taken the opportunity of the tour to do what at least a dozen other Nivara volunteers, both men and women, were also busy doing at the time, which was promoting a model resettlement and rehabilitation (R&R) project that Nivara was designing for the park's eligible slum dwellers.

Nivara, in partnership with a private developer and the state government, envisioned both designing and implementing a model R&R project with full amenities, including low-rise buildings of no more than five floors, ample open spaces, playgrounds, markets, commercial space, schools, and places of worship spread over 45 acres of developable land. Development of the site began in 2002 when the private developer (also the land's owner) began blasting hills that once hosted a series of stone quarries in preparation for construction of a series of apartment buildings. The site is relatively unique. Unlike most other slum resettlement projects erected in the outskirts of cities, this site is a veritable island situated amidst several posh residential and commercial developments well within the city. The site is in a neighbourhood called Chandivali (see Map 1.3), located between two major business and leisure hubs of the city, the suburbs of Powai and Andheri. Under ideal traffic conditions, it is a 12–14 kilometre cab or autorickshaw drive from the southernmost slum of the park.

Nivara considered the location of the R&R project its most notable feature, for it "offered immense scope for employment" for former slum residents ("Nivara Hakk", 2013, under "The long road … "). In accordance with policy directives from the state, Nivara offered each eligible family a 225-square-foot apartment within this site. In 2007, nearly five years after my first encounter with the NGO and two years after completing my dissertation, I received an email from the NGO's founder-leader:

> You'll be glad to know that the first batch of about 3,500 families from the Borivali Natinal [sic] Park have actually shifted to their new home. Lots of roblems [sic] as expected buit [sic] everybody is happy.
> (received July 5, 2007)

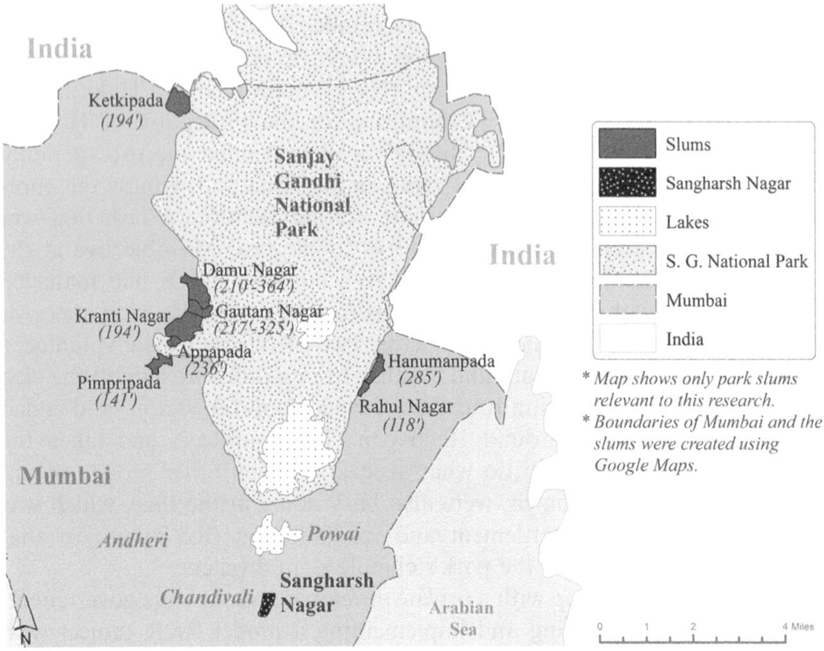

Map 1.3 Sanjay Gandhi National Park slums and Sangharsh Nagar

This brief communication sparked my interest in documenting the "problems", including the expectations and mid-stream reflections, from those affected and set me on several return trips (in December 2007, November 2009, and December 2011) to Mumbai before I started collecting data for this book (in August 2012, November–December 2012, July 2013, December 2014, and December 2016). Witnessing and documenting a major urban R&R process as it unfolded, I soon discovered that the model resettlement site had not been implemented as planned. Nivara had labelled the site *Sangharsh Nagar*, meaning a neighborhood born of struggle, admittedly in recognition of the long, tortuous struggle it had taken to create the site; that struggle was far from over. In late 2007, the NGO and the private developer had a falling-out. During that period, the city's real-estate bubble had burst along with the developer's financial incentive to construct a model development of low-rise buildings with generous open and commercial spaces, and other amenities. The developer sidestepped the NGO, appointed its own architect, and built a site that met only the minimum resettlement guidelines.

Sangharsh Nagar thus grew into a dense assemblage of 200, eight- to fifteen-story apartment buildings with no dedicated areas for playgrounds, places of worship, retail businesses, or other promised amenities. As of December 2011, one year before I started my data collection for this book, 150 of the 200 apartment buildings, all eight stories tall, were ready for occupation. This phase I of the project was to accommodate 12,070 families from the park slums, more than half of the 22,000 families in the park slums who were verified as eligible for alternate accommodation. The remaining 9,930 families were to be resettled in phase II of the project. However, unlike phase I, both the design and construction of the buildings had proceeded without Nivara's involvement. The 50 buildings yet to be completed as part of phase II were each proposed to be 24 stories high, later decreased to 15-story buildings that were constructed by a partnership between the state, the original developer, and a third-party private developer. As of December 2016, all 200 buildings occupied a site shaped like an elongated parallelogram with the longest axis running from the northeastern to southwestern ends of the site. The southern end of the site is lower in elevation than the northern parts. It has far more undulations, making a walk there from one building to the next a workout. The chiselled surface of a massive rocky hill forms the eastern border, with some apartment buildings standing within meters of the rocky cliff. The remaining apartment buildings on the eastern peripheries have significantly more breathing space, at least until all buildings are prepared and occupied as part of the project's second phase. The western portion of the site is the portion that has the most foot traffic and activity. In this part is a very large underground water tank/reservoir that supplies the site's municipal drinking water. A municipal school has also been operating in this vicinity since 2011. An unnamed, paved roadway runs along the southwestern boundary where apartment residents have set up street vending operations on both sides of the road. This is the site's *bazaar* that comes to life each afternoon and teems with activity until 10:30 or 11 each night. To the midwest is an unassuming entrance to Sangharsh Nagar, a paved road with one side lined with small eateries, grocery stores, pawnshops, and the private developer's site office. On the other side is the wall of a private engineering firm. This road runs perpendicular to Chandivali Road where there is a bus stand continuously full of people waiting for one of the handful of city busses that pass through. The road also connects the site to the research and development division of a global chemical company, private banks, marriage halls, film studios, and several upscale housing developments, some long occupied and several others at various stages of completion. Beyond the site's northern end are a public school, a mosque, and a temple, a few slums, and a large plot of vacant land, portions of which appear earmarked for a municipal park and the rest for the construction of more residential housing developments. Right outside the southern end is a small slum on the edge of a neighborhood bursting with a hodgepodge of snack shops, inexpensive hotels, film studios, places of worship, and several small- and medium-size manufacturing companies. The closest railway station is a good 30- to 40-minute autorickshaw drive through this hectic zone. Sangharsh Nagar's location is a paradox. Seemingly well situated, flanked by two popular residential and

Figure 1.1 An inner road of Sangharsh Nagar, as seen from a third floor apartment. In the distance is the chiseled surface of a rocky hill and right beneath it, an incomplete phase II building

commercial suburbs of Mumbai, it stands concealed between upscale housing developments and rocky hillocks (Figure 1.1).

During my weeklong visits to Mumbai, between 2007 and 2011, I would spend most of the week in and around Sangharsh Nagar. I spent at least one afternoon each week in the park slums where the land occupied by the eight slums was far less densely populated than in 2002, although it still housed several thousand new and old migrants. At both the park slums and Sangharsh Nagar, I'd introduce myself as a visitor who had frequented the park as a student and was curious to see how it and the resettlement site had developed. In Sangharsh Nagar, I would usually start my visits around noon with a few minutes in Nivara's site office, a ground-floor apartment unit at Sangharsh Nagar. For the rest of the day, I would loiter around the site making stops by the smaller underground water reservoirs/tanks (situated amidst each cluster of apartment buildings) where small groups of men and/or women, usually in groups of 2–10, would be seated on the tank's concrete surface resting, chatting, or haggling with a passing *saree* salesman. I would also stop if I saw residents waiting in line for water from a private water truck or standing in a line to purchase their ration of wheat flour, cooking oil, and sugar from the site's food subsidy shop. I would chat with vendors at the evening *bazaar* and converse with people at the bus stand while we waited for a ride. In all these conversations, it was invariably the women who would express their satisfactions, complaints, and, above all else, their aspirations about life in the new location. They shared these assessments and desires in response to relatively short questions and probes from me, like "Where did you live before you came to Sangharsh Nagar?" "How is life since your move?" "Did you have good sales today?" "Are you headed to work?" "Did you do the same work back in the slum?" "Does the bus always take this long to come?" "Which building do you live in?" "Does your apartment building have others from your slum?" "How did your family decide to come here?" Occasionally, these and similar questions would generate conversations. Over my visits, I became convinced that this phase in the history of the site was full of stories of struggles and negotiations that should be documented before they faded from individual and collective memory.

These stories about creating a "sense of place" at the resettlement site were rife with details on what their narrators considered possible and imaginable in the lives of themselves, their households, and their neighbourhood (Gray, 2002; Gupta & Fergusen, 1997; Kempny, 2002). They were told with an eloquence that Gadamer (2004, p. 17) refers to as "talking well"; in other words, not just saying something well, but saying it with situated practical wisdom, "the virtue of practical reflection" (Gadamer, 1991, p. 322).

The Methods

I started collecting women's "talk" in August 2012 and continued collecting conversations in November–December 2012, July 2013, December 2014, and December 2016. The data collection process (and the subsequent analysis and reflection) utilized a grounded theory approach (Strauss & Corbin, 1990), like that of the pilot phase of the study (in August 2012), and follow-up visits in the years thereafter. The pilot stage of the research commenced with 40 intake interviews conducted among female participants selected using chain referral sampling procedures. I was particularly careful to not recruit more than one participant from each apartment building in the resettlement site. Participants had to be at least 18 years old and former residents of the park slums. The intake conversation with each woman documented place and date of birth, the year and reason for the move to Mumbai, marital status, level of education, previously acquired skills, current and past employment, and the details of residential moves, if any, within Mumbai. Other household details were also collected, including the inclusion or otherwise of her name in the title to the apartment, how the relocation to Sangharsh Nagar had influenced income and saving patterns and the number, ages, relationships, and employment status of household members. At this stage, all was documented in a written questionnaire I'd developed beforehand.

In late August 2012, once I had recruited 40 women, I visited each at their homes. Every focus-group discussion was to have no more than 10 women. This resulted in 40 women self-selecting participation in one of four discussion groups. Each focus-group discussion lasted approximately 1.5 hours and was both audio- and video-recorded. The discussions centered around five broad questions, with the first four focused on how women recollected their experiences of living in the slum, as well as their more recent experiences adjusting and adapting to life in the resettlement site. The last question invited all participating women to share their future aspirations about life at the resettlement site:

1. How do you recollect your lives in the slums?
2. What was the role you played in your family's decision to resettle in this site?
3. As you look back on the first few months at the resettlement site, are there events that stand out as joyful, puzzling, or challenging? Describe each one.
4. How have you overcome the challenges, if any, that you have encountered since resettlement?
5. What are your key aspirations for life in the resettlement site? How have you come to acquire this aspiration? Have you communicated it to others in the resettlement site? Who are they and what did you share with them?

These conversations were transcribed by a professional firm and I translated the transcriptions from Hindi and Marathi to English. The translated exchanges were then coded three times (using NVivo qualitative data analysis software) by two student researchers and me to ensure intercoder reliability. In data analysis, particular attention was paid to the language the women used to 1) retrospectively describe their lives in the slum,

2) express the nature of their current life in the resettlement site, and 3) articulate their vision or mental model of how to improve or maintain their lives. At this stage of the research process, data analysis revealed that a woman's story about her experiences adapting to life at the resettlement site varied depending on her sociodemographic characteristics (including her age, marital status, level of education, nature and location of past employment, ethnicity, religion, family size, number of earners per household, and/or the size and location of her former residence) as well as household circumstances during the time spent awaiting relocation and the strength of her ties with other residents and external agencies. These characteristics informed future assignment of participants into groups for focused discussions. In other words, each future discussion that took place among women comprised those with different sociodemographic characteristics, varied experiences while awaiting relocation, and different degrees of perceived associations with neighbors and others with a stake in their housing.

When I reentered Mumbai in November 2012, I redesigned the intake interview to collect additional details related to the last two criteria mentioned earlier (i.e. time spent awaiting relocation and the groups and organizations that the participants had associated with during their stay in the slum). I used colorful 8.5-by-11-inch flyers written in Hindi and Marathi to introduce my research project to potential participants and solicit women for focus-group discussions or interviews. I would share the flyers along with a short recruitment speech with women and men I encountered during my regular daily walks around the site, a ritual I maintained through the course of the data collection period. If not immediately available for an intake conversation, the person I met (whether the woman herself or a member of her family) was invited to call me or go to Nivara's office where a sign-up sheet requested their phone number and best time to meet for a short 15-minute intake interview. The office was usually open seven days a week from 9:30 a.m. until about 6 p.m. However, the sign-up sheet stayed blank the whole time I was collecting data. My walks around the site thus became my sole method of recruitment. On occasion, Nivara's three-member staff, especially its two females, would suggest women for the study. I would follow up on their suggestions mostly when struggling to recruit women I wanted represented in each focus group. The older Nivara female employee lived at Sangharsh Nagar. She had migrated from Maharashtra's southern district of Satara and settled with her husband in one of the many slums around the park during the early 1990s. Before relocation, she had served as an unpaid volunteer for Nivara charged with convincing her neighbors to have faith in Nivara's plans to relocate them to Sangharsh Nagar. Nivara had since hired her as a full-time staff member responsible for setting up a savings-and-credit group among the women of Sangharsh Nagar and promoting the many organizations eager to offer vocational training to the site's youth. She therefore knew a number of women living at the site. The other staff member was a Muslim woman from the Sheikh community who originated from Uttar Pradesh in northern India. She traveled an hour to work from a large suburban slum west of Mumbai. She began her association with Nivara as a paid assistant to a physician who ran a children's clinic out of Nivara's headquarters near the park's southwestern corner. Since the inauguration of the resettlement site in 2007, she had worked part time in the office at Sangharsh Nagar, but her exact operational role was less defined. However, she was familiar with other Muslim residents from the park and played a vital role in introducing me to several of them.

The intake interviews with women, held on a date prior to their focus-group discussion, were incredibly rich in detail, especially since I decided to add open-ended questions about recollections of life following the demolitions and the nature of networks that had helped shape participants' lives in the city. The components of subjects' place-related identity following migration to Mumbai were so varied that capturing these details may have been impossible without the tape-recorded conversations during the individual intake interviews. As with the focus-group discussions, I audio-recorded, transcribed, translated, and included the intake conversations in the final data analysis. Once I had recruited about 9–12 women who fit the criteria for selection in a focus-group discussion, I'd visit the recruits' homes to arrange a meeting in Nivara's tiny training room situated across from its office. In this room of approximately 100 square feet, Nivara periodically held training sessions where participants could earn a certificate as a beautician or making beaded jewelry or take short workshops in English conversation. In all, I held 75 intake interviews; 60 of these subjects attended the seven focus-group discussions I held over this phase of the study.

All the discussions took place from 3:00 to 6:00 p.m., on various days of the week. The women—dressed in bright *sarees* or occasionally *salwar-kameez* (loose pants and tunic) or *churidar-kurta* (tight pants and tunic) and maxis, or in *salwar-kameez* and capris or jeans with tops for the younger adults—seated themselves in a semicircle on peach-colored molded plastic chairs with a backrest and arms. I had no control over the nursing child, daughter, sister, or neighbor some women brought with them. I would request them all to be seated but pleaded (rarely with success) that the adult companions refrain from participating during the discussions. The discussion would commence with me circulating five copies of a little photo book of 10 pictures among the participants. The photo book documented my own experiences managing my relocation from India to the United States in 1999. It triggered personal questions about my parents and grandparents, my partner, traffic, snow, the cost of living in the U.S., and especially about my daily routine in Chicago, a city familiar to many as President Obama's hometown. Many hung on to the book and would flip through it whenever there was the slightest pause in the conversation.

After some 10 minutes of talk about life in the U.S. and Chicago, I'd steer the remaining 60- to 90-minute discussion with questions I had asked in the pilot stage (see questions listed above) of the study. Two video recorders placed in different corners of the room recorded each quarter of the semicircle. The audio-recorder sat on a plastic chair in the center of the room (Figure 1.2).

Unlike the group discussions, nearly all of the 20 individual interviews occurred in the homes of the women. Each one-hour chat was audio- but not video-recorded. In three such interviews, the conversations extended well beyond an hour and were scheduled in two or three parts, taking place on days and times the women found convenient. These were also audio-recorded. Many of the women would be doing home-based work while I interviewed them, assembling switch buttons or bracelets. All those present at home at the time would join in, be it a spouse, in-laws, children, grandchildren, other relatives, neighbors, or out-of-town guests. Some of the interviews were held in Nivara's training room, particularly when women admitted to feeling more comfortable getting away from their stay-at-home husbands or in-laws or because the training room was located on their way home from work. The same questions guided these face-to-face conversations. These 20 women were those who, because of their marital status (for instance, recently widowed or separated), their newly moved-in status, or other job- and household-related responsibilities, found it difficult to come to the group discussions. I kept in touch with these 20

Figure 1.2 A focus-group discussion

Table 1.1 Key characteristics of the 120 women whose place-making stories inform this book

Marital Status	*Age group (in years)*	*Religion*	*Self-identified caste affiliation*	*Level of education*	*Number of family members below 18 (average)*	*Family members 18–25 (average)*	*Family members over 25 (average)*	*Family size (average)*	*Earners per family (average)*	*Female earners per family (average)*	*Place migrated from*	*% of those who lived in one of eight slums prior to relocation*
Married = 62.5%	18–25 = 18.3%	Hindu = 66.67%	*Dalit** = 35.83%	No education = 35.83%							From within Maharashtra = 45.83%	Damun Nagar = 20%
Widowed = 20%	26–33 = 4.16%	Buddhist = 20%	Upper caste = 31.66%	Below primary = 11.66%							Uttar Pradesh = 14.16%	Kranti Nagar = 20%
Never married = 13.33%	34–41 = 31.6%	Muslim = 8.33%	OBC** = 21.66%	Completed up to 5th grade = 5.83%							Bihar = 6.66%	Gautam Nagar = 14.16%
Divorced/separated = 4.16%	42–49 = 21.66%	Christian = 1.66%	Muslim = 8.33%	6th–10th grade = 34.16%	1.57	1.39	2.3	5.27	2.15	0.88	Born & brought up in Mumbai = 25.83%	Appapada = 15%
	50–57 = 15%	Others = 2.5%	Christian = .83%	Higher secondary (11th/12th grade) = 6.66%							Other states in India = 7.5%	Ketkipada = 4.16%
	58–65 = 5.83%		Other = 1.69%	Graduate and above = 5.83%								Pimpripada = 1.66%

Marital Status	*Age group (in years)*	*Religion*	*Self-identified caste affiliation*	*Level of education*	*Number of family members below 18 (average)*	*Family members 18–25 (average)*	*Family members over 25 (average)*	*Family size (average)*	*Earners per family (average)*	*Female earners per family (average)*	*Place migrated from*	*% of those who lived in one of eight slums prior to relocation*
	66 and above = 1.7%											Hanumanpada = .83%
	Unknown = 1.75%											Rahul Nagar = 3.33%
												Unclear*** = 20.83%

* Dalit = The oppressed (formerly "untouchable") who fall outside the fourfold Indian caste system of the Brahmin, Kshatriya, Vaishya, and Shudra castes.

** OBC = Other Backward Caste, a phrase coined by the Indian government to refer to a caste above the Dalits but below the aforementioned Brahim, Kshatriya and Vaishya caste. They form the bulk of the traditionally labeled Shudra caste.

***Unclear because they recollected the name of their ward (administrative division of the city's civic body) rather than one of the eight slums. One slum could fall in the jurisdiction of more than one ward.

participants and individually followed up with them during my subsequent visits in July 2013, December 2014, and December 2016. None of these follow-up conversations was audio- or video-recorded.

The data gathered from the pilot phase and the November–December session in 2012 totaled 61 hours of conversations with 120 women. Key characteristics of the 120 women and their families are described in Table 1.1 and are discussed at various points through the course of the book.

Each chapter that follows details the many ways in which diverse women attempted to make sense of their old and new homes. The narratives in Chapters 2 through 5 are chronologically ordered to answer how women recollected their early years as new migrants (Chapter 2), articulated their relationships with external benefactors (Chapter 3), entered their new lives in secure housing (Chapter 4), and reconstructed their livelihoods (Chapter 5). The book concludes by emphasizing the specific and diverse ways in which women expressed a sense of belonging and identification with life after legal tenure. Women are mediating change by communicating to each other their sense of belonging—whether positive or negative—thereby making adjustments, including ones they believe that housing planners and implementers must make on their behalf. A majority of the suggestions in this concluding chapter forward those the participants themselves offered in the preceding pages. They call for the full, continual, and differentiated engagement of affected women in the planning, design, monitoring, and evaluation of place-making processes in cities in general (without) and in their own resettlement colonies (within) in particular.

Note

1 Resettlement and rehabilitation (R&R) are two distinct but closely linked processes and are often distinguished in large-scale development projects, such as those sponsored by the World Bank and other international development funding agencies. *Resettlement* implies physically shifting, for instance, evicted slum dwellers from their homes to a new site. *Rehabilitation* involves the process of rebuilding their lives in the new location. It typically involves adequately compensating households for the assets lost, "[providing them with] the necessary means to restore subsistence and income, to reconstruct the social networks that support production, services and mutual assistance, and to compensate for transitional hardships (such as crop losses, moving costs, interruption or loss of employment, lost income, among others)" (Inter-American Development Bank, 2018).

References

Bombay Environmental Action Group & Others V.A.R. Bharati, Deputy Conservator of Forests & Others, Bom. C.R. 244. (High Court of Judicature at Bombay, 2004). Retrieved from http://cat.org.in/wp-content/uploads/2016/07/WP-305-of-1995-15.09.2003-Encroachments-in-SGNP.pdf.

Desmond, M. (2012). Eviction and the reproduction of urban poverty. *American Journal of Sociology*, 118(1), 88–133.

Forester, J. (1999). *The deliberative practitioner: Encouraging participatory planning processes*. Cambridge, MA: MIT Press.

Gadamer, H.-G. (1991). *Truth and method*. (J. Weinsheimer & D. G. Marshall, Trans.). New York: Crossroads.

Gadamer, H.-G. (2004). *Truth and method* (2nd ed.). (J. Weinsheimer & D. G. Marshall, Trans.). London: Continuum.

Gilbert, M. R. (2000). Identity, difference and the geography of the working poor: Women's survival strategies. In K. B. Miranne & A. H. Young (Eds.), *Gendering the city: Women, boundaries, and visions of urban life* (pp. 65–87). Oxford: Rowman & Littlefield.

Gray, J. (2002). Community as place-making: Ram auctions in the Scottish borderland. In V. Amit (Ed.), *Realizing community: Concepts, social relationships and sentiments* (pp. 38–59). London: Routledge.

Gupta, A. & Ferguson, J. (1997). Beyond "culture": Space, identity and the politics of difference. In A. Gupta & J. Ferguson (Eds), *Culture, power, place: Explorations in critical anthropology* (pp. 1–29). Durham, NC: Duke University Press.

Healey, P. (2002). On creating the "city" as a collective resource. *Urban Studies*, 39 (10), 1777–1792.

Inter-American Development Bank. (2018). Involuntary resettlement. IDB: Improving Lives. Retrieved from www.iadb.org/en/about-us/involuntary-reSETtlement%2C6660.html.

Kempny, M. (2002). Cultural islands in the globalizing world: Community-cum-locality of the Cieszyn Lutherans. In V. Amit (Ed.), *Realizing community: Concepts, social relationships and sentiments* (pp. 60–83). London: Routledge.

The long road from the forest slums to the high rises of Chandivili. (2013). Nivara Hakk Slum Movements, Sanjay Gandhi National Park, Borivali. Retrieved from www.nivarahakk.com/slum-movement-national-park.php.

Mehta, L. (Ed.) (2009). *Displaced by development: Confronting marginalisation and gender injustice*. New Delhi: SAGE.

Menon-Sen, K. (2006). "Better to have died than to live like this": Women and evictions in Delhi. *Economic and Political Weekly*, 41(20), 1969–1974.

Office of the United Nations High Commissioner for Human Rights. (2013). *Report of the Special Rapporteur on adequate housing as a component of the right to an adequate standard of living*. United Nations General Assembly: A/HRC/4/18. Retrieved from www.ohchr.org/Documents/Issues/Housing/Guidelines_en.pdf.

Rein, M. & Schön, D. (1977). Problem setting in policy research. In C. H. Weiss (Ed.), *Using social research in policy making* (pp. 235–251). Lexington, IN: Lexington Books.

Sandercock, L. (2003). Out of the closet: The importance of stories and storytelling in planning practice. *Planning Theory & Practice*, 4(1), 11–28.

Strauss, A. & Corbin, J. (1990). *Basics of qualitative research: Grounded theory procedures and techniques* (2nd ed.). Thousand Oaks, CA: SAGE.

Throgmorton, J. A. (2003). Planning as persuasive storytelling in a global-scale web of relationships. *Planning Theory*, 2(2), 125–151.

2 Vibrant Matter of the Past

A Woman's Theory of Place

> Daily and hourly, from a thousand unnoted sources, there is lodged in Mr. Everyman's mind a mass of unrelated and related information; impressions and images, out of which he somehow manages, undeliberately for the most part, to fashion a history, a patterned picture of remembered things, said and done in past times and distant places.
>
> (Becker, 1932, p. 229)

The aim of this chapter is not to depict a factual history of life in a Mumbai/Bombay[1] slum, but to present a group of 120 women as distinct, individual urban historians, each of whom, in conversation with others, creates and frames a version of her past in her first inhabited space in the slums of Mumbai. This space represents her notion of a home, which she brings to her new, legally tenured home in the Sangharsh Nagar resettlement site. From this vantage point, she assesses her past (and shares her future expectations). Central to the discussion that follows is the argument that a woman's memory of place occurs within networks of relationships that are mediated by objects. This argument is not new. Halbwachs (1992, p. 22) made the same point in his seminal work on the social construction of memory in which he asserted that human memory functions within a collective context and is always selective. It is not surprising therefore that various groups of the women I spoke with expressed different collective memories that produced different modes of behavior at the resettlement site. What were these collective memories? What material forms did they take? The chapter implies that while all the women identified strongly with their lives in the slum, different groups of women responded in different ways—raising many practical issues concerning the design, construction, and use of spaces and places to take into consideration when making accommodation decisions for a multiplicity of urban residents.

Listening to the women's retrospective conversations about their experiences in their former homes in the park slums, I was initially struck by the differences between how various women remembered the "vibrant matter" depending on their age, marital status (e.g. married, single, widowed, and/or separated), the location of their employment (e.g. slum-based or elsewhere), the number of earning members in their household, and/or the location of their slum in the park (e.g. a high- or a low-elevation settlement). The women chiefly invoked routines in their use of particular places (e.g. fetching water from the common well or standpost, using the open-air "toilet areas"), particular items (e.g. a front door, the tarpaulin sheet, the blue drum or plastic *matkas/handaas* to store water) and the natural environment's offerings (e.g. the fresh air, starry nights, greenery). All these were "vibrant matter", potent reminders of both the form that past experiences took and what was subsequently lost, found, and/or desired (Bennett, 2010). The front door that was of marginal utility to some women assumed significance to the widows and still-married women who raised concerns about the safety of their young children. The early morning queue or the disorderly crowd gathered to use the common toilet or to collect water from a municipal standpost were crucial locations for socialization among young girls. However, these same spaces also could be associated with dread of the lengthy process they represented (it could take up to two hours to fill water containers because of frustratingly low water pressure). I was also puzzled by the absence of the bulldozer as a matter remembered from their pasts in the slum. It only came up if I asked about it; surprising, since several chronicles on the resettlement site had characterized the demolition of the slums as a massive, state-led operation executed with incredible brutality (Indian People's Human Rights Commission, 2000, p. 2; Padovani, 2016, p. 121; "Sangharsh Nagar—Slum Rehab", 2017). Actually, the upheaval and displacement was why the resettlement site was christened Sangharsh Nagar (i.e. a neighborhood born of struggle). Why did the women rarely retrieve the demolition or its agent, the bulldozer, as a memory marker of their years in the slum? I address this question in detail in the next chapter, but here I share the "vibrant matter" that revealed the lifeworld of the women pre-demolition.

I begin with a brief overview of Sanjay Gandhi National Park ("the park") based on archival analysis (of Nivara and government records, court documents), scholarly literature, and participant observations undertaken during 10 separate visits to the park, from 2002 to 2016 (three visits in 2002–2003, and annual visits in 2007, 2009, 2011, 2012, 2013, 2014, and 2016). The description that follows treats the hilly park (*dongar* in Marathi) as a legitimate, existing, "vibrant matter" that shaped and is shaped by those who made it their home and the source of their livelihood.

The Dense *Dongar*

Lonely Planet's popular travel guide to India describes the park as a "hard to believe" sanctuary nestled in the northern fringes of Greater Mumbai and extending into the much larger Mumbai Metropolitan Region[2]. The park's undulating topography of hills, valleys, open spaces, and lakes provides an ideal catchment area for the Vihar and Tulsi Lakes that supply Mumbai's drinking water. "Urban development", the guidebook notes, "tries to muscle in on the fringes of this wild region, but its national park status has allowed it to stay green and calm" (Sanjay Gandhi National Park, 2017). The park gained national standing in 1996, a year after a city-based environmental NGO, the Bombay Environmental Action Group (BEAG), filed a petition in the state's High Court against the park's Conservator of Forests in early 1995. BEAG contended that "illegal encroachments and unauthorized constructions had ecologically disastrous effect which had led to massive deforestation" (*Bombay Environmental Action Group & Others v. A. R. Bharati, Deputy Conservator of Forests & Others*, 2004, pp. 7–8). The state's Forest Department responded with an affidavit alleging that 772.82 hectares of the park's 10,309 hectares of forest cover had been encroached upon (*Bombay Environmental Acrion Group & Others v. A. R. Bharati, Deputy Conservator of Forests & Others*, 2004, pp. 13–14). In 1996, 8,696 hectares of the park were declared a nationally protected area. The bulk of the park encroachments were spread over 511 hectares and comprised 75,000 to 86,000 *illegal hutments* (the term used in the 1995 petition for unauthorized slum dwellings). The remainder contained private stone quarries and some government-authorized establishments. The petition sought the eviction of illegal encroachers and the demolition of all unauthorized structures in the park within six months.

Occupation of the park's hilly slopes and interiors was not new. Illegal hutments and other encroachments in the park mushroomed in the late 1970s, during a period of substantial industrial restructuring in Mumbai's central districts. At its peak, this very central area in the city hosted nearly 60 textile mills and employed some 250,000 millworkers (Whitehead, 2008, p. 272), mainly Marathi-speaking men from nearby rural hinterlands of the state. Often, married males would leave their families in the village for work in the city. The workers initially lived in hostels and, eventually, for a small rent in *chawls* (three- to five-story structures with distinctive verandas along the façade at each story). Utilities were shared and each one-room unit measured less than 20 square meters. Designed to accommodate about six men, over time, they came to host 20 to 40 men and, eventually, entire families (Das, 1988, p. 25). These structures were built by the government, mill owners, or private developers; quality construction and maintenance were rarely a priority (D'Monte, 2002, p. 75). The *chawls* soon grew into substandard housing and as labor migration into the central city soared, incoming laborers began squatting on land around the mills, creating domiciles with whatever materials they could gather.

By the late 1970s, the city's textile base had declined precipitously and redundant millworkers turned to the city's rapidly growing informal economy for work.[3] Former millworkers took up home-based small-scale production, hawked vegetables, cooked food, and peddled household items on city streets. Unlike the former millworkers who continued to live and work in the central city, newer immigrants from the state and elsewhere, mainly eastern Uttar Pradesh and Bihar, migrated and found shelter and livelihood in the city's northern and eastern peripheries, about 40 miles from the central industrial district. Starting in the 1970s, the city limits had expanded to accommodate a rapidly growing middle class who settled in new satellite townships that had sprouted outside the park's boundaries (see Map 2). Goregaon, Kandivali, Borivali, and Dahisar to the park's west; Mulund and Bhandup to its east; and Thane to its north hosted manufacturing and production activities, dense middle-class residential areas, newer slums, and an informal economy that supported the city's poor immigrants. By 1980, more than 48 percent of the city's population lived in slums and squatter settlements (Clothey, 2006, p. 88).

The earliest settlers in the park's fringe areas, the immigrants of the 1970s, could be considered its "encroachers" for, as Vaquier (2010, p. 75) notes, they squatted at no cost. As the number of immigrants grew, the park became a "matter" of pecuniary interest to those who grabbed and sold parcels of land at progressively higher prices to new immigrants with little knowledge of "who the genuine owner was" (Vaquier, 2010, p. 75). Like Vaquier, Econet[4] ("Welcome to Econet", 2018) and Zerah (2007, p. 126) also attribute all encroachments, including slums, hotels, restaurants, upscale bungalows, and even government-authorized establishments (like a large government-owned bacon manufacturing unit), situated within the park to a hidden network of private developers, local politicians, government officials, and even the state's forest authorities. By the time environmental and housing rights activists had come to loggerheads in the 1995 petition, the park had grown into a densely populated *dongar* (hills) of hutments clustered into an estimated 54 slums dispersed among the fringes, or buffer zone, of the park. The most densely populated cluster of homes occupied the southwestern border comprising slums such as Damu Nagar, Gautam Nagar, Kranti Nagar, and Appapada. The second densest zone was a strip on the eastern side with slums called Hanumanpada and Rahul Nagar. Another slum in the northwestern part of the park was Ketkipada (see Map 2).[5]

Plenty of sources have richly documented the migratory patterns that fueled the growth of Mumbai's numerous slum and squatter homes—some located right by the city's airport, others alongside railroad tracks, under flyovers, on sidewalks, on hilltops, and by the city's coastline. But few such accounts describe the growth of its slums from the perspective of its female residents. Barring passing references to women's move to the city following a nod from their husbands to join them, there is no discussion of how these women received and were hosted by the city.

Women Encountering Urban Growth

Doors, Taps, and Other Items: Vulnerability and Community

I first met Parineeti early one December afternoon in 2012 when she walked into the 100-square-foot training room in the resettlement site that hosted jewelry-making classes, beautician's courses, and other training programs, mostly for young adult women. She came in panting after a brisk walk from her apartment at the far end of the site, worried that she'd be late for our scheduled conversation. Her 20-year-old daughter, Usha, was with her. By this time, I had completed all my focus group discussions at the resettlement site and had begun recruiting women for individual interviews. I was especially seeking out those I considered more marginalized residents, namely widows with young daughters, divorced and separated women, the elderly, and those with limitations, such as household obligations and/or physical handicaps that inhibited participation in focus-group conversations. Parineeti fit the bill on several counts. She was a young, 40-year-old widow with five daughters. Her husband had died three years before she and her children had moved into Sangharsh Nagar in 2009. She was unable to attend any of the seven group conversations because she was recovering from a painful hysterectomy from six months prior. Since the family's relocation, Parineeti had relied on the earnings of her two oldest daughters still at home. Recently, she had hosted the wedding of her eldest daughter in Sangharsh Nagar, leaving her with an unpaid debt of INR 150,000[6]. Her next oldest daughter worked as a babysitter in a nearby upscale housing complex and Usha, the daughter who accompanied her to our meeting, cooked meals in three different homes in another upscale residential complex nearby. Their collective salary of INR 7,000 supported the household including school fees for Parineeti's two youngest daughters.

PARINEETI: I was born in Bombay itself. My mother used to live in a slum in Goregaon [a western suburb of Mumbai and a 20-minute auto-rickshaw ride from the southwest corner of the park]. But they [my parents] got me married in the village [close to Nashik, a four-hour drive northeast of Mumbai, Maharashtra's fourth largest city]. I was just 13. I would not even understand anything and I was married off [by her parents who arranged her marriage in the village]. I haven't even studied, not gone to one class. He was from Bombay and when we got married, we stayed in the village in my brother-in-law's house. We stayed on rent. My husband did not have any work, nothing. After engagement, he spent two months in my mother's home [in Goregaon, Mumbai]. Then [after our marriage] my father told us that he [my husband] had nothing to do in the village and that he must do some business, some petty business, in the city. That he can start a shop repairing shoes in the corner, the work of a cobbler, you know [an ancestral occupation, under the Scheduled Caste category[7]]. He told him to start a small business in any street corner or on a sidewalk. Then when I got married and went to the village, my mother-in-law started saying that he has married a girl from Bombay and that she does not even know how to fix a *bajra roti* [flatbread made of millet] and this and that. She would tell the whole village that her daughter-in-law cooks this way and that. We lived in the village till I was 15 years old. [We] had a son and he died there. There is no health-care center in the village or anything.

The loss of their son triggered the couple's move to Mumbai and after staying briefly in Parineeti's mother's home, the couple moved to a makeshift roadside shelter (Figure 2.1):

PARINEETI: Over there, by the road, we put up a blanket on four bamboo sticks, put a *saree* and other pieces of cloth over it, and that is where we stayed. I mean, for three to four days, we lived there. The police folks would come at night, the local folks would come, and my husband started saying: 'I can sleep just about anywhere, but as a woman, where am I going to have you sleep? Come, let us look for a room to rent somewhere. I too shall work. We will live as husband and wife'. Then my son [another son] died before birth. My mother-in-law came to Shantaram Talav [an area northwest of the park's buffer zone] and we then took up a room on rent in the hills.

Thus began her life on the steep and rocky slopes of the park. Her husband, who worked as a roadside cobbler, would frequently return home drunk and beat her. When Parineeti got pregnant with yet another son,

Figure 2.1 A family squatting on the city's sidewalk

her mother-in-law insisted that she start earning like all the other "daughter-in-laws that she would see leave for work from their homes in the hill". Parineeti started working as a garbage-picker separating paper and plastic bags discarded into municipal garbage dumps in upper-middle class residential neighborhoods nearby and selling the sorted items to a *kabar-iwalla* (a waste collector). She earned about INR 10–20 a day but had no control over her earnings. "I would work and get 10 or 20 [INR]. I would hide two or three for my belly, to eat on the sly". Undernourishment combined with the health hazards of waste-picking and regular beatings resulted in a second failed pregnancy. Soon after Parineeti delivered her first daughter, in 1992, Mumbai and the rest of the country were rocked by intense clashes between Hindus and Muslims. Slums were hit the hardest. Parineeti and her husband hastily abandoned their rented, one-room shack and sought shelter again with Parineeti's mother. They moved from place to place for about four years—first within the city, then to her husband's native village, next to Nashik, and then back to her mother's home—until their second daughter was born. Worried about space to accommodate her daughter's growing family, her mother approached a gang of four thugs for help securing a home for her daughter's family. The gang promised Parineeti a one-room shack made of bamboo sticks and metal sheets for INR 7,000 in Gautam Nagar, a slum outside the southwestern boundary of the park just two to three kilometers (less than two miles) from her very first rental shack in the park.

PARINEETI: They were Muslim, they were boys, they used to refer to my mother as aunty, aunty. When they would arrive, they would drink water at my mother's doorstep. Sometimes they would ask for food from my mother. They told my mother that if she is your daughter, then she is like our sister. They told my mother not to worry. If I could, they said that I could pay 300 or 500 rupees, that is what they said. We did not have money, so how were we to give it? They treated me like a sister. Sometimes we'd give 200 rupees, I would write in a diary. Sometimes I'd give 300 rupees.

Their one-room shack stayed in its *kuchcha* (unfinished) state for the next 14 years, sheltering Parineeti and her growing family through more hard times. To help pay for the shack, the thugs suggested that Parineeti deliver drinking water to slum households. Several times a day, she would climb up and down the hilly slopes lugging a *matka/handaa* (pot) to fetch water from a "standpost connection" installed by the city's water department at the bottom of the hill to supply 20- or 40-litre drums (about five to 10 gallons) placed outside customers' homes (Figure 2.2).

Parineeti earned INR 5 per 20-liter drum. Their Gautam Nagar slum was located too high up the hill for residents to afford pumping water from the standpost. Parineeti's daughter Usha thought her mother's service was about more than the elevation. She theorized that those "nice thugs" knew that Gautam Nagar had more migrant families from the northern state of Uttar Pradesh (U.P.) than any other slum in the park and were taking advantage of it.[8]

Figure 2.2 Woman carrying a *handaa* of water up the hill in her park slum

USHA: We folks lived in Gautam Nagar. There were all U.P. folks in our neighborhood, they would all drive autorickshaws. Those people could not go fetch water. So, everyone would say, 'Give me two gallons of water' and such.

By 2003, Parineeti and her husband had five girls. She continued supporting the family by collecting and delivering water while her husband stayed home nursing his alcohol-damaged liver. To help meet medical bills, Usha dropped out of school in 2005 after completing her fifth-grade exams and joined her older sister in a sweatshop inserting artificial gems in necklaces. Through it all, Parineeti recalled how her ailing husband never relaxed his tight control over the family.

PARINEETI: He would tell me not to buy rice for the children [because it was far too costly]. I was to cook on firewood and not a stove because he liked the taste of food cooked on firewood. I'd do it just so he wouldn't fight. The door to the house, our rickety door, had to be shut by 6:00 p.m. Five girls, you know. He wanted to save them from the evil eyes of others. There was more danger inside the door than there was outside! He died in 2006 in that very house while we both were at work.

The front door that was literally shut for the supposed protection of Parineeti's daughters was conspicuously open in the memories of other women I spoke with. These women, who were brought up in more economically stable households in the park's slums, referred repeatedly to the now-closed doors of their current homes in Sangharsh Nagar where families sat behind them watching television for hours on end. Their longing for years past was a clear indication of what these women sought in their built environments—a place of togetherness. Consider the nostalgic remembrances of Leela, Preeti, and Alka, all 18 to 25 years old, single, and pursuing baccalaureate studies in college, in comparison to their current relative impoverishment of space and their sense of place:

LEELA: We used to have a home of five rooms there. Each room had a door. To the side was a kitchen and the other side, there was a bathroom. There was everything. When we were about to shift, I did not want to move. I cried so much that I left for the village. I cried so much over not wanting to come here. I didn't want to come here. Only after my father left that home and came here, I returned. I did not want to return because our entire childhood was spent there. And now, here, it does not feel like, I have no interest here. The area we came from, the school [there were several private schools within and many municipal-run schools close to the park's fringe areas], the friends, our neighbors there. If someone were to fall sick, they would come and see: 'How are you? What is it?'

PREETI: They would just come to the door and check up on us and leave.

ALKA: The whole *chaali* [an association of slum dwellers] would come over to inquire: 'Yes, what is it? What happened, how did it happen?' If we fall sick here, no one comes to check up on us.

LEELA: We would even put the television outside and watch it together.

PREETI: Even water was together. They [the slum residents] used to make them into a society and provide them with water in one place. We even had water inside the house, all day, all week.

ALKA: The neighbors from nearby would come and chat outside and the time would pass in the afternoons. Those that don't have work, they could stay at home and now what's happening in the buildings is that you either go to work or you mostly shut your door and keep watching your television. That is how it is. So, that is why it feels that one must directly move from here and head back into the *chaali*.

LEELA: It used to be *chaali* system you see there. Electricity used to be for four houses each. We would go to each other's homes if the wattage in our home was low or the power was cut off.

ALKA: If there was a power-cut in the evenings, then we would all sit outside and sing songs together. I remember that.

Leela had lived in Gautam Nagar while both Preeti and Alka lived in different sections of the Damu Nagar slum[9]. Leela's parents had migrated from U.P. during the late 1980s and ran a grocery store from the lower level of their self-built, two-story home. Preeti's family had settled in the park during the early 1990s after moving from a district nine hours north-east of Mumbai. Her father had worked in a public telecommunications firm and her mother vended vegetables and spices in a local *bazaa*r in the slum. Alka's long-widowed mother, Pooja, had been working as a domestic helper in the same upper-middle-class household for nearly two decades and had raised Alka and her sister single-handedly after her husband's unexpected death.

Leela and Alka first met in the focus-group discussion I hosted in December 2012. At that time, Preeti had been living in Sangharsh Nagar less than a month. All three of them had enjoyed a childhood in a well-consolidated, infrastructure-rich cluster of slum homes, the *chaali*. Unlike the *chawls* built for cotton-textile workers, these *chaalis* could comprise collectives of some 10 to 30 proximate households grouped to qualify for basic infrastructure improvements, such as a municipal water connection. The Municipal Corporation, the city's civic authority, had rules prohibiting slum households from installing individual water connections, but permitted groups of households to apply as a society and to designate one member as a secretary to collect and pay the monthly water bill. Once approved, the association, locally called a *chaali*, could hire a licensed plumber to install a connection from a collective tap near the *chaali* to the nearest standpost paid for by participating *chaali* members. The greater and higher up the distance between the standpost connection and the *chaali*, the costlier it was to install a suction pump to adequately transmit water. Additional costs in the form of pay-offs were involved because none of the park slums were "regularized" by the Municipal Corporation, a process officially recognizing an area as a slum and therefore eligible for improvement or upgrading plans.[10,11] As such, the unauthorized provision of basic infrastructure in the park slums—including water taps, electricity, sewer and storm water drains, community baths and latrines, paved roads, or toilets—depended heavily on the generosity of local politicians who made themselves indispensable in all transactions between slum residents and the city's tedious bureaucracy. The provision of a water connection was often a crucial first step in helping consolidate a settlement for it spurred negotiations for the acquisition of other amenities. Members of the *chaali* would, for instance, band together to unclog drains, secure electricity, pave their alleyway, or dispose of garbage. Each *chaali*, over time, also mobilized its own youth or women's group. The *yuva mandal* (youth collective) would take the lead in organizing religious festivals and sporting events. The women's group, called the *mahila mandal*, engaged in savings and credit activities. The *chaalis* came to host several highly politicized and polarizing groups, some of which are discussed in more detail in Chapter 4.

Former park residents differentiated this kind of *chaali* from what they referred to as *zopadpattis* (squatter settlements or shantytowns). If *chaalis* in the park were a collective of residents who lived in semi-permanent structures built from bricks, mortar, and corrugated iron sheets (many also including amenities like water, toilets, paved alleys, and sewage), then *zopadpatti*s consisted of shacks made of a variety of materials including bits of wood, rag, tin, sheets, mud, brick, and anything at hand. *Zopadpatti*s usually lacked such physical amenities as common toilet blocks, municipal water connections, or garbage disposal systems. The reasons for this lack of amenities could range from technical and operational constraints, such as steep slopes or a lack of space, to the inability of households to raise adequate funds. Women in these locales would often form groups with their neighbors to fetch water free of charge from a standpost some distance away from their slum. Residents from several slums would congregate around these taps, waiting in line as long as three or four hours to collect water flowing at very low pressure. Besides offering companionship, these groupings helped settle squabbles over the acceptable amount of water drawn, by whom, and in what order. Two women from Uttar Pradesh who participated in one of my focus-group discussions recollected their respective struggles. Although discussed amidst laughter and offhand joking, they recalled the physical labor involved in carrying at least two *handaa*s of water every day or two, depending on the size of their household:

BANU: At times, we would go at 1:00 in the afternoon and return at 3:00 or 4:00.

RAJKUMARI: Fight, hit, hit one another. If you hit one another, then you get water faster. Or else, you won't.

Unlike Banu, Rajkumari, and Parineeti, those like Leela, Preeti, and Alka came from homes that through their *chaalis* could afford infrastructure such as a municipal-approved water connection. But other households fit neither type. These were caught in squabbles between political parties in their *chaali*, leaving them only with literal pipe dreams. In addition, others had a municipal standpost but could not afford or were unable to install a suction pump to help transmit water at sufficient pressure. In such instances, four or five households might pool their money for the digging and maintenance of a well, a sewage system, an electrical connection, or a toilet. Such groupings also called themselves *chaalis*.

Most of the women who referenced a past of togetherness with others and having felt more safe and secure had belonged to such *chaalis*. They recollected items and places in the *chaali* that made them feel connected, expressed through phrases, such as neighbors who would come to the "door and check up on us and leave", the water tap "in one place", or the more spacious homes "with everything". But, for Parineeti and some others, these same items and places represented struggles over safety, livelihood, and comfort rather than positive recollections of togetherness.

Figure 2.3 Entrance to the park's Appapada slum, December 2016

Nature: Misery, Freedom, and Fear

> Parks are life's parentheses. … Parks are life's leafy truces, interregnums, pauses for thought; life's instant mini holidays.
>
> (Driver, 1996)

In citing Driver, I do not intend to connote that the park slums encroached on land meant for public leisure, but I present it as green space encircling the residential lives of the women and their families depicted here. To some of these women the park epitomized a village-like backdrop tied to the daily vagaries of the weather. To those brought up on its higher elevations, the breeze and the greenery were a refuge from the concrete city. But for others, who'd lived close enough to the "jungle" regions of the park, encounters with nature recalled situations of distress and drama.

The following extracts from focus-group discussions and individual interviews suggest the diverse ways in which the park and its topography intersected with the everyday lives of these women.

Shaista, a 35-year-old mother of eight children, ages 6 to 20, had relocated to Sangharsh Nagar in late 2007 from the park's Gautam Nagar slum where she'd lived all her life since moving to the city in the same home. She'd migrated from Uttar Pradesh in 1995, joining her husband and in-laws. Her father-in-law had decided to move the family from a slum in central Mumbai to a somewhat bigger plot in Gautam Nagar:

> Allah knows how I did it. There were snakes, scorpions, and I was scared. They would roam around. There were lots of snakes at home. You are, after all, encroaching in their space. Where will they live? They've never bitten me nor anyone in the house. There used to be this one snake without a tail. It would make a quiet entry and quietly exit from the house. It was fat and long. You know, I ask about it [the snake] when I go back [families still live in her former neighborhood in the Gautam Nagar slum]. I think the snake too left after we did. I remember it a lot. Hopefully, it is happy in its home just like I am here.

Kajal, a 35-year-old mother of three, had worked as a domestic helper for an upper-middle-class apartment house near her slum in the park. She recalled what she did not miss about her former life in the park:

KAJAL: In the rainy season, water used to fall from the roof. There used to be water from the ground. That problem is solved now. There used to be tension that we had to put a plastic sheet every year. [It] used to cost 2,000–3,000 [INR]. The house had to be protected for the children, their schoolbooks and bags. We had to get the plastic, get money to file the school fees, and buy plastic to put on the roof. Water used to come from the ground so we had to do that. There was a lot of tension after the rains. We used to get wet as we went to fetch water and that tension is now over.

Pooja, a 42-year-old mother of two teenage daughters, expressed similar sentiments. Like Kajal, she worked as a cook in an upper-middle-class home near her slum in the park:

POOJA: In the slum, we would feel 'how poor are we, what bad days we are going through'. There were times there would be a tiger, other times there would be rats, one would never know. At times it would rain. I would stay alone and in my home, there was no man. The paper would fly away [from the roof]. I would cry a lot and ask God to take me away. 'This life is worse than death. Why are we living this way?'

The self-organizing involved in setting up and maintaining basic infrastructure had also entailed adaptations to the park's physical nature. Recollections of the semi-wilderness of the park itself and the local ecology provoked animated discussions among the women of Sangharsh Nagar. Women who had to leave their homes to earn a living and those with young children who did home-based informal work were most likely to recollect the challenges of the park's environment. Climate factored so prominently in everyday life in the slum that Devi, who used to be a stay-at-home mother of four, with two boys aged 13 and 17 and two girls ages 14 and 19, said: "[In Sangharsh Nagar] we don't get to know [nowadays that] it is rainy. Over there [in the park] during rains, it [rainwater] would fill up [our homes] and [the roof would] break". In fact, many residents from the lower reaches of the park's peripheries recollected how the dreaded sewage would flow all year long, like a river.

An unusually severe monsoon in 2005 brought nearly 37 inches of torrential rain to Mumbai in a single day, causing that river of sewage to flood several homes. If freedom from the drudgery entailed in protecting one's residence from seasonal rains dominated the conversations among some, to other mostly young adult women, these rains were remembered for sullying their clothes and making everything around them "look really dirty". The park slums had no systematic drainage or solid waste disposal facilities other than several hyperlocal drainage lines and solid waste disposal systems set up by select *chaalis* described earlier. As a result, sewage meandered from the steep upper reaches in the hills and pooled into a de facto river that flowed on the park's periphery.

If the park's topography and weather conditions were seen as an occasional or even regular nuisance by some mothers, then for many of the young adult women who'd lived their formative years in the park, it was a source of minor discomfort compared to the positive space it represented, where they had played within nature alone and with friends. Dhruti, 21, and Supriya, 23, recalled the park environment in a group discussion involving five other women. In a different discussion group, 18-year-old Leela could scarcely contain her nostalgia when she talked about her childhood years in the slum, producing smiles from the 10 other women in her group.

DHRUTI: It used to be very hot there. When the electricity was cut off, it used to be very hot.

SUPRIYA: Yes, it would be very sunny there, you see. Lots of sunshine, sunshine, sunshine, sunshine.

DHRUTI: We used to play there a lot in the afternoon time. When mothers and others would sleep, we [friends] used to make a swing on a tree by my best friend's house. We would fetch water from my home, get some *masalas* [spices] from hers, rice from hers, lentils and tomatoes from hers—we used to all get together and eat. It used to be a mess and sometimes the food would get burnt and we would eat the burnt-up food!

LEELA: Where my house was, over there, there was a tree nearby and in front, water would flow, there would be breeze, I would take in a lot of cool air. It would feel very good over there and I had a friend and she would call me to play. If I didn't go, she would pull my cheeks and drag me. She would ask me why I didn't come. I miss sitting together and studying. Tying a rope across two trees and swinging. We miss that a lot. Climbing and jumping on trees like a monkey. Sleeping on trees, going to someone's home and troubling them. Going and eating in someone else's home. We would have a lot of fun.

Recreational and environmental preferences, many scholars note, originate in childhood (Bixler, Floyd, & Mayes, 2002; Chawla, 1998). The recollections of Dhruti and Leela demonstrate the complex combination of meaningful experiences and learning about one's natural environment (including feeling concern for it and acting to conserve it) derived from outdoor play. As young girls, they manipulated objects, climbed, and played alone and with each other in nature. Wilson (1986) refers to children's love of and positive affiliation with nature as *biophilia.* The area around their homes in the slum offered unlimited opportunities for exploration.

Not all the women in this research shared this *biophilia*, however. In fact, for most other women, those who had not spent their childhood in the park, the park emerged as a veritable battleground between the clashing agendas of "brown" (housing) and "green" (forest preservation) advocates and not a place of refuge. The most notable of these clashes came in the form of the High Court's order of 1997 (in conjunction with the 1995 order, namely *BEAG & Others v. A.R. Bharati, Deputy Conservator of Forests & Others*) approving immediate demolition of the homes of those who settled in the park after 1995 or who could not provide proof of residence. Some individual slum residents and their *chaalis*—with support from various entities including social movements, NGOs, or political parties—contested the court's orders based, among other issues, on property titles and the choice of relocation. I address the details of the court order of demolitions and some key contestations in more detail in Chapter 3. Here I highlight the travails of a group of park residents whose determination to remain in the park clashed with "green" advocates.

These determined park residents were the *adivasis* (the tribal/indigenous groups) who resided well within the park's boundaries. There, in tribal hamlets locally referred to as *padas*, residents grazed cattle, gathered firewood and forest products, and cultivated rice paddies on tiny parcels of land. One such *adivasi* filed a petition (with support from a social movement organization with the mission to uplift park tribes) in 2000 claiming that his tribe of *Warlis* had lived in the park for the past 500 years along with 2,500 such tribal families with domicile. Sapte, the *adivasi* petitioner, described himself and other tribal families as neither slum dwellers nor encroachers, but as "the natural allies of the forest and not its enemies" (*Manik Rama Sapte & Another v. State of Maharashtra & Another*, 2003, p. 1). The High Court's response to the petition, issued in 2003, acknowledged that *adivasis,* unlike "slum dwellers, unauthorised occupants and trespassers", were "wedded to [the] forest and they preserve, protest and propagate [the] forest", but judged the petitioners' assertion of 2,500 such families to be "falsified" and a "tall claim" (*Manik Rama Sapte & Another v. State of Maharashtra & Another*, 2003, p. 3). In the court's analysis, no more than 260 such families lived there and they had no more legal right over the forestland than other slum dwellers required to meet the requirements for eligibility and relocation.[12]

A handful of the park's *adivasis* did secure resettlement in Sangharsh Nagar. Fifty-year-old Sita moved there from the tribal hamlet of Chinchpada located within the park. She had come to Mumbai as a 15-year-old bride and recollected her life in the hamlet:

> There used to be snakes in the jungle. In the rains, there used to be tigers that came by our homes. Tiger, tiger … those also used to come by our home. Many tribal children were taken away, eaten. [There were no tigers roaming the jungles adjoining the slums, but participants always referred to the attacking animals as '*sher*' (tiger), not '*cheetah*' (leopard).]

Many of the reported animal attacks occurred in these tribal hamlets or in homes immediately adjacent to the park[13]. One such *chaali* was part of Appapada where Shruti, a 50-year-old migrant from the eastern state of Bengal had lived since migrating to Mumbai as a bride at 19. Her home was on a hillock adjacent to the park's southwestern boundaries. Meenal, 51, had been in Mumbai since age 2. She lived atop a hill in Damu Nagar, a 40-minute walk north of Appapada. The two women related dramatic, implausible-sounding tales of their encounters with wildlife in the urban park:

SHRUTI: There was a tiger. There was a jungle.

MEENAL: It caught me one day. Look here, I have a mark from its nails.

AUTHOR: A *tiger* caught you? [I was confused since the marks, on her right arm, looked nothing like bite marks.]

MEENAL: Yes, early in the morning at 5:00 a.m. I used to go to fill water. Yes, there was an attack one time.

SHRUTI: Only we folks know how we lived. Only those who have lived in the slum would know. It [the leopard] has carried many children away. A scorpion bit, bit in the hand. You know scorpion, right? Yes, it bit. After that, the way it is that I didn't get hurt so much because it caught me this way [gestures where it bit her].

MEENAL: The forest guard would take a plate and beat a plate and would walk around [sounding a leopard alert].

Women's attitudes toward the environment were a function of the location of their slum home and their age. Younger inhabitants who had spent all their childhood in the park had the opportunity to nurture their *biophilia*, an experience not as available to those who'd grown up amidst the city where modern society dominated nature. That tree, that well, and that stream (see Leela's words quoted previously) were significant objects symbolizing freedom and a carefree childhood. Such affective references are essential for the construction of ecological knowledge in urban residents. For women who had migrated from the rural hinterlands or from comparable areas elsewhere in the country, recollections such as the park's clean, unpolluted air and darker nights (when they could "safely" head out to relieve themselves in the open air) were bittersweet reminders of a life they'd once lived in the "native village" (the villages they'd left behind to move to Mumbai).

Although most writers cite Sanjay Gandhi National Park as a prototype of fierce conflicts between "green" and "brown" agendas, I found that the women, at least in retrospect, acknowledged and appreciated both the perils and the pleasures of life there. Eleven women who took part in a spirited focus-group discussion about the highs and lows of life in the slums shared the feeling that Gomati, a 50-year-old former resident of Kranti Nagar slum on the park's southwestern border, expressed to the group: *But whatever it [life in the park] was, it was peaceful.*

The close relationships to and cognizance of nature and their surroundings that women expressed indicated a respect and appreciation for nature, while still recognizing its power to potentially overwhelm them.

Toilet: Public and Private

Most of us reading this take indoor toilets for granted as places where we can "go in peace". I had assumed that Gomati and all the others who'd moved from the park slums would be overjoyed with the new convenience of an apartment with a toilet en-suite. While most did in fact welcome this amenity, it also provoked some intriguing anomalies. As a former student from Russia once told me, "the past has become much more unpredictable than the future". I had assumed that the relocated women would express a sense of relief with having a toilet in the privacy of their homes. Such was the case of 50-year-old Farida who had a witty take on her daily treks to her *chaali's* toilet where members had keys giving them access to a row of three adjoining locked latrines. The toilets were managed by a committee of four male residents who collected money for their upkeep as well as monthly fees for streetlights, garbage collection, and other amenities. She remembered the toilets had been built by state's housing authority, the Maharashtra Housing and Area Development Authority (MHADA)[14], a few years after she'd migrated from UP with her husband during the late 1970s. The couple started their married life in the Kranti Nagar slum, but her husband soon abandoned the family and Farida found work as a casual laborer at a company that made metal picture frames in the neighboring Appapada slum. When I interviewed her at home in Sangharsh Nagar in 2012, she was the sole support for herself and her newly married son and daughter-in-law who lived with her. Her blunt account about the benefits of her new en-suite toilet made us all laugh:

> I would go to the bathroom outside. I had to give a rent, 100 [INR] a month there [her member's fee to the *chaali* committee formed for maintenance]. I had to go out, stand in a line. Over here, there is comfort with the toilet. If I have the urge, then I can go and sit. Over there, you have to stand in a line to go to the toilet. Who knows when it will come out and until then you have to keep it inside. And goodness, you should have seen the long, long line during the rainy months. I am telling you about the comfort. I am telling you that I have this comfort now.

Others who were thankful for the privacy of their en-suite toilets were women from the park's upper reaches. These were locations where constructing group toilets was unaffordable or impractical and who most frequently referred to the lack of toilets as a bane of their past lives. It took their move to the resettlement site for women to recognize the gulf of amenities that had separated park residents with and without the benefits of *chaalis*. Those without perceived themselves as having "suffered" more, which I address in the concluding section of this chapter. The dialogue below illustrates the divide separating more and less privileged slum residents:

SHRUTI: Water, toilet. It was a lot of trouble. I had to take on a lot of difficulty.

RASMI[15]: The water, if the water is far, then we could at least go and fetch it. We used to finish our cooking and then together, we would go and fetch water together. But toilets are really very important for ladies.

SHRUTI: We had to go to a jungle to relieve ourselves.
GOMATI: Where we went, snakes and others would come.
AUTHOR: But I have seen toilets in each *chaali*.
RASMI: No, you saw it in the *chaali*. Not in the *zopadpattis*! [She is saying that I am confusing *zopadpattis* with *chaalis* and that the difference between the two is important.] For those that lived in the hills [in *zopadpattis*], they have gotten it good here [at Sangharsh Nagar].

Pooja, the young widow with two teenaged girls, remembered the dread she'd felt when she headed into the forest at night to relieve herself:

> My girls were very small when we were in the park. I would think about what would happen to my girls. When we would go to the bathroom in the jungles, then strange, very strange men without any purpose would come and sit. I would be so scared for my girls. My girls are at home, what would happen? That kind of fear does not exist here.

In another discussion, 61-year-old Fareesa who was born in Mumbai and had lived in the Kranti Nagar slum since the early 1980s, recalled how she'd use the jungle at night:

FAREESA: We'd go in the dark so men wouldn't see. We'd go together.

Like Fareesa and her friends, it was fairly common to hear participants recollect heading into the jungle in groups at designated, pre-arranged times such as 4:00 a.m. or 5:00 a.m. or after sunset. But to my surprise, some women missed the "public aspect" of their toilet routines in the slum. Sudha, 45, talked about the common toilets of her *chaali* in Appapada as a time- and money-saver:

> Over here [in Sangharsh Nagar], no, we need more water. You know what it is? There is a bathroom in the house, a toilet. So the toilet takes up a lot of water. Now we have to wash this, wash that. Clothes, dishes. That is why.

Sudha had spent all her previous married life in Appapada where her particular *chaali* in the lower reaches of the hillock had had a community toilet block built by the municipality. In 2004, the poorly constructed and ill-maintained toilet block was replaced under the World Bank–funded Slum Sanitation Project.[16] Following the new-and-improved construction, a caretaker lived in a room above the block to maintain the toilets. Some 300 households from nearly three dozen adjacent *chaalis* contributed INR 30 per month for his work. Toilet blocks of various quality and cleanliness were common in the lower elevations of the park's slums.[17] Younger women, including some with a functioning toilet in their *chaalis*, admitted they had preferred going in the open to standing in line to use a rickety *chaali* toilet. They frequently mentioned the positive associations they had enjoyed on these trips, including walking and chatting with friends, choosing what bush to squat behind, breathing in the night air (called "A/C air!" by one woman), and gazing at the stars.

Where women relieved themselves, whether behind bushes in the forest or at the *chaali* toilets, were spaces both cherished for the giggles and chit-chat they called to mind and dreaded for the lack of privacy and comfort they also represented. One does not have to live in a slum to imagine the potential sanitation and contamination problems that untreated, unmanaged human waste can bring. The flooding that followed heavy monsoon rains could send untreated waste running down the hills and into homes. Yet, in trying to isolate what specifically prompted women's positive memories of their experiences with or without toilets in their previous slum lives, I was unable to separate the physical conditions from the emotional or psychological associations in their accounts. The companionship factor appears to have trumped memories of fear and general discomfort.

Conclusions

The women's reminiscences are not of course facts of slum life. In their exchanges of small (but by no means trivial) details and stories, they searched for commonalities and differences in sharing what they considered important markers of a life once lived. Their recollections, of pleasures or horrors, conveniences or nuisances, are likely to fade in significance and be supplanted as time passes. Their stories were colored by the questions I asked them and the circumstances under which they related them. But despite the impermanent significance of the "vibrant matter" from their past—be it conditions of shelter, water supply, toilets, or nature—they were matters that women invoked both collectively and individually in conversations. While the specifics surrounding these memories may become less significant, they offer clear and important indications of what elements in these "core stories" women valued about their lives in the slums and nostalgically missed since moving away (Sandercock, 2003, p. 15). From the perspective of urban planners and designers, they offer practical insight into how multiple women are likely to respond to new housing alternatives.

For the majority of participating women, "community" spaces featured prominently in their core stories. These spaces recalled such things as the open doors to their homes in the slum, the common water tap or well in their *chaali*, the municipal water standpost located downhill from their slum, or the shrubbery that served as de facto toilets. The community networking and mingling that such spaces-within-spaces made possible had created a craving for gathering places, which any future habitation must possess to be considered livable by its inhabitants. Of course, who inhabited these places also mattered. Many of these women had grown familiar with their neighbors over the years, had socialized with them, especially with those who had shared their paved or unpaved alleyway. Neighbors had formed groups around issues like paving, lighting, water networks, and sewer installations. Although perhaps over-idealizing their experiences in retrospect, the longing for a "lost community" that the women expressed post-relocation offers an interesting insight into their sense of segregation and marginalization, particularly those who had come from better-networked slum settlements. (I address that aspect in Chapters 4 and 5.) The networks created in the *chaalis* had helped generate the physical infrastructure, "the vibrant matter", and, in particular, the community that women cherished. This had generated ad hoc groupings of women who fetched well water in their *chaali*, watched television together, and celebrated religious festivals as a group. Whenever expressing some version of "I miss all those who lived next to us", "I miss my friends", "I miss filling water from the well", or "If someone else comes [interrupting friends drawing well water], then we fight to shoo them away", women were referencing a past they considered preferable or in contrast to present circumstances. Not all women shared these sentiments, particularly those who had had to leave their settlements to earn a living or those struggling to make ends meet or with absent or unsatisfying husbands. Time spent standing in lines to use the toilet or collect water was time taken away from making money.

The connectedness that seemed to prevail among women in the *chaalis* was also a salient memory of those from the infrastructure-poorer *zopadpattis*. Long treks to fetch water or trips to the jungles in early morning hours or pitch-dark night were rarely done alone. Ad hoc groupings among women, although not institutionalized like the *chaalis* committees, became increasingly significant sources of safety and security when basic amenities were absent or the quality poor. In these settlements and among these women the emphasis was physical conditions rather than togetherness with others, which engendered different images of life in the park slums. Although they cited similar "vibrant matter" in conversation, in their case the attachments were less positive—leaking roofs, steep and rocky slopes, reptiles and rodents, and raw sewage. After relocation, some women perceived this less positive "vibrant matter" as markers that separated them from those with easier access to water and additional amenities. For women who had lived with few amenities in the past, high-rise living with its physical amenities could arguably be an easier adjustment than it was for those already accustomed to those benefits. Their perceptions notwithstanding, women who had relocated from the *chaalis* were relatively more privileged than those who had never had regular access to amenities, namely the residents of the *zopadpattis* as well as its *adivasis*.

Directing our focus to the constitution of park residents and the park's topography—including the elevation of the slum settlements, the demographic characteristics, and the job locations of its adult female residents—prompts certain questions: How do these dissimilarities among the park's residents influence collective life in their new, legal housing at the resettlement site? To what degree does the site, the design of the self-contained apartments, and the attendant costs of the new amenities satisfy their socializing, networking, and community needs? To address these questions, the next chapter moves a step closer into the lives of these women within the resettlement site. The slum demolitions were historical events that the women I spoke to rarely mentioned unless asked. In retrospect, the women understood the demolitions as a threat that they faced collectively. Demolitions brought a large group of dissimilar park slums under the singular wrath of a city determined to eliminate nearly every "vibrant matter" that had defined their residential lives. Demolitions severed children from their schools, parents and grandparents from their livelihoods, and dislocated all 120 participants from a park they called home. Chapter 3 examines how these women resolved their relationship with the city that struggled to accommodate them.

Notes

1 The name change from Bombay to Mumbai took place in 1995 after the Hindu nationalist party, the Shiv Sena, won the state elections and presided over a coalition that took control of the state assembly. The Shiv Sena had long advocated for a name change on grounds that "Bombay" represented the unwelcome legacy of Portuguese and then British colonial rule and should be renamed after the city's patron deity, the Mumbadevi (Hansen, 2001, p. 1). It realized its agenda in November 1995 when all the federal and state agencies, businesses, and the media were required to make the change. That stated, several of the research participants continue to refer to the city as Bombay.

2 To facilitate urban governance and planning, the large and ever-expanding urban region of Mumbai is divided into two zones: Greater Mumbai and the Mumbai Metropolitan Region. Greater Mumbai comprises the island city and suburbs and is considered the core of the Mumbai Metropolitan Region (MMR). The municipal authority, the Municipal Corporation of Greater Mumbai (MCGM), is responsible for governing Greater Mumbai. Per the 2011 census, Greater Mumbai was home to 12.44 million people ("Census", 2011). The Mumbai Metropolitan Region consists of Greater Mumbai plus seven other municipalities, nine municipal councils, and several thousand villages. MMR has a total population of 18.39 million and is governed by the Mumbai Metropolitan and Regional Development Authority (MMRDA). The park is spread over both the Greater Mumbai and the MMR and its protected forest cover is managed by the state government, the Maharashtra Forest Department.

3 The de-industrialization of Mumbai is attributed to a number of factors, many of which resemble the changes unfolding in cities such as London, Detroit, and Mexico City. These include the growing obsolescence of Mumbai's textile mills, which had transitioned to using high-tech technologies worldwide. At the same time, mill owners refused to negotiate with worker unions over better wages and improved living and working conditions on grounds that cheaper and less militant labor could be mobilized if mills moved from the city center to peripheral areas and smaller towns in the state (a move that did indeed materialize). All of this resulted in a sea change in the city's economic landscape,

transitioning it from a manufacturing hub to a service-based economy rife with jobs in banks and other financial institutions, domestic service, restaurants and hotels, the film industry, educational institutions, street hawking, and real-estate development.

4 Econet is an NGO that focuses on forestry and environmental policy-related issues and is headquartered in Pune, the second largest city after Mumbai in the state of Maharashtra ("Welcome to Econet", 2018).

5 The households that moved in phase one of the two-phase relocation process to Sangharsh Nagar were former residents of these eight settlements.

6 INR is short for Indian Rupees and written also as Rupees and abbreviated Rs. As of January 19, 2018 the exchange rate was USD $1 = INR 63.83.

7 The Scheduled Caste (SC) is a phrase first coined in 1935 when the British listed the lowest-ranked Hindu castes of untouchables in a schedule appended to the Government of India Act for the provision of employment and educational assistance. Since adoption of Indian constitution in 1950, Scheduled Caste is similarly a phrase utilized as a legal designation for the historically disadvantaged castes. It is used to manage positive discrimination for recruitment and promotion in government jobs, admission to higher-education institutions and to extend financial assistance in a variety of development and welfare programs.

8 Women from the northern Indian states of Uttar Pradesh (U.P.) and Bihar are known to have far more restrictions on their mobility than do migrants from other states or those from within Maharashtra. These restrictions on mobility can, at least in part, be attributed to fears for their safety and are imposed by the husbands and/or other senior members of the household. For a more detailed discussion on the reasons attributed to the north-south differences in female autonomy in India, read Dyson and Moore (1983); Basu (1992); Jeejeebhoy and Sathar (2001); and Miller (1981).

9 These slums were located in the southwestern fringe of the park. Damu Nagar was the farthest north of the three, Gautam Nagar was immediately south of it, and a slum known as Mathangadh was situated some distance away in the southwestern-most corner of the park's periphery.

10 Even when not officially recognized as a slum, it was common for groups of slum residents in the park to find ways and means to get the rules of the Municipal Corporation to work in their favor. This worked in neighborhoods with the financial means and stronger networks among its residents.

11 Regularization of slums was a process that commenced in Mumbai in 1976 to protect the rights of slum dwellers to alternate housing. They earned this right through a fairly haphazard census conducted in a mere 24 hours on January 4, 1976 with the help of 7,000 enumerators who were also residents of slums on land owned by the Municipal Corporation, the state's housing board, and the state government. Each slum household was issued an identity card, called a photopass, which they could use to verify their right to alternate housing should their land be needed for a public purpose. Their homes were numbered and circulars issued to concerned officials to keep an eye for (and when reported, to demolish) any new structure built, enlarged, or altered. The 4th of January 4, 1976 thus became the first "cut-off date" for protection against demolition without alternate accommodation. This date has since extended to 1980, 1985, 1990, and 1995. According to the policy at the time of data collection for this book, the cut-off date was January 1, 1995. That stated, project-specific exceptions were made for relocation to Sangharsh Nagar (i.e. those with documentation proving residence on or before January 1, 2000, were eligible for relocation to Sangharsh Nagar resettlement site).

12 My conversations with tribal residents during visits in 2002–2003 and in 2012 revealed that over time, especially in the 2000s, these hamlets had become

home to a heterogeneous mix of *adivasi* and non-*adivasi* settlers. The various *adivasi* groups spoke conversational Marathi and *Bombaiyya* Hindi (Mumbai's slang version of Hindi). The girls and women wore contemporary Indian frocks, skirts, *salwar-kameez*, and sarees, and the men wore the usual shirts, pants, and *lungis*. Their seeming assimilation contradicted legal claims of the types made by Sapte requesting that they "not be disturbed from the National Park, Borivli and their possession and occupation at the same place be regularized by granting and extending all facilities an amenities" (*Manik Rama Sapte & Another v. State of Maharashtra & Another*, 2003, p. 2). For more details, on the case of the *adivasis*, see Sen and Pattnaik (2016) and Elison (2010).

13 The Guardian's (Soumya, 2014) U.S. edition identified 176 leopard attacks on humans between 1991 and 2013. Some sources blamed the attacks on slum encroachments, linking the attacks to the nighttime defecation in the open by slum residents living on the park's peripheries (Bhale, Bhatti, & Mayes, n.d., p. 89).

14 These were toilets constructed by MHADA and the city's Municipal Corporation through grants made out of the discretionary funds of state and local elected officials and some times by funds allocated to the state by the central government. They were constructed across the city's slums since the 1970s and were free of cost to the slum dwellers. They were "a populist measure for mobilizing votes by political parties in power" and were notorious for overuse, poor maintenance, and perpetual state of disrepair (Sharma & Bhide, 2005, p. 1785).

15 Rasmi was a 40-year-old resident of Sangharsh Nagar, who had migrated to Mumbai in 1994 soon after her marriage. She had lived in Damu Nagar, and at the time she participated in this discussion, had two sons, ages 17 and 12, and an 18-year-old daughter.

16 The World Bank, as part of its condition for releasing the funds for the Slum Sanitation Program, required the involvement of NGOs and community-based organizations in aspects such as the selection of households willing to participate in the program, the training of participants in toilet maintenance and sanitary practices and the handing over of completed blocks to users. Sudha did not recollect the name of the NGO that managed her toilet's construction, but suffice to state here that her toilet block, or at least her recollection of it, was an exception. See Sharma and Bhide (2005) for an assessment of the Slum Sanitation Program.

17 I have used such toilet blocks in my visits to the park over the years. I found some of them to be exceptionally well kept mostly because they were managed by a network of homes in the settlements. Some such networks were formally registered organizations that employed cleaners, and some were informal groups that hired their own cleaning staff. However, many were downright revolting but used out of sheer necessity.

References

Basu, A. M. (1992). The status of women and the quality of life among the poor. *Cambridge Journal of Economics*, 16(3), 249–267.

Becker, C. (1932). Everyman his own historian. *The American Historical Review*, 37(2), 221–236.

Bennett, J. (2010). *Vibrant matter: A political ecology of things*. Durham, NC: Duke University Press.

Bhale, P., Bhatti, I. & Mayes, R. (2017). *Sanjay Gandhi National Park (SGNP): A concise report*. doi:10.13140/RG.2.2.14953.49768.

Bixler, R. D., Floyd, M. F. & Hammitt, W. E. (2002). Environmental socialization: Quantitative tests of the childhood play hypothesis. *Environment and Behavior*, 34(6), 795–818.
Bombay Environmental Action Group & Others v. A. R. Bharati, Deputy Conservator of Forests & Others, Bom. C.R. 244 (High Court of Judicature at Bombay, 2004). Retrieved from http://cat.org.in/wp-content/uploads/2016/07/WP-305-of-1995-15.09.2003-Encroachments-in-SGNP.pdf.
Chawla, L. (1998). Significant life experiences revisited: A review of research on sources of environmental sensitivity. *The Journal of Environmental Education*, 29 (3), 11–21.
Clothey, F. W. (2006). *Ritualizing on the boundaries: Continuity and innovation in the Tamil diaspora*. Columbia, SC: University of South Carolina Press.
D'Monte, D. (2002). *Ripping the fabric: The decline of Mumbai and its mills*. New Dehli: Oxford University Press.
Das, S. K. (1988). The chawl in Bombay. *Architecture Plus Design*, 4(2), 25.
Driver, P. (1996). Parenthesis on parks. In K. Worpole (Ed.), *Here comes the sun: Architecture in the public space in twentieth-century European culture* (p. 9). Islington: Reaktion Books.
Dyson, T. & Moore, M. (1983). On kinship structure, female autonomy, and demographic behavior in India. *Population and Development Review*, 9(1), 35–60.
Elison, W. (2010). "Bonafide tribals": Religion and recognition among Denisens of Mumbai's forest frontier. *Journal for the Study of Religion, Nature & Culture*, 4 (2), 191–212.
Halbwachs, M. (1992). *On collective memory*. Chicago, IL: University of Chicago Press.
Hansen, T. B. (2001). *Wages of violence: Naming and identity in postcolonial Bombay*. Princeton, NJ: Princeton University Press.
Indian People's Human Rights Commission. (2000). *Crushed homes, lost lives: The story of the demolitions in the Sanjay Gandhi National Park*. Mumbai: P.A. Sebastian. Retrieved from www.unipune.ac.in/snc/cssh/HumanRights/08%20STATE%20AND%20HOUSING/10.pdf.
Jejeebhoy, S. J. & Sathar, Z. A. (2001). Women's autonomy in India and Pakistan: The influence of religion and region. *Population and Development Review*, 27(4), 687–712.
Manik Rama Sapte & Another v. State of Maharashtra & Another, Writ Petition No. 925 (Bombay High Court, 2003). Retrieved from www.casemine.com/judgement/in/5767b108e691cb22da6d139f#.
Miller, B. D. (1981). *The endangered sex*. Ithaca, NY: Cornell University Press.
Mumbai (Greater Mumbai) Metropolitan. (2015). *Census 2011*. Retrieved from www.census2011.co.in/census/metropolitan/305-mumbai.html.
Padovani, F. (2016). *Development-induced displacement in India and China: A comparative look at the burdens of growth*. Lanham, MD: Rowman & Littlefield.
Sandercock, L. (2003). Out of the closet: The importance of stories and storytelling in planning practice. *Planning Theory & Practice*, 4(1), 11–28.
Sangharsh Nagar—slum rehab, Chandivali, Mumbai. (2017). P. K. Das & Associates. Retrieved from www.pkdas.com/sangharsh-nagar-slum-rehab-chandivali-mumbai-project-11-1-35.php.

Sanjay Gandhi National Park. (2017). *Lonely planet*. Retrieved from www.lonelyplanet.com/india/mumbai/attractions/sanjay-gandhi-national-park/a/poi-sig/1149073/356405.

Sen, A. & Pattanaik, S. (2016). Politics of biodiversity conservation and socio ecological conflicts in a city: The case of Sanjay Gandhi National Park, Mumbai. *Journal of Agricultural and Environmental Ethics*, 29(2), 305–326.

Sharma, R. N. & Bhide, A. (2005). World Bank funded slum sanitation programme in Mumbai: Participatory approach and lessons learnt. *Economic and Political Weekly*, 40(17), 1784–1789.

Soumya, E. (2014, November 26). The leopards of Mumbai: Life and death among the city's "living ghosts". *The Guardian*. Retrieved from www.theguardian.com/cities/2014/nov/26/leopards-mumbai-life-death-living-ghosts-sgnp.

Vaquier, D. (2010). *The impact of slum resettlement on urban integration in Mumbai: The case of the Chandivali Project* (Occasional Paper No. 26). New Dehli: The French Research Institutes in India Centre for Social Sciences and Humanities. Retrieved from www.mumbaidp24seven.in/reference/Document11822010569_565371E_02.pdf.

Welcome to Econet. (2018). *Econet India*. Retrieved from http://econetindia.org/.

Whitehead, J. (2008). Rent gaps, revanchism and regimes of accumulation in Mumbai. *Anthropologica*, 50(2), 269–282.

Wilson, E. O. (1986). *Biophilia*. Cambridge, MA: Harvard University Press.

Zérah, M. H. (2007). Conflict between green space preservation and housing needs: The case of the Sanjay Gandhi National Park in Mumbai. *Cities*, 24(2), 122–132.

3 Deliberation Over Legitimate Benefactors in a Neoliberal Bazaar

Massey (1994) argues that "we should question any characterization of place which is singular, essentialist, which relies on a view of there having been one past of this place [and] one story to tell" (p. 114). The park, as described in Chapter 2 and reasoned by Massey (1994), was indeed a space emplaced differently by different women. Different senses of place among different women were based on the particular relationships and the geographical difference forged through daily practices. In other words, each slum had its own identity with which its women formed a relationship. What happens when the long-emplaced space is threatened with demolition supported by powerful interest groups? In this chapter, I argue that the threat of and actual demolition of slum settlements as carried out in Mumbai's Sanjay Gandhi National Park—often portrayed as a process that accentuates "pauperisation" of the already poor (Dupont, 2008, p. 86), a "brutal" act done with needless force (Weinstein, 2013), the "most appalling of social injustices" (Slater, 2013, p. 384)—must also take into consideration the practices of women who make sense of the demolitions and its consequences on their lives and livelihoods.

In particular, the chapter finds that participating women made sense of the demolitions as an inevitable, even exploitable outcome of a city space undergoing reorganization. The demolitions had invited a bevy of players—city-based NGOs, government functionaries, international human rights groups, and political parties—each laying claims to broker transactions between the slum dwellers and their "right to the city" (Lefebvre, 1905-/1996). For 10 years the park slum dwellers awaited resettlement while various stakeholders competed to portray themselves as the more legitimate guarantor of their right to legally recognized housing. Women admitted that they weathered this deluge of "saviors" by hedging their bets or by shifting their allegiances among the competing organizations and individuals.

Legitimacy is used here to refer to a woman's normative belief that institutions deserve trust and, like individuals, possess goals, styles, and intentions that are decent, wise, and have their recipients' best interests at heart. From 1997–2007, the subjects of this book oscillated among multiple competing sources vying for legitimacy and support within a new slum housing policy context. With authorization from the High Court, the state's legal apparatus, *environmentalists* alongside the *Forest Department* surveyed slum residents in an effort to convince them that their homes were illegal encroachments worthy of demolition; *the housing rights advocacy NGO* attempted to mobilize residents to fight the legal system until an acceptable resettlement site was found; the *state government* (also on orders of the High Court) sought their consent to resettle in government-issued plots at a distant site; various *political parties* urged them to reject relocation and insisted on construction of apartment housing in the park's fringe areas; and, finally, a collaboration between a *private developer, the state government,* and the same *housing rights advocacy NGO* endeavored to develop a housing alternative to resettle former park-slum dwellers willing to pay a fee to the Forest Department and agree to relocate to their proposed high-rise apartment development.

Amidst the arrival of several, often-competing saviors on park terrain vying for their favor, the very "voices" of residents whose homes and livelihoods were in jeopardy were not heard. All the women I spoke to admitted to being voiceless spectators in decisions regarding the location, size, set-up, and design of their future homes. Among themselves, however, they were far from silent or passive bystanders. In this chapter, I present and describe the opportunistic claim-making that women used to safeguard their individual interests amidst a volatile, uncertain *bazaar* of slum redevelopment claims. This individual claim-making created distinctions as perceived by its female residents and highlights how participating women came to consider themselves, and others like them, more deserving than some others of their first legally recognized homes in Mumbai.

Following an overview of the political–economic context surrounding the park's slum housing in the 1980s and the 1990s, I present, in their own voices, the recollections of the women who were at the receiving end of the changing housing-policy context. Their experiences over the 10-year resettlement waiting period generated a series of judgments about deservingness among the women themselves. Distinctions arose out of the perceptions of the hardships that the displaced residents had endured and witnessed before their move to the resettlement site; from the presence or lack of connections they each had with NGOs and others with a stake in their resettlement; and from the timing of their resettlement (early versus later occupants). The expression of these distinctions represent the years they had spent reorganizing their lives and livelihoods, often without hope of being heard.

This period of limbo (which in many other documented cases of slum evictions is permanent, not temporary) is rarely problematized as a crucial time influencing the psychological as well as economic hardships of its residents. I consider this period between insecure and secure homeownership a variable that assumes disparate states among those displaced rather than as an indeterminate and general condition in which everyone who qualified for legal tenure was willing and able to afford the costs of gestation and lay claim to their new lives at the resettlement site. To understand a change in housing conditions, from illegal to legal or from insecure to secure home ownership, it is important to consider the criteria the women evoked as important in determining whether they and others deserved or were entitled to secure homeownership.

A Bazaar of Players and Strategies: Old Saviors in New Garb

During the late 1980s and early 1990s, the housing-policy environment governing the park slums shifted significantly. The changes had their roots in the new policy thrust advocated by the World Bank and supported by the United Nations Centre for Human Settlements (World Bank, 1993; UNCHS–Habitat, 1991). Both encouraged the governments of developing countries to withdraw from their traditional role as providers of public housing and become "enablers" who supported and facilitated the provision of housing through the private, for-profit sector (World Bank, 1993). To accommodate market delivery of housing, this strategy recommended the removal of demand- and supply-side barriers to participation, maintaining that markets could be made to work for all including those residing in slums and squatter settlements (Pugh, 1994, p. 358; World Bank, 1993, p. 2).

The 1980s also witnessed the emergence of "democratization" as a key theme in development discourse worldwide (Clark, 1991; United Nations Development Programme, 2002; Crook & Manor, 2000). Building on this discourse, the enabling strategy encouraged the involvement of different stakeholders—including NGOs, community-based organizations, political parties, for-profit players, and government agencies—as the way to realize the strategic goal of reducing the "institutional monopoly of government over the lives of the urban poor" (Sanyal & Mukhija, 2001, p. 2043). As early as 1991, most countries had begun integrating enabling strategy goals into their respective national housing policies (UNCHS–Habitat, 1991, pp. 7–8). India's national housing policy of 1994 encouraged private sector participation and defined the government's role in housing as removing legal and regulatory constraints toward the expansion of housing supply and increasing the development of infrastructure. The policy promoted greater access to housing and other basic services (such as water and sanitation) for the poor and mobilized additional resources through public–private partnerships (Government of India, 1994).

In keeping with global development trends, the ruling Congress Party of Maharashtra inaugurated the Slum Redevelopment Scheme (SRD) for the Greater Mumbai region in March 1991. The program deviated considerably from earlier schemes by expressly seeking private developers who could provide on-site housing to slum residents while profiting from the sale of extra, allowable floor space at market rates. Slum dwellers who formed cooperative housing societies could join builders to promote and develop slum rehousing provided the slum resident's household head was a registered voter in the 1985 state electoral rolls and the family contributed INR 15,000 (i.e. USD $23.49 per the exchange rate on January 19, 2018). These eligible slum families could then qualify for a 180-square-foot (16.75 square meters) apartment home. The SRD offered an attractive new incentive in the form of an expanded total floor area ratio (FAR) of up to 2.5[1] for slum redevelopment. This allowed developers to earn a profit by building additional units to sell at commercial rates. But the potential profits were limited to 25 percent of the developers' investment in a given project.

The SRD was soon succeeded by the more ambitious Slum Rehabilitation Scheme (SRS). Preceding a new round of Maharashtra state elections in 1995, the opposition Shiv Sena Party and its ally, the Bharatiya Janata Party, launched a massive propaganda campaign promising "free" housing for slum dwellers. The opposition alliance won the elections and immediately put together a "high powered study group" to realize its campaign promise (Government of Maharashtra, 1997, p. 2). The group recommended the creation of a state-level housing program distinct in several key aspects from its SRD predecessor of 1991. Like the SRD, the SRS utilized slum land as a resource by offering FAR incentives for sale at commercial rates. Also as before, on-site FAR was restricted to 2.5. But unlike the SRD, the SRS took advantage of a booming Mumbai real-estate market and allowed developers unlimited profits on SRS investments. It also introduced transferable development rights (TDR), which permitted the transfer of any FAR greater than 2.5 elsewhere in the city. The scheme assured a 225-square-foot (20.9 square meters) home for each slum family listed on state electoral rolls taken on or before January 1, 1995. In December 1995, the state government amended its Slum Areas Improvement, Clearance and Redevelopment Act to create the Slum Rehabilitation Authority, or the SRA, a new state-level agency charged with sanctioning and monitoring all slum rehabilitation projects.

This flurry of developments in the slum housing–policy field in the early 1990s—spurred by a thriving real-estate market, a newly elected state government eager to fulfill its campaign pledge to provide "free" and legally recognized housing in slums and squatter settlements, and developers attracted to an ostensibly favorable policy environment—set the stage for considerable drama within Mumbai's housing sector. The metaphor of the *bazaar* vividly conjures up the swarm of saviors—builders, developers, and landowners—intent on outcompeting and overwhelming each other that arose within Mumbai's market-driven, neoliberal housing-policy environment in the early 1990s. Not every actor, however, was enthusiastic about these developments. That included Nivara, a Mumbai-based housing NGO. Although not a registered NGO[2], Nivara was a loosely structured federation of local organizations skilled at mobilizing slum and squatter dwellers and in using tactics of protests, mass demonstrations, and litigation to challenge state-led housing demolition and forced relocation proposals. Since its founding in the 1980s, Nivara interpreted the government's use of demolitions and relocations as a violation of the poor's right to safe, adequate, and secure residence in the city[3]. Through much of the 1990s, Nivara actively dissuaded slum dwellers from participating in the SRD and SRS programs, arguing that private developers were using the redevelopment of the slums to "sell off the commercial units, grab the proceeds, and make off leaving the slum-dwellers high and dry" (Singh & Das 1995, p. 2481). Nivara's skepticism attracted more media attention than similar NGOs largely because of its leaders, a who's who of the city's elite: Its president (1997–2013) was the popular Bollywood actor and member of Parliament, Shabana Azmi; the vice-president, P. K. Das, was a prominent Mumbai architect; and founding member and chief organizer Gurbir Singh worked as a journalist for a national daily. Others of its volunteer leaders were well-known Mumbai-based professionals, including a prominent social worker, a human rights lawyer, and a controversial documentary filmmaker.

But Nivara's highly visible stance against the state government would reverse dramatically in relation to the park slums. As described in the previous chapter, the Bombay Environmental Action Group backed by the state Forest Department petitioned the High Court to clear the park slums of all encroachments. The state housing policy had designated all park slum residents appearing on state electoral rolls by a certain date eligible for legal tenure at an alternate site[4]. The court ordered that all those found eligible would be relocated just outside the boundaries of the park within a stipulated time frame. Those determined ineligible were to have their homes demolished and their belongings confiscated. Nivara supported this relocation proposal on the grounds that it would cause the least displacement to residents. But Forest Department officials challenged the proposal, which was later rejected by the court. In July 1999, the High Court ordered those eligible for rehousing to be relocated to a site about 60 kilometers (about 37 miles) north of the park. This site was spread over five villages and divided into 10-by-15-foot plots. The land was to be allocated according to eligibility criteria set by the prevailing SRS program and the High Court. The criteria included (a) the listing of the head of household and the dwelling address on electoral rolls of 1995 or earlier; (b) the listing of all occupants of the household on the household's ration card, a document entitling holders to free or subsidized foodstuffs from fair-price shops; and (c) a receipt from the Forest Department confirming full payment of INR 7,000 (payable in installments by a deadline that the court repeatedly extended). The state argued that this fee was needed to cover the electricity, water, and other infrastructure installed at the resettlement site.

According to Nivara, an estimated 12,000 of the 33,000 eligible slum[5] families had paid the Forest Department the required INR 7,000 from July 1999 to late 2002, but less than a dozen families had relocated to the site situated 60 kilometers north of the park. Opposition centered not just on the distance but also on the open hostility of the host community who claimed they were entitled to "grazing land" on part of the site allocated for relocation. Park slum dwellers' hesitation to move to the designated site became a block to the demolitions until the holders accepted a relocation site. In my treks up the park hills, I saw many homes displaying a copy of their paid-up receipt outside their still-standing homes.

While the state government did its part in selecting a far-off relocation site for the park dwellers, the NGOs and political parties operating in the area stayed busy too. Nivara, the best-known NGO working in the slums in the southwestern portions of the park, unleashed its practiced protests and demonstrations and filed court petitions challenging the state's proposal to relocate slum residents. Nivara continued to argue that slum dwellers preferred in-situ rehabilitation because it interfered least with their lives and livelihoods. But Nivara's efforts were unable to halt a series of demolitions that began in May 1997 and continued in fits and starts into 2001. The seemingly unending conflict concerning the fate of the park slums took a new turn in November 2001 when the state housing minister invited Nivara to a meeting with a Mumbai-based private developer named Sumer Corporation (henceforth "Sumer") eager to develop 80 acres of land he owned to house slum dwellers. Under the SRS program, an owner of vacant, unencumbered land could construct dwellings for "project affected persons" (in this case the project was the "clearance" of park slums) and be compensated with transferable development rights both for land and construction. The land Sumer offered was in the Chandivali area about 10 kilometers southeast of the park—today's Sangharsh Nagar (see Map 3). At the time, it contained decrepit stone quarries and a slum housing several former quarry workers and their families. Surrounding it was a posh residential area of condominiums, penthouses, bungalows, and commercial complexes whose upmarket residents vehemently resisted the proposed rehabilitation project. They complained that blasting the quarry hills would generate noise and debris and would strain area roads.

The commotion surrounding the proposed relocation of park residents to Sangharsh Nagar had sparked activity among political leaders with electoral constituencies in the park slums. They began making their own promises to relocate slum dwellers and urged them to disregard Nivara and wait to get resettled closer to the park borders (see Ramanath, 2005, pp. 301–303 for details). Amidst all this maneuvering, I reentered Mumbai in 2002 to collect data for my doctoral study on the relations between NGOs and the government in slum and squatter housing. Accompanied by two Nivara volunteers, I first saw the park slums on a hot December morning in 2002. Five years of demolitions had left visible scarring on the landscape. I saw abandoned homes under lock and key, partial homes with a broken wall or a missing door, and many structures completely collapsed, with only bricks and stones marking their former location. Black or blue tarpaulin sheets held up by bamboo sticks or constructions of recycled bricks created makeshift dwellings. The residents still present were unsure of their housing futures. Representatives from the state government, Nivara, political party workers, journalists, photographers, and outsiders like me had all come bearing promises, threats, or information, listened to residents' tales, and then left. During my visits to the park from November 2002 to August 2003, I was invariably introduced to Nivara loyalists or to residents at least familiar with Nivara (it was Nivara volunteers/park residents who accompanied me around the hills of the park). It was in December 2007, six months after the first batch of families relocated to Sangharsh Nagar, that I independently became acquainted with the relocated slum residents. From August 2012 (until December 2016), I started to systematically record the memories of diverse women. The remainder of this chapter revisits the post-demolition years, from 1997 until relocation to Sangharsh Nagar in 2007 and later, captured in the words and phrases of the women who spoke to me. They shared their memories of those years with not only me but with each other from the vantage point of their new, legally tenured apartment homes in Sangharsh Nagar.

Perceived Degrees of Suffering

Eleven women had gathered in Nivara's training room in Sangharsh Nagar in November 2012, the seventh of 11 focus-group discussions I hosted that year. In the discussion that followed that afternoon, I became more familiar with Gomati, 50, a former resident of the Kranti Nagar slum on the park's southwestern border. She had migrated from Uttar Pradesh soon after her marriage in 1987. At the time of our discussion, she was living with her husband and four children who had come from a slum located within the disputed park boundaries. Also there for the discussion was Sharada, 45. She had migrated to Mumbai in 1983 from the Ratnagiri district of Maharashtra to find work and lived with her uncle's daughter initially. She soon married a construction laborer living in the Ambedkar Nagar slum of the park. The couple had been loyal to Nivara since the agency entered the park in the early 1990s. Another participant, Mumbai-born Suhana, was a 32-year-old widow with two boys and two girls, ages 8 to 15. They had lived in the Damu Nagar slum. We started out talking about life pre-relocation and the subject of demolitions did not come up until I raised it, using questions like "Was your home demolished [by the Forest Department]?" "How did you manage your household during and after demolitions?" It was in response to these questions that three women in the focus-group discussion compared how they experienced the demolitions in their respective slums:

GOMATI: They did not even let us take out our fan [ceiling fan]. They did not allow us to remove our dishes. They kicked us out. They would say,

'Show me proof'. We have given Rs, 7,000 in full, and showed them the proof. Then he [the officer in charge of the operation] said, 'Good, now yours will not be torn down'. But they had removed my wall. I had my younger daughter; I told them that my girl will die.

SHARADA: Were you in Damu Nagar?

GOMATI: No, no, in Kranti Nagar. Next to Appapada.

SHARADA: They did a lot more destruction over there [in Kranti Nagar]. They did not do as much on our side [in Ambedkar Nagar]. Where did they do it in Ambedkar Nagar [she asks this of the other members in her group, three of whom had come from the same slum]? Those folks that are by the temple, near Vageshwari Temple. You know, once you leave Nivara [its main office is a relatively short walk from the southernmost slum of the park], that side faced a lot [of demolition loss]. They [the demolition crews] took their goods, their dishes, and all the rest. But on our side …

AUTHOR: They picked it all up?

GOMATI: Yes, if on our side …

AUTHOR: They picked it up. You mean, they took it and left?

SHARADA: Yes, they took it.

GOMATI: Oh, they took it all. So many folks had kids. In Appapada, that lady was having a child, her medicines [were destroyed]. There were ladies police. 'It is my duty, you get out. It is our law and you are breaking it' [quoting the officer leading the demolition]. Whether you have a kid or anything. She was a Maharashtrian, poor thing, her child was hurting so much. In Appapada, they put on that gas, the gas that burns the eyes [tear gas], they let that out. There was a riot in Appapada [a demolition on November 11, 1997 that ended in a riot].

AUTHOR: They let out tear gas then?

GOMATI: Yes, the way they let it out. My younger son was three months old. Those folks, we folks were blinded. Where will the children go? Where would we folks go? We are very fortunate to be alive.

SUHANA: It is the women who were to deliver that suffered the most.

AUTHOR: Who?

SUHANA: The ones who were about to go into labor. They suffered the most. They would deliver right on the way.

GOMATI: So much, so much difficulty.

SUHANA: They would remove their sarees and do it [deliver] right there. [The woman in question, according to Nivara, delivered stillborn twins on November 8, 1997.]

SHARADA: The folks who are living in my area, where I lived, do you know, you know in our area, they did not do anything. They did not lift any of our goods. They did not break our bamboos; they just broke some of the homes. They did not take it. They did not. They did not fight with us. Our homes, no one raised a hand against them.

AUTHOR: Why did they not do it?

SHARADA: Most of us had settled down many, many years ago. We have lived there together for 18 to 20 years, you see. We lived on top and they started the demolitions from the bottom. By the time they came to our area, we knew what to do to stop them. I have worked for Nivara, you know, I have. I told everyone to get ready, called Nivara activists. They only touched homes that were not eligible.

Homes located on the park's lower elevations tended to be those with access to basic services like water, electricity, paved alleyways, and sanitation (an aspect detailed in Chapter 2). Because these homes with amenities were more easily accessed by foot, their owners had developed stronger ties to agencies such as Nivara and with political parties. They were able to mobilize timely resistance of the type that Sharada mentioned. Networks connecting the residents and external advocacy agencies were critical sources of information, including knowing when to gather proofs of residence, mobilizing assistance of their kith and kin in paying the INR 7,000 to the Forest Department, and learning how to give their consent to relocate to Nivara's recommended site in Chandivali. These were all critical steps in protecting one's home in the slum from demolitions and earning the right to alternate housing. Memories of the intensity and frequency of demolitions appeared far less severe to women like Sharada who were "in the know" about these steps. At the same time, however, women like Sakshi considered a move to the resettlement site, where each would be allocated a 225-square-foot home, a step down from their "big", "lovely" homes in the park. Fifty-year-old Sakshi was born and brought up in Mumbai and had moved to the park's Kranti Nagar slum 20 years prior to her move to Sangharsh Nagar in 2007:

SAKSHI: And our homes were so [incomplete sentence]. Where we lived, we had such lovely homes there. This [Sangharsh Nagar] is nothing. They were *pucca* [solid] homes. And before they tore it down, everything was inside. Toilet, taps, everything. In comparison, this is, this is nothing in comparison.

AUTHOR: It was a big home?

SAKSHI: Yes, it was a big home. It was big and, see, this is a *chaali*. If this is a *chaali*, then they broke this and what is here. What is at the back, still stands. And people are still living there. If you were to price those homes, those homes go for no less than 15 [INR 15,000]. Even after the demolitions, they go for a good price.

But memories of comparative comfort were not everyone's experience of life in the slum, including those who couldn't afford improvements to their homes and more recent park residents who lived closest to the site of a proposed boundary wall to separate the park from the city. Those living closest to the border also faced a demolition squad increasingly determined to clear land for construction of the boundary wall. Still incomplete as of December 2016, the wall was meant to prevent any further encroachments on parkland. The parts of Gautam Nagar slum located closest to the planned boundary were subjected to repeated demolitions. Deepali, aged 53 when I interviewed her in late December 2012, settled in Gautam Nagar with her husband and three daughters in 1993. She said her family's home was bulldozed as many as three times, far more than her new neighbor in Sangharsh Nagar, Sakshi, who had lived in the lower elevations of the park:

DEEPALI: These folks were beneath, right? They [Sakshi and her neighbors] did not feel it [repeated demolitions] as much. We were on top. They tore down ours so many, so many times.

AUTHOR: How many times?

DEEPALI: They broke it two to three times.

AUTHOR: You put it up again, they tore it down, and you put it up again?

DEEPALI: Yes, we put it up again. The third time they gave us down there [downhill] in Ramgad. We had proof of January 1 1995, no, so they had to give it to us.

SAKSHI: It got very crowded downhill near us. That is where they were put up.

The Forest Department encouraged eligible residents like Deepali to utilize the lower-elevation settlements like Ramgad as a temporary transit site (where they could set up shacks on any land they found vacant). However, most participants either stayed amidst the rubble of their demolished homes, rented a home in a slum nearby, doubled-up with a relative, or migrated to cities, towns, or villages where they'd lived before. Preeti, who was introduced in Chapter 2, recollected the difficult times her family experienced following the demolition of their home in Damu Nagar:

PREETI: We stayed on rent. Over there [in Damu Nagar] the environment became really bad, all drinking and all. Everyone had started to drink. My father had taken up a lot of anxiety. Father had fallen ill at that time. My brother was in the village, and older sister too was in the village. Only four of us, me, my sister, my mother and father were there. It all fell on her [my mother]. She ran helter-skelter. The poor thing, we were all tiny. She would bring all the goods. The room in front of us was torn down, but they told us that ours will not be torn down. We paid up [the INR 7,000] after our house was torn down.

AUTHOR: What happened then?

PREETI: We went to Hanuman Nagar where my father's friend stays. He considers her a sister. She helped us a lot. She had a number of people in her house and she hardly had any space. The rooms were all real tiny. She would sleep on top of our goods in the living room and she would let us both sleep in the room. I had to give up my college education. Three, four years wasted.

There were also cases like Vijaya's whose family was split up when she and her husband sent their three school-going children to live in charity youth hostels near trusted relatives in Krishnapuram village in Telangana state in the southeast. The couple lived in Appapada, a slum where residents protested demolitions and filed court cases contending that their land belonged to a private trust. As these protests and court cases progressed, Vijaya recollected the challenges her family endured:

VIJAYA: We went on rent. Now, where would I go with the children? Their schooling would get spoilt. For one year, for one year [they rented quarters in a slum within walking distance of Appapada but outside the park]. [My] husband's earning was not enough, the rent costs money. He [the older son] came back [after completing his 12th-grade exams]. Now I brought him back to Appapada, but then [once demolitions began] I sent him back [to the village] to stay with my sister. We constructed a small one [home]. And sent all the children to the village.

AUTHOR: So, you constructed a small one?

VIJAYA: Yes, constructed a small one. We would get water from the hills. No electricity either. We would light an oil lamp, an oil lamp.

AUTHOR: All these three [her three children] were in the village?

VIJAYA: The three of them were in the village. Over here, we would have kept running [from one spot to the other within their slum or in different slums in the area]. After so many years, we got this. After seven years, we got this [the apartment unit at Sangharsh Nagar].

Some residents permanently left the park after demolitions, returning to their original villages, towns, or cities, or they moved north of Mumbai into their own homes. Their departure was closely watched by those eager to own an apartment unit in the city. Deepali and Sakshi, the women who told me about their demolition experiences, said several settlers headed to the places they'd migrated from and were never seen in Mumbai again or returned to the city as soon as they got wind that apartments were being allocated to eligible residents. Some returned to Mumbai in time to get legal titles in their name; others learned that someone else had forged their identities in the ration card and presented it as evidence to fraudulently gain ownership of a unit in Sangharsh Nagar. The interim period between the start of demolitions and the inauguration of Sangharsh Nagar had created a chaotic R&R environment that the women characterized as hard but possible to monitor. Having more organized eyes and ears on the ground to monitor conditions might have prevented the many alleged instances of fraudulent dealings in which residents got their hands on more than one apartment unit and made a profit off selling or renting them:

DEEPALI: What do you think will happen [to those eligible who were absent at the time of allotment]? Someone else will get a home in their name!

At the time of demolitions, they left to the village and they did not return [when apartment allotments were announced].

SAKSHI: 75 percent of them!

AUTHOR: 75 percent of them are not right [are not the rightful owners]?[6]

SAKSHI: They are not, isn't it?

DEEPALI: Hmm. Yes, it is so.

SAKSHI: It is so.

DEEPALI: They have taken someone else's [identity] and are sitting in their place or have sold the unit and disappeared.

SAKSHI: The corruption [in apartment unit allotments] starts from right there.

DEEPALI: Yes, if they [the Forest Department] had not given it to them [certified their documents], then nothing would have happened. If not for me [being present], mine [my allotment] is given to someone else. If that other one does not get it, then with some monetary transactions, a third one gets it. That is how it is.

Depending on the circumstances of their household, women evoked what they perceived as hardships ranging from minimal disruptions to having to split up the family in order to survive the post-demolition waiting period. During this period, 1997–2007, each woman was both subject of and spectator to the transitions unfolding in the built environment of her slum. As storytellers later recounting what they experienced, the women spoke with some distance from the events of these years. That distance gave them a perspective on the relative hardships of those years and on their abilities to cope. My questions about demolitions during the 11 focus-group discussions invariably evoked more references to the years spent waiting for a housing alternative than to the demolitions themselves. These perceptions shed light on the methods of valuation the women used to describe what they and others they knew faced during these years and the clarity or otherwise in the resettlement process.

At one end of this perceived continuum of hardships were families who remained in the park, living amidst the rubble of the homes of their neighbors. Based on the narratives I gathered, homes were spared from demolitions because either (a) the household met the three eligibility criteria (the head of the household was listed in the electoral roll on or before January 1, 1995, had a government-issued ration card, and had a receipt for the INR 7,000 paid to the Forest Department); (b) other eligible households adjoined the spared home (the more the number of adjoining households eligible for resettlement, the less likely the demolition); or (c) the household and adjoining houses were well-connected to a political party and/or Nivara. But living amongst rubble without the previous physical amenities or social infrastructure was a source of considerable anguish, especially to those with school-going children, pregnant women, and people who worked out of their homes. Those perceived to have undergone less hardship were slum residents who could afford restarting life in middle-class housing developments in far-off suburbs "outside" the city or could return to their hometowns or villages. According to the women interviewed, many of these families also sold or rented out their apartment units in Sangharsh Nagar, unfairly profiting from the state government's negligent monitoring of housing entitlements. In between these two extremes were those who moved downhill, rented a room, split up their households to avoid interrupting their children's education, or doubled-up with relatives in another slum in the city. Still others returned to their villages or towns temporarily to await news of a state-approved apartment unit. The extent of the women's suffering through the demolitions and the years before they relocated to Sangharsh Nagar influenced the degree of solidarity they felt toward others at the resettlement site. It surfaced in conversations about who did or did not deserve homes; who had cause to complain about their new homes in the resettlement site; and the extent of satisfaction they felt over their new living conditions.

Another potent criterion that some participating women used to judge deservingness for homeownership at Sangharsh Nagar was the extent of loyalty that they (and those like them) felt toward external agents like Nivara. This perceived difference between a small group of loyalists and the much larger number of those unfamiliar with Nivara or its motives and methods became clear when women talked about what they felt they deserved or were entitled to receive after they'd consented to resettle at Sangharsh Nagar, an option that Nivara led, designed, and promoted.

NGO Loyalists and Others

Official reports (Sushil & George, 2003) date the start of the demolition of the park slums to May 1997, two years after the High Court issued the authorization order. For four years, from 1997 to 2001, city-based NGOs like Nivara squared off against the demolition squads. Since commencing its work in 1981, Nivara had considered the twin tactics of struggle and education "watchwords for Nivara Hakk building a peoples [sic] movement of housing and citizens [sic] rights in the city". Recalling the NGO's earliest attempts to stall the demolition of "dongar bastis" [hilltop slums] of the park, founding member Gurbir Singh referenced a demolition exercise from 1993, two years before the High Court issued the demolition order (Nivara Hakk Suraksha Samiti, 1995, p. 7):

> There are over 40,000 families residing in bastis along the Borivali National Park [Sanjay Gandhi National Park's former name] stretching from Malad to Kandivali. Soon after the riots, the forest authorities launched an "operation demolition" of the bastis. NHSS [Nivara] has taken a lead in fighting this policy, and the agitation is still on. In Jambrosi Nagar, in September 1993, in fact one BMC [Brihanmumbai Municipal Corporation, the city's governing body] demolition worker

was killed in the stone throwing. A big slum melawa [assembly] was held on August 30, 1993 on this issue in Malad. This was followed by a massive morcha [protest march] on 16th September 1993 of nearly 10,000 slum-dwellers.

I located the speech that Nivara's Singh delivered on July 8, 1995 (in a seminar at an unspecified location and event) after some of the women I met mentioned similar episodes concerning Nivara. Some associated their first encounter with Nivara's prominent leaders with the use of tear gas, *lathi*-charges [a lead-weighted bamboo stick carried by police], and the government-led demolition squads' harsh treatment of the leaders. That was the experience of Divya, a well-known volunteer activist who had migrated to Mumbai as a two-year-old with her parents from Gujarat in west India north of Maharashtra. After living in rental apartments as a child, Divya met her husband Saif at a garment factory where she said, "I would do the measurements and he would do the stitching! That is how we met". Upon marriage in 1992, the couple bought a plot of land for INR 10,000 in the Kranti Nagar slum to build a house. The land was full of holes: "We spent over two lakhs [INR 200,000] to make it livable and home-like". They also rented a small space a 20-minute walk from their slum home, where they worked as subcontracted tailors making shirts for a city-based fashion house. At their peak, they employed up to 20 other tailors. Their two children, now 21 and 28 years old, grew up amidst this compact workshop where their parents and their employees put in long hours of work. The demolitions began in 1993, less than a year after they'd made their Kranti Nagar home livable:

DIVYA: We [she and her husband Saif] were volunteer workers [for Nivara] since 1990. In the slum when they threw tear gas, Shabana Azmi and Gurbir Singh fought, they got beaten up. And then, then we had a connection with Nivara and they would call us to go there and go here during demolition. We also got to know the forest officials too. We got involved in stopping them [the bulldozers]. And in all that helter-skelter work, I couldn't pay attention to them [my children]. Even we did not know where we shall eat or sleep.

AUTHOR: But how did you get to know Nivara?

SAIF: I knew it from earlier.

AUTHOR: How so?

DIVYA: There was a fire in Paanch Bawadi [an industrial area southwest of Kranti Nagar slum and the park].

AUTHOR: During the time of the riots [Hindu-Muslim riots of 1992–1993]?

DIVYA: No, much earlier than that.

SAIF: Madam [Shabana Azmi, the Bollywood actor and Nivara front woman] was brand new [to slum activism] at that time. You know, it is me who sent her [Divya] to Nivara or else she wouldn't have gone to them.

AUTHOR: Really?

SAIF: I told her to go.

AUTHOR: Why?

DIVYA: I wanted to move forward by working hard on my own.

SAIF: I told her that they are good people and that you must go. As a woman, you will get some help for a room [an apartment] and such.

DIVYA: For 10 years, for 10 years we fought for this [home], no? For 10 years. Wherever they told us to go, if they called, then I would go.

SAIF: I had proof of 1994 and I would have gotten a home somewhere or the other, but yet I told her to go and that others too need to get it.

As an upper-class Muslim woman and film actor, Shabana (participating women consistently referred to by her first and not her last name) often portrayed "authentic" Indian characters. In the early 1990s, she joined Nivara's chiefly male leadership and quickly became the most recognizable face of the organization. Her overt endorsement of Nivara's opposition to the state-led slum evictions, whether from the front lines of a mass protest or through other activities to stall demolition, helped mobilize slum dwellers, especially women in their 30s and 40s. Residents like Saif well understood the potential benefits that might be gained by ingratiating his family with NGOs such as Nivara whose elite leaders had access to government officials and a host of other development brokers. Encouraged by her husband, Divya was one of a handful of women in the park slums who became hyper-visible supporters of Nivara's activities. In late 1993, Shabana led a "slum dwellers' morcha" ("Slum-Dwellers' Morcha", 1993) to protest the frequent demolitions of slum dwellers living on forestland and demanded "regularising of all slums on 'forest land' and the provision of basic civic amenities to the inhabitants". Joining her protest were nearly 10,000 slum dwellers from "shanties situated on forest land". The event attracted considerable media attention, including published photographs of slum women surrounding Shabana who brandished a banner proclaiming, "Stop demolishing slums; the poor have a right to their shanties". However, slum women's higher visibility in such public protests did not automatically translate into more equal power relations between residents and Nivara or give them a say over Nivara's plans for the design and development of their housing solutions. If anything, the new visibility created a perception in the slums that Nivara loyalists stood to gain the most from resettlement, thereby creating distinctions among the women.

Divya, for instance, was later convinced that someone in Sangharsh Nagar had filed a complaint with the Forest Department claiming that she and her husband had been allotted more than one apartment and had made money off their sale:

DIVYA: Over here [in Sangharsh Nagar] having one [apartment unit] is difficult. In my name, there were so many rumors. [Rumors like] 'she works in Nivara and has taken 10 homes', and this and that.

AUTHOR: Really?

DIVYA: Yes, the forest folks came here 10 times. They checked my papers 10 times. They checked all the rooms [all the apartment units], the original papers. I told them [the forest officials] that I'd file a case of harassment in the court.

SAIF: I was very angry.

As volunteer workers with Nivara, she and her husband were suspected (whether justifiably or not) of getting more than their fair share as payback for their loyalty. Whatever the circumstances, they were privy to details concerning Nivara's vision for the design and development of the resettlement site[7]. In Nivara's head office, a 20-minute walk from the southernmost slum of the park, a three-dimensional model of the project was on display in a fiberglass case. Sometime after November 2002, Sumer won approval to develop the site for slum resettlement and appointed Nivara's P. K. Das as project architect. The model that Das and his team designed showed a cluster of five-story (ground plus four) apartment buildings comprising some 550 units in all. Of those 550 units, 16 were earmarked for common use as *balwadis* (government- or NGO-run preschool centers for the economically disadvantaged), cooperative housing society offices, crèches, a women's center, and other social amenities. It also featured a central courtyard for shared use. On the wall adjoining the model were poster-size displays of the site design and layouts of each apartment unit, all of the same size, consisting of a living room/bedroom, a kitchen, a balcony, and a bathroom.

Nivara, according to the women, developed the site's layout and the design of each individual apartment unit without any apparent input from the potential occupants of the buildings. Divya and other volunteer workers like Fareesa, who came to the office for Nivara's customary Sunday night meetings, were more familiar with the general details of the project than other eligible residents of the park slums. But this insiders' knowledge could also create problems of unmet expectations and disgruntlement like that expressed by Fareesa:

> I have also seen it [the plan] with my very own eyes; each and every aspect. We were all volunteer workers. As volunteer workers we have seen this in proximity. We have seen everything. All the aspects that were in that plan, why don't we see it here today? The folks who were volunteer workers, they got to see it. You [Nivara] showed us a school, you showed us a school, you showed us a municipal hospital, you showed us a garden for children, where is all that? You showed us a market, there will be a market, and stated that you folks will have a right over it.

Those less familiar with Nivara's intentions had little, if any, pre-knowledge about the resettlement site and therefore were less likely to overtly express negative feelings about Sangharsh Nagar. Shakuntala, 60, had migrated to

Mumbai in 1976, roughly two years after her marriage. She, her husband, and their two sons lived in Hanumanpada, a slum on the eastern side of the park. Residents there were not as familiar with Nivara as those in the southwestern slums. Although she had paid the Forest Department the required INR 7,000 in 2000, she only submitted her proof to Nivara's office in 2008 when she signed her consent for the Chandivali resettlement proposal. I first met Shakuntala in December 2012 when she and her grandson walked into Nivara's Sangharsh Nagar site-office looking for someone in charge. She wanted to know when her kitchen faucet would be set up but made a point of stressing that she was in no hurry to have the problem resolved. She left after being told to go to Sumer's site-office, a stone's throw away. Intrigued to see what she did next, I left with her and made an appointment for a conversation (Figure 3.1), held soon after and excerpted below. She told me about her hesitancy in approaching Nivara with her problem:

AUTHOR: Did you know Nivara?

SHAKUNTALA: Yes, yes, yes, and this boy's father [her son who had lived near her in the slum] too knew. He would come here and go there [to the Sangharsh Nagar site]. He knew everything.

AUTHOR: He knew?

SHAKUNTALA: Yes, driving the rickshaw [his job]. Good folks would sit in his rickshaw. They would tell him. Like you, now you tell me and I felt good, so this way, someone would sit, no? And would say, it is very good there [at the proposed Sangharsh Nagar resettlement site], there is nothing wrong there, it is alright. 'Over here, your house will be torn down, so you must come there'. They would say that.

AUTHOR: So you did not know Nivara directly and hadn't come here to check out the site?

SHAKUNTALA: No, no, not then. I got to know them [Nivara] slowly. Without them, I wouldn't have gotten this house. Shabana fought to give us this, but there is one thing I want to tell you: I thought 10 times before I came to Nivara's office today.

AUTHOR: Why?

SHAKUNTALA: You know, I don't know them, they don't know me. I don't want them to think I am ungrateful. I am happy, very happy here. We should take whatever we get. What is our right? They'll say to me, 'We gave you an apartment and now you are complaining?' It is not nice to hear such things.

AUTHOR: Have they said such things to you?

SHAKUNTALA: No, no, not such things, but I just can't ask. I used to go to the corporator in Mulund. That Maske [Vishwanath Shankar Maske, a local corporator[8] who won the T Ward's municipal elections in 2007].

AUTHOR: Why would you go to him?

SHAKUNTALA: If I had to do some work with my ration card, I would go. I have shaken hands with him. Something to do with the house, I would go for that. If I had a need for papers, I would go for that. Here too I do the same with Tayade [the corporator for the L Ward representing Sangharsh Nagar]. I went to him about a place in the market [the open-air bazaar adjoining Sangharsh Nagar which I'll discuss in more detail later].

Figure 3.1 Shakuntala in her apartment demonstrating her former home-based work in the slum. She assembled caps for cooking gas cylinders

People like Shakuntala who were less familiar with Nivara learned about the Sangharsh Nagar option through their familial networks or from neighbors. Driving an autorickshaw offered Shakuntala's son the opportunity to both hear about and verify Nivara's relocation and resettlement claims. But Shakuntala's unfamiliarity with details about the site or Nivara's vision for its design left her more inclined to be satisfied than Fareesa, who saw discrepancies between what was promised and what was eventually delivered. Shakuntala was reluctant to blame Nivara, which she believed had fought for her right to an apartment. Reactions like hers illustrated the relationships between transparency, accountability, and the effectiveness of service delivery. In the usual chain of causation, awareness carries the possibility of community empowerment and ultimately accountability and learning. In the case of Sangharsh Nagar, the lack of community participation in Nivara's proposed design had set in motion a generally opaque R&R process. Later on, when Sumer removed Nivara as project architect, the design-and-construction process, which never was community-driven, became even less visible. Despite it all, participating women considered their apartments the product of the largesse of Nivara, the NGO that had "fought" to "give" them their homes. Those who did not count themselves among Nivara's small coterie of loyalists feared complaining about the quality of their homes lest they appear ungrateful. I interpret such attitudes as an impediment in the R&R process. It could hinder Nivara, Sumer, and other concerned stakeholders from addressing problems, making mid-course changes, or streamlining the ongoing resettlement of park residents. Sharada, 46, a former resident of the park's Ketkipada slum, brought up the problems she saw and suggested a solution during an intake conversation we had at her apartment:

SHARADA: Before the buildings [were constructed], this side [pointing to the side next to her apartment in the site's southeastern corner] was full of hills. After we moved here, in three years, they have torn down the hills and these buildings have been put up. They would saw the hills with a drill and the noise from the machine would be so much, so much. It would give us a lot of pain. If the hill broke, then all the dust, the mud would all come in. One time they put a dynamite, a big piece of stone came. It came from afar, hit the [sewer] pipe and tore it up. We then complained to the builder. We called him and showed it to him. I told him that if there were a man there, then his head would have burst. There was no one outside in the afternoon. It could have hurt someone. That Nivara gave us is good. We are not saying that it is not. But they should have given it to us after the work is complete. They should have broken our homes and then shifted us here. There are so many challenges here now. There is a lot of difficulty. It feels like [incomplete sentence]. That is why we think of the slum so much.

AUTHOR: Who is 'they'?

SHARADA: Everyone. Nivara, the state government, the Forest Department, the builder. Everyone that said they're giving us a home. This is a site still under construction.

Early and Later Occupancy of Sangharsh Nagar

Another perceived wedge among participating women was when they had moved in. There were basically two groups of residents in Sangharsh Nagar, the earliest occupants, who had consented to the relocation site and received apartment allocations within the first two years of its inauguration in May 2007 and those who followed, who had waited longer. These two groups of early versus later occupants harbored distinct grievances and perceptions about the advantages in the timing of their relocation. For instance, those that signed their consent earlier and received their apartments in the first two years considered themselves deserving of the choicest spots to do business in but were homeowners who had endured living in a site that was devoid of several amenities, especially drinking water (an aspect shared in detail in Chapter 4). It had taken nearly a year and a half after the site's inauguration, in 2007, for kitchen faucets in each apartment home to have running water. These early occupants believed that those that relocated later had little cause to complain about the quality of their new homes in the resettlement site. In contrast, those who moved into their apartment homes in the years following them found it impossible to afford the unofficial payments demanded by early occupants who had now resorted to "selling" their spots in the site's *bazaar* to other aspiring vendors.

The origins of a perceived gulf between early and later occupants lay in a process that commenced in 2003. On 9 March 2003, Nivara issued its first notice among the park residents, a notice that initiated the process of mobilizing slum residents for relocation to the then undeveloped Sangharsh Nagar. Circulated in both Hindi and Marathi, the notice invited eligible dwellers to sign their consent for resettlement in an apartment unit in the suburban neighborhood of Chandivali. The invitation went to those who had already paid the required INR 7,000[9] to the Forest Department and had proof of receipt. To get on the chronological wait list for apartment allocations, each eligible family was told to report to Nivara's office ready to pay an additional INR 100 for a pre-printed revenue stamp. This receipt would guarantee holders the right to a 225-square-foot apartment unit in Chandivali.

Shakuntala was a late occupant who moved into her unit five years after the resettlement site opened. She was unaware of Nivara's involvement, but took a leap of faith based on word from her son and signed up for a Chandivali apartment in 2008, five years after Nivara had initiated the process of gathering slum dwellers' consent for the resettlement site. She only committed to the process after her son reassured her that the proposed site was legitimate and safe.

Preeti's household, on the other hand, lacked a trusted source that could validate the promises they were hearing from two different NGOs—one for a home right outside the park's peripheries and a second for an apartment well within the city. Before they could sign up for either one or pay the Forest Department the INR 7,000 resettlement sum, the family needed proof themselves of an impending demolition. Had the demolition squad not parked its bulldozers and dump trucks by the open-air *bazaar* near her house in Damu Nagar, the family would have boarded a train to Preeti's native village only to return to find their home in ruins.

PREETI: Yes, everybody was paying, but some told us not to and some told us to [pay]. 'There are so many homes, let it go' [i.e. don't worry]. If we get, we get.

AUTHOR: So you paid?

PREETI: Yes. 7,000 rupees each.

AUTHOR: And yet the house was torn down?

PREETI: No, I mean they [unspecified] had first put up a board telling us to pay 5,000 [INR], but someone had removed the board. So, we folks did not even know that we had to pay. Some folks had paid up and theirs was still there [not demolished]. So we paid 7,000 [INR] *after* [emphasis the speaker's] ours was torn down.

AUTHOR: You knew that they were going to tear it down?

PREETI: No, we had made a [train] reservation to go to the village. It was for the 10th of May. We had our vegetable stall [in a roadside *bazaar* in the park].

AUTHOR: A reservation for the 10th of May?

PREETI: 10th of May. We had to leave for the village in May. We had a vegetable stall then. Bulldozers came and stood there [by the stall]. We thought that they were going to tear it down and that is why the bulldozers were there. There were some five or six bulldozers. There is no construction after all [her family's 'stall' was a wheeled cart]. Then we all guessed that something or the other is going to happen. We cancelled our reservation. It is good that we cancelled it because those that had gone to the village had all their goods destroyed.

AUTHOR: Everything was completely gone?

PREETI: All gone.

AUTHOR: Oh no! All the ones next door?

PREETI: They are right there in their huts, some of them. Among us, only three [households] had paid up. And three of us got our numbers [an allotted apartment in Sangharsh Nagar] now [in 2012]. The others have just [recently] paid up. Some of them had a problem proving their ownership, some had problems in their name.

AUTHOR: So they will get their numbers [allocations] slowly?

PREETI: Yes. The time when our home was torn down, they worked overtime to tear down our home. They would stop at 6:00 p.m. each day

> and that day, they worked until 6:30. Once they tore down our room [home], that is when the work stopped. The ones to the right and left of us, their homes were broken. Just ours was remaining. We felt like it might remain, but he hit it such that it all broke. We had a story building [two-story home]. Permanent. Tiles and all of that was put.

The source of the contradictory information that had so confused Preeti was a fevered competition between area NGOs for the attention and trust of park evictees. Vidya Chavan, a local corporator and founder-leader of the NGO Zopadpatti Bachao Parishad (Save the Slums Assembly in Hindi/Marathi, hereafter called "ZBP"), was popular in Preeti's Damu Nagar slum. Chavan was also the city president of the Janata Dal (Secular) Party. Backed by lawyers, ZBP accused the Forest Department of unjustly demolishing homes on roughly 200 acres of land over which it had no jurisdiction. In a conversation I had with Chavan in April 2003, she alleged:

> Why not allow the slums to be where they are? Their land has nothing to do with the forest, so how can the forest demolish the settlements? The poor should not be deprived of their dwellings just because the government is not clear about its maps and land records.

She won the support of the late Vishwanath Pratap Singh, a former Prime Minister of India (1989–1990) and eminent politician. Singh first got involved with the park slums at Nivara's invitation but soon sided with ZBP. He supported ZBP's petition to the Mumbai High Court demanding another survey of the park's boundaries. The Nivara supporters I interviewed claimed that Nivara and ZBP started out as allied NGOs. They remembered Shabana introducing Chavan to the park dwellers in a massive rally in April 2000 where Nivara, Chavan, and Singh collectively urged residents to stay put until the state government had resettled them on land on the park's periphery. This unity unraveled in November 2001 when Nivara made public its negotiations with Sumer to resettle slum dwellers in Chandivali. Nivara's about-face—from opposing to favoring off-site resettlement and from opposition to support for private-sector participation in slum housing—offered ZBP artillery to launch a counter-campaign. Chavan publicly questioned Nivara's motives and redoubled her efforts in court for resettlement on land that ZBP believed was incorrectly interpreted as falling within the park's boundaries. Circulars like the one below, distributed by her NGO in April 2002, became commonplace:

> No Chandivali [site of the Sangharsh Nagar resettlement]. We shall stay in Malad-Kandivali [the disputed area where Damu Nagar, Ambedkar Nagar, and several other park slums were located]. Do not

fill the Chandivali form! If you have filled it out, then contact us and get it cancelled! If you fill the Chandivali form, then you will lose your rights over land in Malad-Kandivali.

Through much of late 2002 and 2003, Nivara negotiated the many technical details of the resettlement site and project with the state government and Sumer while it simultaneously disputed rumors and what it claimed was an incessant stream of misinformation spread by ZBP. Vijaya from the Appapada slum recalled the many nights that Nivara staff and volunteers spent at her house in the slum after distributing notices door-to-door and meeting all day:

AUTHOR: How did he [her husband] know of Nivara?

VIJAYA: About Nivara? Nivara would come to us. Lots of them, lots of them would come. I have fed many of them for many days.

AUTHOR: Really?

VIJAYA: Really. A lot of them would come. Lots of them would come. This way or that, lots would come and eat and leave. Some would at times sleep there. If it got late, then they would sleep, they would sleep right there at my house. My husband was the main person in the slum.

AUTHOR: What did he do?

VIJAYA: He would do all the talk about being together. He would carry messages from here to there. Many of them had not heard about paying money. He would go to the Nivara meetings. They would have meetings and would call him and he would go attend them.

AUTHOR: Did you not tell people [to pay the INR 7,000 and sign up for Chandivali?]

VIJAYA: I told them so many times. We held meetings and told so many people, and my husband told them too and I told them too. A lot of people did not trust. They thought that Nivara would take [the] money and not give us a home, so they did not pay the money.

To dispel rumors and prepare eligible residents for resettlement, Nivara circulated a written announcement (in Hindi and Marathi) in September 2002, which read in part:

> If we were to stick together, then the 10-year-long struggle under the guidance of Nivara Hakk Suraksha Samiti [referred to as Nivara throughout this book] will reach a favorable ending. We have to draw inspiration from the sacrifices of thousands of those whose homes have been demolished by bulldozers and those who have lost their lives on account of atrocities of the police. … If eventually the court orders a resurvey and designates the [200 acres of] land to lie outside the peripheries of the park, then we welcome such a resurvey. The slum residents of Ambedkar Nagar can decide to continue to stay here and

> commence lives with their families right here. The Chandivali scheme is meant for those whose homes are on land belonging to the Forest Department and who are under constant threat of being evicted. ... The government has appointed Nivara as the promoter for the Chandivali project. This has strengthened our position. Soon, you shall be receiving notice of when to arrive to come forward to sign your consent for this scheme.

Nivara expected residents to queue up in droves when, in March 2003, it began the process of collecting consent from slum dwellers for the Chandivali resettlement site. After all, the site was located right within the metropolis (significantly closer than the far-flung Malad-Kandivali site) and Nivara had portrayed the proposed constellation of residential apartment blocks as a self-sufficient "city within a city", awash with amenities. To verify the credibility of those seeking relocation to Chandivali, Nivara deployed volunteer workers to collect detailed information from those who came to sign their consent, such as when the head of household had migrated to the city (with or without family), what had brought them to Mumbai, where they first settled, how they had acquired their park hutments, the full address of the hutment, employment, reason for opting for Chandivali—30 questions in all. To facilitate joint ownership of their apartments, passport-size photographs of both the husband and wife (when applicable) was collected and pasted to the filled-up questionnaire. The intent, at this stage, was that Nivara would advocate that the state grant tenure in the name of both members of each household. As this process of collecting data proceeded, a majority of the approximately 12,000 families who had already consented to resettlement in general (and not specifically to resettlement in Chandivali) by paying INR 7,000 to the Forest Department appeared in no rush to follow through on Chandivali. In fact, in July 2003, while I was doing my dissertation work, less than 5,000 families had submitted their consent for resettlement in Chandivali. I had attributed the sluggish response to Chavan's tireless efforts. As Nivara gathered signed consents, Chavan and members of several political parties (including Congress and Bharatiya Janata Party) began busily encouraging families to withdraw their consent. Chavan organized a human protest chain held on March 27, 2003 of several hundred slum dwellers holding placards proclaiming, "Chandivali is a conspiracy of the NGO. We demand Malad-Kandivali".

Much later, in 2012, Nivara employees told me that the trickling-in of slum families was largely the result of the upward mobility of the park's long-time residents. Kamala, 45, a former resident of Ketkipada slum in the suburb of Dahisar outside the park's northwestern borders, strongly believed that a majority of her neighbors were unlikely to relocate to their allotted apartments at Sangharsh Nagar because they already had secured homes elsewhere.

KAMALA: Madam you must know this. Some people have as many as four homes! One home here, one home in another building [in the city], another way north in Nalasopara, Naigaon, and a fourth in their village. Do you know why? A lot of people have developed [done legitimately well for themselves over the years]. Those that are fortunate have done well, earned well, and their families have progressed. Those that are fearful have been left behind. They had a home in the slum when they started out in Mumbai, but then they did well. They rented their home in the slum and moved into buildings and now that the SRA is offering them a home here, they are coming back to claim their unit. They were late in paying [the INR 7,000] because they were in no rush to come. They already have homes. They won't live here in Sangharsh Nagar, you know. They'll sell it or rent it out [to an 'undeserving' family]. These are joint families; these homes are too tiny for them.

To improve its resettlement response rate, Nivara also promised to lobby the Forest Department to reimburse residents the INR 7,000 (according to the participants, Nivara is still fighting the case and seeking reimbursement in the High Court). On weekends in June 2003, Nivara arranged to bus slum dwellers to Chandivali where the quarry hills were being blasted to prepare the site for resettlement. Following these visits, many who had already paid all the required fees became worried that making a living in the new locality would be daunting without a planned marketplace. They admitted keeping this information to themselves so they could claim the choicest spots to squat and set up shop. Sometime in the first two months of 2007, a few months before the site opened, those familiar with the layout of Sangharsh Nagar secured their business spots. Shanti, 42, from the Appapada slum, recollected how she rushed to find a spot the minute she knew that her household would be among the first to get keys to an apartment in Sangharsh Nagar. When I interviewed her in November 2012, Shanti was vending fish from a stall erected on top of a drainage canal that ran behind her apartment block:

SHANTI: We [those squatting along the road that fronts Sangharsh Nagar] started working even before we got our room. When we filled our form. When we got our Rupees 100 receipt, then we started to work.

AUTHOR: Really?

SHANTI: They began to sell [goods] using that receipt. We came a long time ago, and if we haven't gotten a spot [in the market], then how will the others get?

AUTHOR: So, do you get this space for free, this space?

SHANTI: No, we folks sit behind our building, just like that, it is temporary.

AUTHOR: So, the BMC [Brihanmumbai Municipal Corporation] can come any time and remove you?

SHANTI: No, forget about the BMC. The building folks will tell you to move, saying that we litter the place, it gets dirty, get up and we would then have to run.

Conclusions: Benefactors and Beneficiaries

In the years following the High Court's 1997 directive to clear the forest-land of residential dwellings, the park's atmosphere resembled a crowded hospital waiting room where the slum families anxiously awaited word on the future of their housing. As a multitude of self-proclaimed "benefactors" busily worked on a treatment out of earshot of their intended beneficiaries, the slum dwellers were left to themselves and provided with few updates about current or eventual conditions. This waiting period had created perceptions about who deserved and was undeserving of legal tenure at Sangharsh Nagar. This does not mean that women living in the park's various slums had previously considered each other equals. However, pre-demolition, each participating woman had based her identity on the *chaali* or the *zopadpatti* in which she lived. Following the demolitions, new types of distinctions emerged, including one based on the cut-off date of January 1, 1995 (extended in March 2014 to January 1, 2000) that determined who was eligible for resettlement in a new legal apartment. In instituting the cut-off date, the ruling state government had effectively divided many *chaalis* and *zopadpattis* (communities within slums without *chaalis*) into categories of the deserving and undeserving. Regular, frequent interactions in the park had facilitated collective decision-making around such vital matters as securing a municipal water connection, a toilet, digging a well, getting an electrical connection, and even mobilizing resistance to demolitions. The feelings of community and association engendered in the slum contributed to members' sense of distinctiveness and belonging. With the demolition of their homes, this place-centered group identity that had characterized slum dwellers' everyday lives was also erased.

Other new distinctions surfaced in the narratives I gathered. There were perceived differences between those from lower and upper elevations of the park slums (also discussed in Chapter 2); in degrees of hardship women reportedly experienced in the period between demolition and relocation; in women's descriptions of their networks or their attachments to external agencies, particularly Nivara; and differences in how long it had taken women to consent to relocate to the new site. Could their resettlement in Sangharsh Nagar mimic the pre-demolition set-up of their homes in the *chaalis* and *zopadpattis*, recreating feelings of community and association? Was the assignment of apartments random or was an attempt made to engineer residential homogeneity (or diversity) in the name of successful cohabitation? The upcoming chapter takes on these questions and concerns while recounting the years immediately following relocation to Sangharsh Nagar from the perspective of some of its female residents.

The memories of these women residents bring up their perspectives on whom they considered deserving or otherwise of legal tenure in the resettlement site and, in turn, influenced their perceived levels of satisfaction with life following relocation. The women shared these perceptions almost as asides. They included decisions about where and with whom to reside, whom to trust, which NGO or political party meeting to attend, and whether to invest resources in an apartment unit in Mumbai.

Some of these decisions occurred even before Nivara announced its resettlement option in March 2003. As Gramling and Freudenburg (1992, pp. 217–218) have observed,

> in the biological or physical sciences, it may be true that impacts do not take place until concrete alterations of physical or biological conditions have occurred. With the human environment, however, measurable impacts begin as soon as there are changes in social conditions—often from the time when information about a project first becomes available. … Speculators buy property, politicians maneuver for position, interest groups form or redirect their energies, stresses mount, and a variety of other social and economic impacts take place, particularly in the case of facilities that are large, controversial, risky, or otherwise out of the range of ordinary experiences for the local community. These changes have sometimes been called "predevelopment" or "anticipatory" impacts, but they are far more real and measurable than such terminology might imply.

Empowering slum dwellers to use and manage their legal tenure to mutual satisfaction entails significantly more than decentralizing the responsibility for slum housing to a combination of public–private players. If slum resettlement initiatives like Sangharsh Nagar, which involve the physical transplanting of residents into alternate housing locations from a variety of different communities, are to be accepted and settled by their intended beneficiaries, then recognizing and working through the demolition and pre-relocation impacts and processes are crucial. The far more challenging task of resettlement and rehabilitation, according to participating women, involves the enlisting of eyes and ears on the ground to identify and understand the patterns of acceptance and rejection of relocation; the multiplicity of types and needs residing within slum communities; and the various interests and relationships that shape decisions about what constitutes livable housing. The memories and perceptions of women have far-reaching implications for they predict the forms of social cohesion and general functioning of the resettlement site.

Notes

1 Normally the FAR in Mumbai, depending on the location within the city, ranged from .75 to 1.33. Prior to 1991, it was fixed at 1.33 for the island city and 1.00

for the suburbs (as noted in Chapter 2, endnote 2, the city is comprised of the island city and its suburbs). The SRD expanded the FAR on slum land by a substantial 150 percent.

2 To receive state and foreign funds, Nivara operated the Nivara Hakk Welfare Centre, an NGO created in 1988, seven years after Nivara Hakk Suraksha Samiti (referred to simply as Nivara in this book) was formed.

3 The founding of Nivara is detailed in Ramanath (2005, pp. 130–158).

4 State policy in effect since 1971 (Maharashtra Slum Areas Improvement, Clearance & Redevelopment Act, 1971) forbid the demolition of any structure whose occupants met the eligibility criteria for alternate accommodation until they were allotted an alternate dwelling (or transit accommodation). The alternate accommodation had to be agreed-upon by both the resident and the developer/promoter of the slum rehabilitation proposal.

5 When data collection for this work was completed in December 2016, only 22,000 of the 33,000 families were found to meet SRA requirements for eligibility. Additionally, 12,070 of the 22,000 families had paid the INR 7,000 to the Forest Department and had been allocated homes under phase I of the Sangharsh Nagar resettlement project. The 3,500 families mentioned in the founder-leader's email (see Chapter 1) were part of the 12,070 families who were allocated homes under phase I of the proposed two-phase resettlement process. Another 9,930 (of the 22,000) families stayed either in the park or moved to other city slums or to their native towns or villages to await their turn to move into Sangharsh Nagar's phase II buildings. Phase II was being developed by two for-profit builders, Sumer Corporation and DB Realty. Despite objections from Nivara, the two successfully negotiated with SRA to construct 15-story apartment buildings in phase II, seven stories taller than the phase I buildings.

6 Shocked by this high statistic, one difficult to verify, I brought it up in other discussions and individual conversations with participants. Women generally agreed that several residents from their respective slums had engaged in fraudulent dealings like selling or renting out their new units to non-eligible slum residents (they were neither eligible residents from the park nor residents of the slum that had housed former quarry workers who lived on the land now called Sangharsh Nagar) and from areas unknown. According to the rules of the Slum Rehabilitation Authority, once resettled, "project-affected people" could not rent or sell their unit for 10 years.

7 Nivara's role in Sangharsh Nagar began as a *facilitator*, a term used in the first letter of intent issued by the SRA in November 2002 (see Ramanath, 2005, p. 293). Per this official letter, Nivara was to do the "ground work" towards shifting "encroachers of forest land" from the forest to the proposed rehabilitation site of Sangharsh Nagar. Besides mobilizing slum residents' consent, Nivara was eager to control the design of the project and lobbied the SRA to appoint Nivara's P. K. Das as the joint-developer and architect for the Sangharsh Nagar resettlement project. Sumer eventually did appoint Das whose architecture firm quickly worked out a detailed site layout and building plans for the project. This all took place between November 2002 and July 2003 during the course of my data collection for my doctoral research completed in 2005. Thus, not only did Nivara work to mobilize encroachers of forestland to sign their consent for Sangharsh Nagar as a resettlement option but it also actively sought to shape the design of the resettlement site. Much to Nivara's stated disappointment, the result was not the self-contained, low-rise resettlement expected.

8 Corporators like Maske are elected members of the city's municipal corporation. Mumbai is divided into 227 wards (as of May 2017), each headed by a corporator (and a ward official who serves as the corporator's administrative counterpart), elected every five years. Although some corporators are independents, a political

party nominates most. Each has a budget to provide essential ward services, including water, sanitation, education, roads, and health care. Maske was the Bharatiya Janata Party's candidate in the 2007 elections for the Mulund Colony-Tulsi Road (the T Ward), which included the Hanumanpada slum.

9 After lobbying the Forest Department and seeking the court's consent, Nivara secured approval to also include those who had not paid pre-demolition, the INR 7,000 for the Chandivali resettlement. The sole requirement in such cases was that the family submit proof of their residence in the park slum as of January 1, 1995, or before. A majority of the women who participated in this research had paid the full INR 7,000 beforehand and the others, who could not afford to or were late payees, followed the court's relaxed requirements and paid the INR 7,000 in several installments. All of the park residents currently in Sangharsh Nagar eventually paid the full INR 7,000 at some point prior to their relocation.

References

Clark, J. (1991). *Democratizing development: The role of voluntary organizations.* Sterling, VA: Kumarian Press.

Crook, R., & Manor, J. (2000). *Democratic decentralization* (OED Working Paper Series No. 11). Retrieved from World Bank Operations Evaluation Department website http://lnweb90.worldbank.org/OED/oeddoclib.nsf/DocUNIDViewForJavaSearch/2365D3D73CFE619D8525697700729143/$file/Demcratc.pdf.

Dupont, V. (2008). Slum demolitions in Delhi since the 1990s: An appraisal. *Economic and Political Weekly*, 43(28) 79–87.

Government of India, Ministry of Urban Development. (1994). *National housing policy.* New Delhi: Author.

Government of Maharashtra, Slum Rehabilitation Authority, Housing and Special Assistance Department. (1997). *Guidelines for the implementation of slum rehabilitation schemes in Greater Mumbai* (SRA Publication No. 002821). Mumbai: Author.

Gramling, R., & Freudenburg, W. R. (1992). Opportunity, threat, development, and adaptation: Toward a comprehensive framework for social impact assessment. *Rural Sociology*, 57(2), 216–234.

Lefebvre, H. (1905/1996). *Writings on cities* (E. Kofman & E. Lebas, Trans.). Malden, MA: Blackwell.

Maharashtra Slum Areas Improvement, Clearance & Redevelopment Act (Mah. XXVIII of 1971). Retrieved from http://sra.gov.in/upload/Maharashtra_Slum_Areas_Improvement_Clearance.pdf.

Massey, D. (1994). *Space, place, and gender.* Minneapolis, MN: University of Minnesota Press.

Nivara Hakk Suraksha Samiti. (1995, July 8). Nivara Hakk over the years. Retrieved from www.nivarahakk.com/pdfs/Nivara-Hakk-over-the-years.pdf.

Pugh, C. (1994). The idea of enablement in housing sector development: The political economy of housing for developing countries. *Cities*, 11(6) 357–371.

Ramanath, R. (2005). From conflict to collaboration: Nongovernmental organizations and their negotiations for local control of slum squatter housing in Mumbai, India. *Institute for Policy and Governance: Student Research.* Retrieved from https://vtechworks.lib.vt.edu/bitstream/handle/10919/28167/RamyaRamanathDissertation.pdf?sequence=1&isAllowed=y.

Sanyal, B., & Mukhija, V. (2001). Institutional pluralism and housing delivery: A case of unforeseen conflicts in Mumbai, India. *World Development*, 29(12), 2043–2057.

Singh, G., & Das, P. K. (1995). Building castles in air: Housing scheme for Bombay's slum-dwellers. *Economic and Political Weekly*, 30(40), 2477–2481.

Slater, T. (2013). Expulsions from public housing: The hidden context of concentrated affluence. *Cities*, 35, 384–390.

Slum-dwellers' morcha against demolitions. (1993, September 17). *Indian Express.*

Sushil & George, R. J. (2003). *Eviction watch India: A report on evictions in India's major cities* (National Forum for Housing Rights, India). Mumbai: Compact Law Publication Pvt.

United Nations Centre for Human Settlements-Habitat. (1991). *Global strategy for shelter to the year 2000: Sub-regional seminars to support national action.* Nairobi: Author. Retrieved from http://mirror.unhabitat.org/downloads/docs/3642_39011_HS-C-13-3.htm.

United Nations Development Programme. (2002). *Human development report: Deeping democracy in a fragmented world.* New York: Oxford University Press. Retrieved from http://hdr.undp.org/sites/default/files/reports/263/hdr_2002_en_complete.pdf.

Weinstein, L. (2013). Demolition and dispossession: Toward an understanding of state violence in millennial Mumbai. *Studies in Comparative International Development*, 48(3), 285–307.

World Bank. (1993). *Housing: Enabling markets to work (with technical supplements).* Washington, DC: Author. Retrieved from http://documents.worldbank.org/curated/en/387041468345854972/Housing-enabling-markets-to-work.

4 Hazards of a New Fortune

A cacophony of voices, Mumbai, 2002–2003:

> This area is already over-populated and cannot take further load of unauthorised slum dwellers from the national park. We request you to kindly consider this representation on merits and reconsider the proposal received from any private parties or NGOs, who are trying to destroy the environment in this area.
>
> Memorandum sent by residents in and around Chandivali to the Chief Minister of Maharashtra, published in the *Times of India* daily on June 24, 2002

> The first time in history that instead of being thrown to the fringes of the city, slum dwellers are being rehabilitated further south of the city. This is not a private scheme done by a builder, it is a government scheme done in partnership with Nivara.
>
> General Secretary, Nivara, speech delivered to park slum dwellers, February 16, 2003

> She [Shabana Azmi, president of Nivara, Bollywood actor and Member of Parliament] wants to go beyond her image from an agitationist to someone who is doing a concrete intervention in development. Imagine, 16,000 people with homes—a great social contribution!
>
> Convenor, Nivara, interview held on May 25, 2003

> It is not possible to live in the forest. Court has to settle this. Court has to decide—it will take another 4–5 years to build. Court has to issue orders that some more time be given. The blasting will commence from Monday.
>
> Convenor, Nivara, community meeting held in Nivara's office May 25, 2003

> Most of those in my area are those in support of Nivara. It's those without proof who are still with Vidya Chavan. There is widespread

> nervousness about the scheme. It's people from Gautam Nagar who are the most adversely influenced by Vidya's anti-Chandivali campaign. They were to come [to this meeting], but then retracted. They want to hear Shabana speak, at least twice, and then an announcement in the papers that Chandivali is official.
>
> Resident, Gautam Nagar slum, community meeting at Nivara's office, May 25, 2003

> The TDR prices now have stabilized at Rupees 800 in the last six months. If prices were to crash, would Sumer stick around to complete? He would make his booty and run away! Are people in the park willing to come here? Does Nivara have previous experience in housing? Can they do it?
>
> Joint Program Director, Mumbai Metropolitan and Regional Development Authority[1], May 23, 2003

Aversion, pride, doubt, anxiety, skepticism: Over the course of two years, for all of 2002 and 2003, the Sangharsh Nagar R&R project generated divergent sentiments, voiced with much passion and gusto by those with a stake in its execution. They were expressed in newspapers, interviews, and personal observations that I had collected in 2003, the year I finished my doctoral work and returned to the U.S. to analyze my data. Through correspondence with friends I had made in Mumbai and newspaper clippings that my grandfather religiously mailed to me from India, I became aware of the tensions surrounding the move to Sangharsh Nagar—disputes between Nivara and Sumer, between Nivara and the state government—that shrouded the four-year construction of the first phase of the resettlement site. On July 5, 2007, the convener/founder of Nivara emailed me this note:

> You'll be glad to know that the first batch of about 3,500 families from the Borivali Natinal [sic] Park have actually shifted to their new home. Lots of roblems [sic] as expected buit [sic] everybody is happy.

"Really? Awesome" I quickly wrote back. Although unsure whom I was excited for, I knew that accomplishing this much wasn't easy for Nivara. The success of the slum rehabilitation project depended not only on size and location but also on the behavior of the city's housing market. Through email correspondence with Nivara's convener/leader and conversations with slum and resettlement site residents and Nivara staff in 2007, 2009, and 2011, I learned that the joint agreement that Nivara and Sumer had entered into in June 2003 started coming undone when the Mumbai real-estate bubble began deflating in the second half of 2003. As the Mumbai Metropolitan and Regional Development Authority's (MMRDA) Joint Program Director noted in the quote above, Sumer wanted to make hay while the going was good, but expressed less interest in living up to Nivara's ideals of a low-density, low-rise development with ample open spaces and other amenities after the housing market started failing. On its webpage created almost a decade later, in 2013, Nivara derided Sumer as "little better than a goon". Nivara feared that Sumer would redraw site plans, increase the height of the apartment buildings, and eliminate amenities like parks, marketplaces, and playgrounds, setting the stage for just "another 'multi-story slum'" ("Nivara Hakk", 2013). Scholars continue to document such fears as they argue that unless planned with sufficient room for leisure activities and other "civilized facilities" like gardens and garages (Smart, 1987, p. 15), high-rise, low-income housing projects rapidly deteriorate. The emergence of "vertical slums" from new high-rise developments was observed in New York (Ickes, 1935), Bangkok (Yap, 1996), Johannesburg (Frenzel, 2014), and Kuala Lumpur (Aziz, Hussain, & Ujang, 2016), among other cities.

Joining the developer were the municipal and state government agencies that wholeheartedly supported the use of slum transferable development rights (TDR)[2] as a mechanism to make resettlement programs like Sangharsh Nagar affordable for the government. From 1997, the year slum TDR was first issued in Mumbai, to late 2003, large sums of slum TDR were traded, resulting in a steep rise in the construction of upscale housing in suburbs like Andheri and Santa Cruz, considered prime-real-estate territory. This construction activity, utilizing slum TDR, aroused responses from others. Concerned citizens, like the anti-corruption crusader Anna Hazare, filed public interest litigation in the city's High Court accusing the SRA of prematurely issuing slum TDR certificates to a slew of private developers for projects to rehouse slum dwellers ("Hazare Loses Case", 2004). Under the state's slum rehabilitation policy, builders were to be issued TDR certificates depending on their progress. A builder would receive 65 percent of the TDR on completion of ground-level construction and get the remainder when the project was finished. But public interest litigation like Hazare's and media reports from late 2002 until 2004 (Balakrishnan & Bharucha, 2002; Bharucha, 2004) reported a slew of "fraudulent transactions", including one in which a builder (not identified in the newspaper article[3]) had utilized his connection with a state-level Congress Party leader to persuade the SRA to release slum TDR certificates regardless of building progress. After unscrupulously procuring TDR certificates, the builder allegedly resold them to another buyer for a whopping INR 1 billion. Private builders/developers like this one were eager to exploit the city's rapidly plunging slum TDR market[4]. From October 2003 to September 2004, slum TDR prices fell from INR 800–850 per square foot to INR 540–575, not auguring well for timely completions or high-quality construction of projects like Sangharsh Nagar whose developers were counting on slum TDR for handsome profits. But when TDR transactions were poorly monitored[5] by civic authorities and tightly guarded by a handful of builders, it was unsurprising when investors tried to maximize gains by holding on to their stock of TDR to restrict supply and inflate prices. This caused city property prices to rise to levels where only the rich could afford to buy a home. Sumer Corporation, a member of this "secret" cartel of insiders, held on to TDR certificates issued by the Municipal Corporation despite no evidence of corresponding progress in construction activity.

Sumer's surreptitious dealings infuriated Nivara. In mid-2005, Nivara's elite leadership urged the SRA to issue no more TDR certificates to Sumer without demonstrated progress in construction of the promised apartment buildings. This tactic signaled the beginning of the end of a partnership that rival politicians like Vidya Chavan had not hesitated to label as dubious from the outset (see Chapter 3). Sumer retaliated aggressively and prevailed on the SRA to remove Nivara as the joint developer and Das as the architect. Where Nivara had proudly pointed to its plan's low-rise construction as a first in the city's slum resettlement projects, the redesign of Sangharsh Nagar following Nivara's removal called for ground-plus-seven (eight-floor) apartment buildings, three stories higher than originally planned. Sumer also eliminated features such as balconies for each unit, playgrounds, and the marketplace. It further insisted that in order to build the five-floor design Nivara favored, each slum family should pay INR 40,000. Speaking on behalf of the slum residents, Nivara refused and maintained that if Sumer wanted to construct taller, eight-floor buildings then the SRA policy required it to contribute INR 20,000 per apartment unit to the SRA for future maintenance costs. Nivara succeeded, but the two parties—Nivara and Sumer—never saw eye to eye again. According to Nivara, the situation reached "a low point when the builder [Sumer], revealing his true, violent face, demolished the Nivara Hakk project office in Chandivali on 17 January 2006" ("The Long Road", 2013). Their partnership disintegrated roughly 18 months before I received Nivara's self-congratulatory email message excitedly announcing occupancy of nearly 3,500 homes in the first phase of the resettlement project.

This information came from city newspapers, email, and in-person conversations, and updates from Nivara's leaders and staff during my visits to Mumbai (in December 2007, 2009, 2010, and 2011). During all these short visits, I found the women residents to be far more vocal than the men in raising their dissatisfactions with life at Sangharsh Nagar. They offered me a privileged window into a process that Archer (2007, p. 73) describes as an "internal conversation" that revealed how these women from the slums reconciled their built environment—their hopes, expectations, fears, and misgivings.

Chapter 3 showed that women were mostly victims of an R&R process that they had to negotiate by their own wits. During this prolonged phase of "received knowing" (Belenky et al., 1986), women acknowledged feeling like spectators who faced just two likely scenarios: continue with life as is (whether living in the park amidst the rubble of their former *chaalis* and *zopadpattis*, in a relative's house in another slum in the city, in a village with relatives, start over in another city slum), or move to a legally tenured apartment in the city, if offered.

This chapter concerns the next phase of the conversation, which occurred when women were allocated an apartment unit at the Sangharsh Nagar resettlement site. For the first batch of resettlers, the relocation experience presented them with copious amounts of unexpected data on what was available and accessible in the built environment and what was not. This period demanded[6] that they rebuild their lives without the amenities they knew to expect through legal tenancy in a city building—continuous drinking water, electricity, elevators, transportation, and safety. During this time, the newly resettled women evaluated the information they'd received over the past several years and found that it lacked the details that mattered to them. Each woman assessed the habitability and implications of her potential new home at the resettlement site either by inspecting the unit in person or through discussions with neighbors, relatives or other connections who'd seen it or who had chosen to move in. This deliberation included considerations such as: "Is it worth it to occupy the apartment unit when the children are still completing their school year? Perhaps not" or "How will I earn a living? Will it be enough to support this new life here? Likely not". "Maybe I should take on a new job, but what kind of job? Should I keep my job? I think I have to. How else will we pay for the expenses at this new location?" "Should I accept the allocated unit on the eighth floor? I can barely walk and the lift [elevator] in my building isn't working yet". "Can I afford to commute to and from work? I can't, but maybe I can ask madam to hike my wages so I can continue working for her and don't have to look for a new job".

Dialogues like these moved from the extremes of what was unthinkable to considerations of several likely future courses of action. This chapter details what occurred in this exploratory stage in which dissatisfactions and the costs needed to overcome them were the chief focus. What the women pursue, with whom, and why are all questions that provide invaluable insight into the means mobilized to realize a "better life". I begin by focusing on these women's first forays into legal homeownership.

The First Few Years (Batch 1, Phase I of Relocation)

By March or April 2007, 48 of the proposed 150 apartment buildings of phase I (the first of two construction phases) were complete, and on May 1 2007, the still-unfinished site was inaugurated amidst much fanfare, including a welcoming committee made up of politicians and housing VIPs, with a speech by the Chief Minister of the state. A resident I met at the marketplace in Sangharsh Nagar recalled what he and several thousand other slum dwellers heard that day: "The Chief Minister urged us to maintain a clean site, not run petty shops from the windows of homes on the ground floor, or sell our units for the next 10 years. He did not want Sangharsh Nagar to become another slum". The settlement was framed, yet again, as a key milestone in the lives of long-suffering slum dwellers, who, on this occasion, were counseled to mimic the lifestyles and habits of the "building people" of a well-groomed suburb. Following the speech, house keys were symbolically distributed to the female heads of 15 park slum households. It took the state government another five months to put forward a list of the tenants whose homes were ready for occupancy. The 3,500 families (and the other 8,570 authorized tenants under phase I) had to wait until their individual apartment units passed SRA inspection (approved for occupancy) and tenants had to submit the appropriate documents proving residence in the park slum (given to Nivara) for verification by forest officials. Both Nivara and Forest Department officials, working in tandem, had to then select which qualifying slum household would get a unit ready for occupation[7]. At the time of collecting consent for the Chandivali project, Nivara intended that each unit be jointly owned by the husband and the wife. However, eventually, the allotment letter from the state, a document that serves as the title to the property, assigned each unit solely in the name of the male head of the household. This was a major lacuna in the apartment allocation process and one that Nivara, much later in 2014, regretted not noticing and fighting for with the state. In practice, a separation or divorce after allotment of a unit in Sangharsh Nagar meant that the title to the apartment did not automatically transfer to the wife but entered a bureaucratic maze of paperwork[8]. In addition, residents faced much that was still unfinished in the apartments, buildings, and common areas, including water connections, elevator installations, and the construction of a planned marketplace, two municipal schools, a hospital, a community hall, playgrounds, and places of worship.

The fitful journey to resettlement finally culminated in October 2007 for 3,500 phase I families[9]. Despite the site's relatively close 10-kilometer distance from the park, the 3,500 families of phase I trickled in to the site, taking their time to move in. Many families with children waited until the school year ended, particularly those with children in their 10th or 12th years of school. Those with children in the 11th year or already enrolled in one of the many colleges near the park slums left their children with relatives to avoid disrupting their education. Those free to move crammed their goods and themselves into *tempos* (the four-wheeled light trucks used to carry goods commonly seen on Indian roads) hired for the day or made several trips back and forth in autorickshaws filled to capacity with the families' prized television set, DVD player, kitchen stove, wall-clock, clay *handaas* (pots), and the occasional desktop computer. For most of the women who relocated between October 2007 and 2008, when life at Sangharsh Nagar meant no drinking water supply and few opportunities for jobs, the move may have seemed premature.

What Is Life Without Water?

One such resident I interviewed was Gowri, 50, a mother of two teenage boys, 15 and 16, and a 20-year-old daughter. I met her one warm December evening in 2012 after she returned from her factory job at a nearby manufacturer of metallic lids for glass *achaar* (pickle) jars. We sat down to talk on a lopsided, worn sofa in Nivara's office and Gowri's grief over the past and fears for the future spilled out through more tears than words. She described an overwhelming and unhappy first year after the move and the continuing struggles involved in managing her family's life. Less than a week after relocating, her husband insisted that she and their children temporarily move to her maternal home while he stayed in their new apartment to look for construction work. She agreed, not only because no apartment building in the new site had running water but even more to help reduce the family's living expenses. She took their three children out of a municipal school near the slum to accompany her to Kheda village located in Maharashtra's Aurangabad district, situated 322 kilometers (about 200 miles) northeast of Mumbai. Her husband continued looking for contractual work in Chandivali while making frequent visits to a nearby private hospital to relieve his chronic leg pain. His brother and his family moved in with him, but within less than two months, Gowri received a call informing her that he had died.

> What was I supposed to do? They [her husband's brother, wife, and their son] did not take him to the hospital [that day]. I was told that my nephew fed him his meal that day. He fed him a fruit and he passed away while eating it. No savings, no job, nothing. I rushed back and I started staying here. So much work, so much trouble. I couldn't get work. I have worked for 50 rupees or 40 rupees a day. I picked papers from garbage dumps. That is all I know, that is all I could get. This place is so expensive. What could I do, where can I go from here?

Her husband's untimely death may have been unrelated to the relocation, but death and disease among new homeowners, especially the men, fueled impressions among residents that the under-developed site was physically dangerous and the move itself was ill-advised. Similar to Gowri's experience was the much-discussed story of Diya, 23, a mother of two children, ages 5 and 3, whose husband died 18 months after they moved to the resettlement site in 2010. She introduced herself in the focus-group discussion by saying:

> It has been four to five months [since he died]. He was unwell. His kidneys collapsed. The kidneys went bad after we got here. We had problems with water. We used to bring water from Khairani Road

[a road located a few meters southwest of the resettlement site that is dotted with snack shops, three-star hotels, film studios, places of worship, and numerous formal and informal factories]. They [her husband and father-in-law] used to bring it from there.

The lack of running water in apartment units (and the still-empty elevator shafts) brought back memories of a life residents thought they'd left behind. Walking in quest of water, queueing up, and lugging *handaas* (pots) full of water up flights of stairs were reminiscent of the activities that had filled their lives in the slum. They recalled the days when the women had pilfered unregulated amounts of potable water from the city's pipeline or drew water from an authorized government standpost put up under a slum improvement or upgrade program.

SUMITRA: After coming here, the earnings have gone up but so have our visits to the doctor. The air and the water here is not good. The builder's work is always in progress. All the time, so much dirt.

SHARADA: When we folks came we fetched water on our own for seven to eight months, going up and down the stairs.

SUHANA: Yes, we would carry water to the very top.

SHARADA: Where was there any water [in our apartment faucets/taps]?

SUMITRA: The tap was all dry.

SHARADA: We, we people got water from MHADA [the Maharashtra Housing and Area Development Authority; it had built a residential project nearby in 1992 that was occupied by middle- and lower-middle-class residents].

SUMITRA: We got water from MHADA. And that too, listening to a ton of curses [from its residents].

AUTHOR: Listening to curses?

SUMITRA: Yes [laughs]. No fun to be reminded that you shall remain a begging slum dweller.

Sumitra, 39, had five daughters and a son. She worked as domestic help in an upscale township near the resettlement site. Sharada, introduced in Chapter 3, made a living selling *pooja* (prayer) items in the alleyway adjacent to her apartment building. She was contributing to her household's income for the first time since her arrival in Mumbai in 1983 and often attended events hosted by Nivara. Suhana, 32, the third woman quoted in the conversation above, was a widow. She too had lost her husband after relocating to the site and began working as a domestic help to support her three sons and a daughter. Their comments were extracted from a focus-group discussion of seven participants. Conversation about the settlement's water problems continued, and Gomati, one of the group's seven participants, introduced in Chapter 3, also chimed in:

GOMATI: Oh, for two years, we would go to fetch water in a vehicle, in a rickshaw [the three-wheel autorickshaw] and we had to climb five floors. We have taken on so much difficulty as a result.

SHARADA: When the builder's work started, we would get water from there.[10]

SUMITRA: We would go to that quarry to wash our clothes for so many months after coming here [the uneven gradient created by all the blasting of hills and construction work around the site had created several makeshift ponds, including one particularly large one on the northeast portion of the site that became a *dhobi ghaat,* an open-air laundry, and a water-park for boys seeking relief during the hot summer months]. We filled water [drinking water] for more than a year and a half.

SUHANA: The water thing [the problem of no drinkable water] was for two years.[11]

GOMATI: Yes, madam, the builder released such [bad quality] water here, the water he released to the tank, you know. We faced such sickness here that the whole body would itch, it would feel like that and sickness came. We have had so much difficulty here.

SUHANA: Earlier, the situation, sister, was that the water does not suit everyone and that is why they are falling sick. Water is not tasty here. It does not taste right and the stomach is always full of gas. Can't digest the water, don't even feel hungry. And it digests slowly, something or the other. We fall sick. In the beginning, in the first year, everyone got malaria. Everyone. There is work going on in the surrounding areas. All the dust from the construction causes a lot of sicknesses.

Of course life in the slum had not been free of death and disease. But a settlement put together by a high-profile NGO and located near prime urban real estate carried with it expectations that things would not go too wrong. I questioned remarks frequently made in two previous discussions associating death and disease with the resettlement site in contrast to the slum. This launched five of the six women taking part in one discussion into a comparison of the physically different environments and different behaviors witnessed at the two sites:[12]

REEMA: Yes, of course [we'd fall sick]. Those who lived next to the drain would, but here we fall sick again and again.

KAJAL: We did not fall sick like that there.

REEMA: *(vigorously nodding in agreement, along with Hamsika and Gayatri)* There, only during the rains. We used to fall sick only during the rains. There it used to be dirty but here, there are mosquitoes.

AUTHOR: So, where did the mosquitoes over there [in the slum] go?

KAJAL: Yes, only they [the mosquitoes] would know! You see, there our rooms were all separate. My room is here, your room is there. So, she cleans just in front of her room and I clean in front of mine.

HAMSIKA: Yes, clean it.

REEMA: If she doesn't litter, then how can mosquitoes come? But here, you throw garbage from up above so there are mosquitoes ... [a cacophony of voices].

A poignant analysis of post-relocation conditions emerged during my intake conversation with Kajal three days before she took part in the previous discussion. We talked while her husband and 15-year-old daughter were also home. Her husband had lost his day job working for a tourist-taxi company located near their former home in the Ambedkar Nagar slum in Malad. As I filled out the intake form, he began narrating how hard it was for him to manage time for his job until Kajal jumped in and vociferously steered the conversation to a different concern:

KAJAL'S HUSBAND: I had to reach Malad by 7:30 a.m. in the company's car. The traffic was horrible, horrible. It took me two hours to cover the distance.

KAJAL: And by the time he got home, it used to be 11:30 or 12 at night and then he'd have to be at work by 7:30! His manager and he had so many spats and then he was finally let go. It's been three and a half years, but he's helping me manage our flower shop here in the market.

KAJAL'S HUSBAND: We are managing okay. This is a good season [Ganapati festival][13] but ...

KAJAL: But the serious issue is that of water. Water is life. Our biggest problem in the slum was water from the roof and water from below. During rains, water would seep in from everywhere. Now we have a roof but no water. We would get water 24/7 from that municipal tap near our home. But here, we have four taps: one in the kitchen and three in the bathroom, and no water! This is a big problem. We can't go on vacations because someone has to be home to store water when it does come through the taps. Our family and friends are desperate to spend time with us but won't come because they know of the water problem. Any agency handling resettlement like ours must not accept a site where there is no consistent supply of drinking water. If you can't give 24 hours of water supply, then eight hours of continuous supply is a must; that must happen. What is life without water?

Water was (and remains) a major concern throughout Sangharsh Nagar. Borewells were drilled into the earth in 2009, but fearful of steep electric bills, most of the cooperative housing societies (CHSs) in charge of building expenses only ran their borewell motors five to 10 minutes a day. During this scheduled period, women would rush home to fill drums with water or hand-wash their clothes at a speed rivaling the rinse-and-spin cycle of an automatic washing machine!

Prestige Is Up, But So Are Expenses

The high cost of apartment living came up unfailingly in the research-conversations. On average, each household paid INR 300 per month to the CHS managing committee. This covered the expense of pumping water from the underground tank[14] to the roof-top tanks of their respective buildings as well as general building maintenance, including the cleaning, lighting, and upkeep of common areas (Figure 4.1) and the frequent elevator repairs. In addition, monthly electric bills could be as high as INR 1,200 per household. But considering that many of these women had worked in upper- or middle-class homes with elevators, private water, and electricity, should these costs have come as a surprise? According to the participants, it wasn't so much the expenses of owning a home in a pricey neighborhood but their size. One motive to help explain slum dwellers' willingness to assume the costs of homeownership (even if they lacked adequate means) was the opportunity to raise their social standing:

AUTHOR: Before you got here, was there discussion about how you shall pay for maintenance? About 'How are we to do all of this'?

SUHANA: All that was decided by the committee [the managing committee of the CHSs] after we came here[15].

SHARADA: People needed a home. Instead of dying there in the heat over there. … People would refer to us as those who live in the slum. That one black spot on us is wiped off. We now live in the building. Now they cannot say that we live in the slum. Now they do not.

SUHANA: Forget about people, now relatives in their speech are saying, 'They say come, come [and visit us]'!

[The participants laugh]

SUHANA: I am telling the truth. Prestige has gone up. Just by climbing four floors, the respect for us has gone up!

It was soon apparent that they had transitioned into a lifestyle significantly beyond their previous means. All financial budgeting, as one participant put it, revolved around the monthly maintenance dues. Non-payment carried a fine of INR 50:

RANI[16]: Then there is the cable [television], the fee for the cable … see, we have to keep at least 1,000 Rupees a month somehow.

AUTHOR: Payment for cable?

RANI: Yes, cable is 200 Rupees. For the three together [maintenance, electric bill, and television cable bill], equals about 1,000 Rupees. If there is no cable, then the children [would complain]. We also get to see some of the news. If the children can see a little …

NIRMALA: To reside, we get a lot [of bills]. There is trouble with money, there are challenges with money.

Figure 4.1 An underground water reservoir/tank in the courtyard area of a cluster with residents seated on its concrete surface. As seen in December 2012

RANI: There are some good people here [good earners]. The ones that are good and those, there are some, sister, what do I tell you? There are challenges to eat each meal because none of the husbands are good. Some drink, some do whatever, so the women have to run the household. If there are children, then you have to make sure they go to school, and then we have to watch their work. It is a lot of trouble. Some of us have so much …

AUTHOR: This challenge existed in the slum too, no?

RANI: In the slum as well.

RAJKUMARI: That is everywhere. If we don't earn, how are we to eat?

AUTHOR: So, what is it that you do not like about here?

RANI: The place is good. The ones who are literate, get a job, but the ones like us …

Participants repeatedly mentioned that proximate jobs commensurate with their skills could help make what Rani called a "good" place better. This sense of hope that jobs matching their skills could be brought to the site is the subject of the next chapter. In their initial months at Sangharsh Nagar, many residents spent long hours commuting back to workplaces near their former homes in the park. But within a year, many of them had left or lost those jobs due to the time and expense it took to get back and forth. As with many other relocation experiences, there were exceptions, however. Pooja, 42, lived at Sangharsh Nagar with her two daughters, ages 21 and 15. She was the only one among all the participants working outside the home who had retained her job near the slum beyond a year. She had worked as a domestic helper for an upper-middle-class household for more than two decades. Initially, her daily journey by public transportation took a good two hours each way at a price hardly affordable at her existing income. The commute was the worst in the first two years when Sangharsh Nagar was poorly served by transportation. In 2009, the city opened a bus line running between the site and the park for a relatively high fare of INR 40 each way[17]:

POOJA: And after coming here, there is a lot of peace. She [her employer] was nice. I waited, waited for a year to ask her for more money [to cover transportation costs]. They've been good to me and my daughters and I owed her money [borrowed money]. She gave me [INR] 3,000 as salary [while I lived] in Malad and after I came here to Sangharsh Nagar, she is giving me [INR] 5,000. She is giving me an extra 60 Rupees [a day] for transportation. My girl would make [INR] 1,000 as salary in Malad and now my daughter [the same 'girl' who works as a domestic helper in an upmarket township near Sangharsh Nagar, contributes to the household and has no transportation expense getting to work] is making [INR] 8,000 because the area here is more expensive. Because of Hiranandani [an upmarket township within walking distance of Sangharsh Nagar].

She was far more fortunate than Kajal, whose husband had lost his job because of the same long commute. Access to transportation by autorickshaw, the popular black-and-yellow motorized three-wheelers, was limited as well. Early on, Sangharsh Nagar gained notoriety for some thefts. According to the participants, autorickshaw drivers hesitated to enter the area after sunset for fear they'd be robbed. Instead, they would drop passengers off at an intersection that was a 20-minute walk away. Gayatri, 55, an unemployed widow who lived with three of her sons, a daughter, two daughters-in-law, and two grandchildren, became visibly upset when she spoke about the lack of transportation available. She had left behind her previous domestic helper job in the Damu Nagar slum for health reasons. She had been silent for most of the 65-minute focus-group discussion, but near the end she moved to the edge of her chair as if about to stand and announced: "Just getting a roof over one's head does not make for a home". She continued:

GAYATRI: It was the second month here and my grandchild had an accident. His hand completely broke and I had to take him to the hospital late at night. No autorickshaw, just no autorickshaw. Then finally one [autorickshaw] man said yes to coming and I had to pay him extra to wait at the hospital to bring us back. Can you imagine? No one wanted to come here.

The resettlement site's reputation only began to improve after a majority of the phase-I allottees had moved in (i.e. by about 2009). But even in December 2016, during my last visit to Sangharsh Nagar, I found getting an autorickshaw for the half-hour ride to my hotel in Andheri to be a daily struggle[18]. My experience contextualized participants' conversations about a third area of disappointment at the new site: safety. I had thought this would be no concern in a place with as much foot traffic as Sangharsh Nagar, but women passionately described a different situation. They traced their concerns about safety to the very nature of cooperatively owned, multi-story housing and its rules. They said the design of the buildings allowed observers to peer down over the site from windows, balconies, hallways, and parapets. They also blamed the lack of open spaces and community cohesiveness. And they criticized the intermingling of residents from dissimilar slums in the same apartment buildings for creating what they characterized as an uncomfortable hotchpotch of inhabitants. I address these aspects in detail in Chapter 5.

So Many Rules and yet Unsafe

Sangharsh Nagar's 225-square-foot, three-room apartment units comprised a bedroom/living room, a kitchen, and a bath/toilet, regardless of the size of the household. In addition, there were few open spaces of the type that women were accustomed to. Women were used to walking up and down the hills of the park slums to take children to school, taking evening strolls to buy fresh meat or vegetables for the family's meals, or to killing time among the trees, shrubs, wells, and water standposts; all were cherished spaces beyond the walls of their slum homes. Their new outside spaces at the resettlement site became the hallway, lobby, elevator, stairway landings, building rooftop, and courtyard benches of their apartment buildings[19], atop the water tank in their courtyard (Figure 4.1), or the sites of the makeshift *bazaar*, bus stand, or English and computer training classes that had mushroomed throughout the site. But when these women felt that they could not stroll freely through the courtyard or utilize other spaces in and around their buildings, their "living space" shrank to the walls of their three-room apartments and perhaps to Nivara's training room where vocational training classes were periodically held. These became their only "safe" and "sanctioned" spaces for leisure and growth activities.

Shailja, 19, was an unmarried girl living with her mother, two brothers, a nephew, and a sister-in-law. After moving to Sangharsh Nagar in 2008 from the Gandhi Nagar slum, she found work at a jewelry-plating company in the city's export processing zone, a special economic zone created to attract foreign investment and technology situated in the suburb of

Andheri. On Friday evenings she and six other young adult women attended the two-month beautician training course held in Nivara's training room (the site of all the focus-group discussions). Here Shailja shared her version of safety:

SHAILJA: No one could say anything over there [in the park slums], but over here, since we have come here, we have gotten somewhat bored here. Meaning, once you go inside, you cannot go out. You cannot make a noise in the building, you cannot form a group with friends and head to the terrace. Boys can definitely not be seen in groups together in the entrance of the buildings. You can't sit around chatting with others outside the buildings or in the stairwell or even use the elevator at certain times of the day and cannot be seen chatting with boys for too long. After coming here, there are lots of [rules and restrictions]. It used to feel very good over there.

AUTHOR: And it doesn't feel good here?

SHAILJA: No, no. If you call your friends to play here, then their parents will call them to study or to eat. They will make some excuse and will call them home. So here, despite living close to one another, we folks cannot talk. It's good to have some, but so many rules?

AUTHOR: Really? You can't talk?

SHAILJA: When we go out, that is when we can talk. When we get together, when we go walking together, only then [can we talk to one another]. My own friend who lives right by me, I don't talk to her as much because you cannot do this and that in the building. When we come here [to the beautician training course], that is when we talk. Despite living close to one another, we cannot talk.

The rules and restrictions Shailja referred to constituted an integral part of the Slum Rehabilitation Schemes' vision of "making slum dwellers tax paying citizens of Bombay" (Slum Rehabilitation Authority, 1997, p. 10). In order to share in the "growth, status and prosperity of this great city" (Afzulpurkar, 1995), the Authority decided that the former slum residents who now lived in one building (or a combination of buildings proximate to one another) were to register themselves as a CHS[20]. This society would be responsible for maintaining the built environment at the new site[21]. Cooperative ownership was a mandated means to help build and sustain a viable place, but transitioning from the generally informal group arrangements of the slums to the formal model of cooperative ownership wasn't seamless. (See Chapter 2 for more about the committees residents had organized in the slums for getting and maintaining such amenities as roads, wells, water standposts, and garbage disposal.) Young adult women like Shailja, who had spent the first two decades of their lives in the slums, found the rules imposed by the CHS managing committees to be constricting.

The resettled residents of one apartment building cluster were registered as one or two CHSs. The CHS managing committees created rules regulating the use of spaces and amenities in and around their buildings, with some rules more draconian than others. This was in sharp contrast to the nearly unbridled freedom of movement residents were used to in the slum. In many buildings I visited, strictly enforced rules controlled elevator operating hours, intended both to keep children from mis- or over-using them (elevators broke frequently) and to keep down electric bills. CHS committees restricted access to the roofs, fearing suicide attempts or tampering with the building water tanks; to stair landings, mostly to prevent hanky-panky between the sexes; and to courtyards where the concrete lids on the borewells were fenced-in and locked to keep residents from drawing or contaminating the water (Figure 4.2).

Residents complained about the rules governing the relatively safe interior spaces of the building clusters and about the unsafe conditions existing outside their clusters. Amrapali, 20, summarized it best when she spoke of the rowdies who stood outside waiting to tease or attract passing women:

> The way it is here is that when you get down out of your building, all the boys are staring. In the slum we could disappear, disappear in those alleyways of Prem Nagar [her neighborhood]. They [the alleys/lanes] were tiny. You would get out of here, and enter there. We friends would race in them. We were not allowed to run [in our particular lane], but we ran. We could pick and choose the shortest route and here, they [the rowdies] are everywhere. There at 10 or at 11 at night, we could go, but here it is hard to get out of the house because the rowdies keep coming and they all have their own areas. At 8:00 at night it feels like midnight. No girls step out. You have to keep thinking who might be standing in the next corner. There were also no [street] lights in the first few months. My brother wouldn't let me get out of the house after 7:00.

Those concerned about rowdies had grown into young adults after relocation and might now view perceived attention from males from a different point of view. Some vehemently argued that there was more to their concern. "The boys", Ruchi argued, "had changed".

RUCHI: Now they look at you like they have never seen you before. They stare away. If you step out of your house …

AUTHOR: Because you have grown older?

RUCHI: Here, whether you are big or you are small, they stare at you all the time.

SHAILJA: Yes.

RUCHI: And if a girl, if she is just a 10-year-old girl passing by, then they will stare at her, whether it is a big or a small girl.

I posed the same question to Leela and others in another discussion. She had a different explanation for what she and her circle of friends considered the source of the problem:

AUTHOR: So what do these boys do?

LEELA: If they find someone by themselves, they'll say something [nasty], if they find a gold necklace [she gestured the snatching of a necklace].

AUTHOR: Which [building] number do you live in? No. 20, right?

LEELA: 19.

AUTHOR: So, it has happened there?

LEELA: Yes, many times. I mean, the people from the MNS (Maharashtra Navnirman Sena)[22] Party have a group. There is a lot of rowdyism from there and you must have seen them. Most of it happens right by the gate, by the main gate [of building 19].[23] We need a ladies' police station here. So many people and no police station?

Leela blamed the rowdyism on a particular political party and the absence of police protection. But to two young women introduced earlier in this chapter, the perceived change in behavior was due to the corrupting influence of men from "other" slums in the park and the dearth of jobs and positive recreational opportunities at the resettlement site:

Figure 4.2 The same underground water reservoir/tank shown earlier (in Figure 4.1) but with a fence erected around it. As seen in December 2014

AUTHOR: Boys have gotten spoilt here?
SANGEETA: Yes, they have gotten spoilt.
AUTHOR: The girls haven't been spoilt? The boys have? How come?
AMRAPALI: Girls too have gotten somewhat spoilt.
AUTHOR: The boys that were there, have come here and become rowdies?
SANGEETA: Yes. Over there, wherever the boys were, they were separate. Now, from Appapada, Damu Nagar [park slums], they have all gotten mixed here. A boy that wasn't a rowdy, has become *shaana* [Mumbai-style Hindi for "loafer"] here. No one is interested in studies.
AMRAPALI: You will only see girls heading out to work. The boys have become lazy, real lazy.
AUTHOR: Why do you say that?
AMRAPALI: No, you need money and money comes steadily. The mother earns, the father earns. And once the wife comes, she will earn and we can loiter around with our friends.
SANGEETA: Like us girls, boys get bored too, you know. No jobs here for anyone. There [in and around the park slums] there were so many [jobs].

The rationalizations expressed by some of the young, unmarried participants revealed the many factors influencing their perceptions of safety at the site. Like themselves, they saw young adult men with too little space for recreation or nearby jobs that matched their skills. They concluded that this induced rowdy behavior not seen in the slums. These young, unmarried women thought that their rise in status that came with their move into a high-rise would raise the standards of behavior all around. But for their young male counterparts, it seemed to have changed their behavior for the worse. Following Sangeeta's remark about the lack of livelihood options Amrapali expressed her disappointment with what she observed:

> We have now started living in buildings. How should we stay? We should live here like professionals. Some people are just like rowdies. They live like it is their birthright. We are born this way and we shall die this way. That is how these people continue to behave.

The topic of unsavory male attention generated a range of suggestions about what can and should be done to remedy behavior and improve gender relations within the resettlement site, aspects I address in more detail in the following chapter.

A second factor explaining participants' perceived lack of safety was the influx of political parties, politicians, and young male loiterers, many of who worked, often for small sums of money, as street-level brokers for local politicians. These brokers were usually unemployed youth of Sangharsh Nagar who were deployed as the eyes and ears of the many aspiring candidates running in the municipal elections. Corporators—members of the city's Municipal Corporation—are elected every five years and are critical agents of the city's poor. They mobilize an often tangled and opaque constellation of actors who have a stake in bringing services to the ward that elects them. Key among the corporators' many formal and informal networks (from personal, political, bureaucratic, financial, and criminal to NGO and CBO networks) are the street- or neighborhood-level brokers. These unemployed youth help distribute money for votes prior to corporation elections, exact rent for services rendered to the ward's population (for access to any public service, water supply, or public distribution system), attend to complaints, and open lines of communication between complainants and the city's bureaucracy. They serve as brokers between the corporator, the neighborhood's elected chief, and the residents of his or her ward.

The rowdies that Leela and others complained about were active year-round, but were especially visible in the months preceding the municipal elections held in February. During my visit to the site in December 2011, preparations for the February 2012 municipal elections were in full swing. Bamboo-pole arches covered with streamers, flags, banners, and campaign posters displaying headshot zooms of the candidates surrounded by miniscule headshots of their loyalists flooded the main and arterial roads of Sangharsh Nagar. The pestering youth that Leela had pointed to were hardly particular to the Maharashtra Navnirman Sena (MNS) Party. People from several political parties had descended on the site since its inauguration in 2007 to compete for the favor of its occupants. Each party had been quick to plant its local informers (or recruit informers from) youth and sports clubs, *mahila mandals* (women's groups) and *bishis* (rotating credit and savings associations). Assembling such networks of informants was not unique to Sangharsh Nagar. The slums the participating women had left were highly politicized; many considered them more politicized than the non-slums (Kimani, Zulu, & Undie, 2005; Ghertner, 2010; Laquian, 1983). The women said that voter mobilization occurred throughout the year in their slums, but gained fervor and urgency in the months leading up to election day. Community groups (whose members usually shared the candidate's caste, religion, or ethnicity) would receive small sums of money from the candidate with the implied understanding that it would be used to deliver votes on election day. The young men who were loitering (and harassing women) were most likely brokers affiliated with area youth and sports clubs. Such brokers had been ubiquitous in the slum, but crammed within a site like Sangharsh Nagar, with few open spaces and fenced-in clusters of apartment buildings, women may have perceived their presence as a greater deterrent to their safety and mobility. As Amrapali saw it, the resettlement site didn't offer the freedom of the slum to "pick and choose the shortest [and safest] route" in and out.

The task of voter appeasement and mobilization continued post election. The victors (and their competitors) spent the years in office trying to control the area and win reelection. This took place through varied means, both legitimate and devious. It largely involved obtaining, maintaining, and/or expanding physical infrastructure and services that residents needed.[24] In August 2012, when I visited Mumbai to start collecting data, posters supporting Ishwar Devram Tayade, the winner of the 2012 municipal elections, were abundant. He won as candidate of the recently formed MNS Party, defeating the former corporator and Shiv Sena candidate, Chitra Sangale. Once residents like Shakuntala and Leela had relocated to Sangharsh Nagar and found an absence of job opportunities and such critical amenities as water, public transportation, paved roads, and street lighting, the women eagerly sought candidates' help in securing what was missing. For instance, the absence of an authorized marketplace gave Tayade's brokers de facto license to assume the role of agents (of the corporator and patrons of the resettled population) who could exact generous payments from residents who wished to set up business in the unauthorized roadside *bazaar*. Residents willingly paid these de facto bribes to protect their businesses and sustain life in an increasingly expensive habitat.

Conclusions

Lack of water, the higher cost of apartment living, and loitering youth on street corners and at building-cluster gates represented sources of significant dissatisfaction for the participating women. These disappointments were unpleasant reminders that, despite the transition to legal tenure, "we shall remain a begging slum dweller". In the words of Chatterjee (2004), were they still part of the "population" and not "citizens"? As members of a "population", the participating women recognized the long waits and repeated efforts still required for every incremental improvement in their living conditions at the resettlement site. Like Bayat (2010) observed in the context of slums (*ashwaiyyats*) in Middle Eastern cities, participating women (sometimes by themselves but often with their neighbors) quietly shaped their everyday lives in the park slums into a semblance of order and routine. Securely tidying themselves up in the wee hours of the morning or under cover of darkness, carrying *handaas* after *handaas* of water from the nearest source, saving money on the sly to give their children a better meal, and protecting their homes from the torrential monsoon rains made up the relatively silent but daily struggles to succeed within the "very zones of exclusion" called slums (Bayat, 2010, p. 6). Yet, each woman had a different place-making story (Chapter 2), her own individual saga of struggles that reflected the elevation of her slum home, her age, marital status, the type and location of her employment, and the size of her household income. All were accounts of amenities and routines earned through *sangharsh* (struggle), an intense tug-of-war between them as "population" versus the rest as "citizens".

A transition to the assumption of legal housing tenure had not yet ferried them into *citizen*ship. Questions demanding spatial justice[25] emerged repeatedly in focus-group discussions and individual interviews, centered on questions like, "When shall we get water?" "Why is there just one bus between our old and new homes?" "How will we manage to pay the bills?" "When will they assign us a place where we can conduct business?" "Why isn't there a ladies police station for such a large settlement?" For "citizens" who are engaged with governance apparatus demanding their rights for clean and sufficient water, public transportation, livelihood opportunities, or security–these questions would be prominently exposed and solutions explored. But for the women of the slums, these were still mostly questions and wishful conjecture.

I end this chapter somewhat more positively with a poignant observation about the changes women experienced upon relocation, namely that of socio-spatial exclusion. Although a sense of non-inclusion could be listed alongside women's other significant disappointments in their new environment, I also heard this resonate more as a solution, faith in the resettlement site's "perfectable" future with adequate amenities, livelihood options, and safety. In one focus-group discussion four women responded to my query about whether and how they regarded their daily routines and habits to have changed after five years of life at the resettlement site. This same question in other focus groups had produced discussions about problems with water, living expenses, and safety. In this one discussion, however, the women connected it to the closed-door habit they saw residents take up post-resettlement:

GAYATRI: The doors there [in the slums] were never shut. They were open [loud chatter among the participants]. There was constant movement, in and out, here and there, through the night and day. There were 50 homes [in her *chaali*], and the child would play there. If he cried, then we could run and go there. That is how it was there. All open.

VAIJAYANTI[26]: If a [political leader/candidate] leader comes to give a speech [at Sangharsh Nagar], or to do something, then people will see from atop. They will not come down. They won't come down. They must. Unless people come, only then.

SITA: Yes, we are comfortable here. That is why our bellies have swollen. We are putting on weight. There is no strength in the body, just fat in the belly. We are good to look at, but there is no strength. There we were thin and here we have become fat; that is the only difference.

VAIJAYANTI: But you know what has happened is that humanity has come down. Why do we think of those times? Because, we think of our humanity, because we were together there, it was one *chaali*, if anything happened then we came together.

GAYATRI: Here there is an elevator, you see. Let's take the example of my neighbor next door in the slum. They may have lived there for five to ten years, but here it is not so. Here, we have all been separated, are far apart and hence we don't know our neighbors. There we were on a level ground [at the same elevation], so we got to know. How are we to know now? Everyone's doors are closed. They stay inside, so how do we come to know? That is why we don't come to know anything.

In addition to the complaints about physical amenities, women noted a decline in collectivism and the emergence of a more individualized, atomistic lifestyle due at least in part to the disaggregation of those who'd lived near one another in their respective *chaalis*. However, this was a complaint shared not as a permanent or unchangeable condition but as a means to generate a healthier balance between privacy and community, between individuality and a sense of common purpose. Efforts to break through the more private, imposed architecture of apartment living amidst strangers to satisfy a professed need for greater social contact and ultimately a "better life" are the subject of the next chapter.

Notes

1 The Mumbai Metropolitan Region is spread over 4,355 square kilometers (1681.475 square miles) and consists of eight Municipal Corporations including Greater Mumbai, Thane, Kalyan-Dombivali, Navi Mumbai, Ulhasnagar, Bhiwandi-Nizamapur, Vasai-Virar, and Mira-Bhayandar; and nine municipal councils, namely Ambarnath, Kulgaon-Badalapur, Matheran, Karjat, Panvel, Khopoli, Pen, Uran, and Alibaug, along with more than 1,000 villages in the Thane and Raigad districts. MMRDA is responsible for transportation, housing, water supply, and environmental concerns in these areas and for long-term planning, the promotion of new growth centers, implementation of strategic projects, and the financing and development of infrastructure.

2 In Mumbai, there are various types of TDR comprising heritage, reservation, road, and slum TDR. In the case of slum TDR, slums are the "sending areas" and anywhere north of the slum (except areas that fall within the island city) are "receiving areas" where construction of housing for sale at market rates is permitted. Under the state's Slum Rehabilitation Scheme inaugurated in 1995, the owner of the slum land surrenders it to the state government and agrees to rehouse slum dwellers or project-affected persons (PAPs) for free. In the case of the park, the sending area comprised a dilapidated quarry land that was home to several hundred former quarry workers as well as the park dwellers who had to be resettled from the park lands. The landowner and the developer in this case were the same. Per slum rehabilitation regulations, the developer was required to get the consent of at least 70 percent of the former stone quarry workers who met the state's eligibility criteria for rehousing and these former quarry workers were required to organize themselves into a community-based organization. These rules did not apply to the park dwellers who were being rehoused on the former quarry land. Thus, Sangharsh Nagar was developed under two types of slum rehabilitation regulatory schemes offered by the city: 33.10, whereby slum dwellers are rehabilitated on the site of their original slum, and 3.11, whereby the owner of vacant, unencumbered land agrees to use the land for public construction involving project-affected persons (PAPs). Although the slum dwellers in the park's fringe areas are not the prototypical PAPs, such as people displaced by road or dam construction projects, the SRA exercised its right to declare this former quarry land a slum rehabilitation area to resettle those residing in park slums. In the 3.11 scheme, the owner is

compensated by TDR for both land and the construction of tenements for slum dwellers. The TDR obtained from the 33.10 and the 3.11 schemes gives developers the right to construct units in higher-income areas, but only north of where the TDR originates.

3 Nivara staff told me that the unidentified "private developer" (Bharucha, 2004) was none other than Sumer.

4 This plunge was the result of an anticipated release of several hundred thousand square feet of slum TDR generated by the ongoing Mumbai Urban Transportation Project and the Mumbai Urban Infrastructure Project. Both projects involved the resettlement of slum dwellers and were significantly funded by the World Bank (Nainan, 2008, p. 31).

5 The city's Municipal Corporation was ill equipped to maintain records and administer the high volume of TDR transacted in Mumbai during this period. Mumbai's TDR market is notorious for its corrupt dealings controlled by a small, tightly guarded group of buyers, sellers, and the municipal authority in charge of mediating these transactions. According to general wisdom, records indicating where the TDR originates and where it is ultimately utilized need to be maintained so that the Municipal Corporation can realistically assess the capacity of the area to adequately support physical infrastructure commensurate with the housing construction made possible by use of slum TDR.

6 Once allotted a home at the resettlement site and per the state government's slum rehabilitation policy, the slum resident was required to vacate their home in the slum so that the state may proceed with demolishing and clearing the collapsed structure.

7 According to the women who participated in my research, units were allocated through a lottery system that interspersed residents from the various slums and neighborhoods among the different buildings. The High Court had ordered residents from the same "area" to be resettled in one or proximate building(s) and specific units within the building(s) to be assigned by lottery. However, women frequently complained that they were put alongside people from several different "areas" of the park.

8 In my intake conversations with the women, one of the questions asked concerned the title to the unit. Everyone, barring those who'd been divorced or separated before signing consent, mentioned that their unit was in the name of their husband, father, or father-in-law. Some participating women, as is highlighted later in this chapter, lost their husbands soon after relocation and some separated from their abusive husbands. All such women never brought up the issue of having lost their legal rights to homeownership, but when I inquired further, some women mentioned that they were working on it with the Forest Department and others were yet to initiate all needed paperwork to claim their equal rights to the property. I shared this with Nivara's leaders once I completed my 2013 stay. After a few months, Nivara's Singh responded stating that this was an unfortunate omission and something that it hoped to correct in future allotments. "Maybe", wrote Singh, "your report can be the basis for demanding a revision in [future] allotment letter[s]".

9 The May 2007 inauguration saw the handing over of keys to 15 families still residing in the slum, but this was only a symbolic gesture. October 2007 was when the process of physical relocation from the park slums to Sangharsh Nagar actually commenced.

10 As part of its deliverables, Sumer installed a large-capacity water tank to hold municipal drinking water. It was located at the southwest end of the site at an elevation lower than land in the southern parts. The women strongly felt that this tank had been misplaced. The reason for its location, however, had to do with the location of the municipal water pipeline adjacent to the site. Perhaps Sumer

could have negotiated the extension of the municipal line to a more suitable location within the site. A booster pump had to be installed to channel water from this large water tank to several smaller, underground tanks that Sumer constructed in the open spaces adjoining the clusters of apartment buildings. (These were the spaces that Nivara had described in its plan as "courtyards" for community gatherings and other leisure activities.) A second booster pump had to be installed to lift the water from the ground-level tank to tanks on the roofs of individual apartment buildings. To pay for the electric cost of pumping water (from the large tank to their cluster tank and from the cluster tank to their individual apartment buildings), residents were required to form Cooperative Housing Societies. A cluster of 14–18 apartment buildings formed one or more societies, and all the societies created across the resettlement site subsequently became part of a federation, a society of societies. The cluster societies were responsible for paying the electrical bill for their respective booster pumps and the federation collected payments from cluster societies for yet another electricity bill that came from running the pump attached to the large-capacity tank. Until these societies and their federation were registered, participants stated that the tank held water sourced from a nearby pond for the use of construction work on the site and to supply water to the construction workers temporarily housed there. The first resettled residents would use a rope and bucket to draw this tank water, which was unsuitable for drinking. They had to fetch potable water from outside the settlement or hire a private water tanker to supply drinking water to their building(s).

In 2009, borewells were dug to draw non-potable underground water, which the women described as reddish-brown colored and only fit for flushing their toilets. Like with the drinking water supply, information is unclear on when the drilling of borewells to supply non-potable water to each household occurred. For at least a year (i.e. from October 2007 through September or October 2008), Nivara's staff affirmed that non-potable water was fetched from several makeshift ponds around the site, including the one large pond situated in the site's northeast corner.

11 I heard contradictory information about when the drinking water supply began. Some women said their kitchen taps were dry for the first six months; others put it at 18 months to two years. Although I can't say when the drinking water supply in Sangharsh Nagar commenced, it is safe to state that sometime in early 2009, after many of the cooperative housing societies were registered and their managing committees formed, Sangharsh Nagar was officially connected to a municipal water pipeline and the booster pumps were in place.

12 Reema, 42, worked as one of two full-time staff members in Nivara's office at the resettlement site. She joined this discussion as Hamsika's translator, but couldn't resist contributing herself. She had moved from the Appapada slum into an apartment unit with her husband and two daughters just steps from Nivara's office. Hamsika, who only spoke Marathi, 44, lived with her husband, two sons, and two daughters. Unlike most other participants, her unit belonged to her brother (her family did not meet the eligibility criteria since they'd migrated to Damu Nagar slum in 2000, after the deadline). Her brother had moved back to their native home in Ghotil village in the southwestern district of Satara in Maharashtra. Gayatri, 55, came from the same slum as Hamsika. She lived with her three sons, two daughters-in-law, and three grandchildren. Kajal, 35, had lived in the Ambedkar Nagar slum since 1993 and now occupied a 225-square-foot apartment home with her husband, two children, her mother-in-law, as well as her brother-in-law and his family of four.

13 Kajal's husband is referring to an annual, publicly observed 10-day Hindu festival that is particularly extravagant in Mumbai. Idols of the elephant-headed

deity Ganapati, or Ganesha, are placed in makeshift, community-sponsored tents called *pandals* that are decorated with varying amounts of flowers and lights depending on the neighborhood's resources.

14 For the first two or two and a half years, all the electricity utilized to get water from the large water tank (not the underground tank close to the apartment buildings) to the various other tanks on the site went unpaid. The women claimed that bill was issued in Sumer's name, who said it was the residents' expense. They refused to pay the outstanding bill (INR 6.8 million as of December 2012), arguing that Sumer had used much of the billed-for water for construction purposes. In the resulting deadlock, the private power utility company would cut off electricity, causing the unpredictable water conditions that Kajal and others complained about.

15 The size of the CHSs varied considerably. As many as 14–18 different apartment buildings might register as one or two societies, or one society might represent a single apartment building. This inconsistency in how tenants grouped themselves to pay their monthly maintenance expenses created a logistical challenge in apportioning charges for operation of the site's large water tank.

16 Rani, 35, had migrated to Mumbai from the state of Bihar. She had joined her husband in 1991, roughly 10 years after their marriage. She made earrings and earned meager wages as a sub-contracted home-based worker in Gautam Nagar. She had set up her own shop selling *saree* falls (a strip of fabric that is sewed on to bottom hem of a *saree* so that its pleats fall well), and thread in the makeshift *bazaar* in Sangharsh Nagar. Her husband worked as a street vendor and her son did temporary work at a nearby medical store. Nirmala, 35, with two children, ages 10 and 18, had worked as a home-based sub-contracted worker making earrings in the slum. She did the same job after moving to Sangharsh Nagar. Her husband repaired furniture. Rajkumari, 32, had migrated to Mumbai from Uttar Pradesh in 2002. She started her life in the city as a renter in the park's Hanuman Nagar slum and two years later the family purchased land and set up a *pucca* home in the park's Damu Nagar slum. She, her husband, and their four children, ages 7 to 16, moved to Sangharsh Nagar in 2009. She made a living tailoring *saree* blouses from her apartment and her husband, 38, worked as a mechanic in an auto garage.

17 Source: Bus No: 498LTD (2016).

18 During the focus group discussions and interviews held in August and November–December 2012, I stayed in a serviced apartment, a short 15-minute walk from Sangharsh Nagar's entrance. In all my future visits, I stayed in the same hotel in the suburb of Andheri. There was just one direct bus to Andheri, and autorickshaws rarely agreed to take me all the way back there after sunset. Cabs were significantly more expensive than autorickshaws and less frequently seen at Sangharsh Nagar. The struggle to get daily transportation meant that Sangharsh Nagar's roads were regularly filled with people waiting for a bus, an autorickshaw, or a cab. There was no direct train from the nearby Ghatkopar station to the hotel or direct service from the Ghatkopar station to the park slums.

19 Each building contained 48–55 units and, on average, eight buildings shared a courtyard. This courtyard was intended to be arranged like a garden, with benches, to serve as an open space for recreational and leisure activities or a playground for children. In reality, each courtyard was partially taken up by a water tank and less than half the buildings in a typical cluster directly faced it. The rest overlooked alleys or roads within or connecting the clusters to one another. The courtyards and the darker alleyways between buildings were considered a menace to young women who were periodically accosted by men who assembled there.

20 Once registered, each CHS would apply to the Superintendent of Land Records of Mumbai Suburban District to change the record of property rights from Sumer to the society. The Municipal Corporation then assessed each building for property, water, tree, and street taxes plus fees like the education cess, a tax levied to cover the cost of government-run secondary and higher education. In light of the inability of slum dwellers to pay such taxes, the state government reduced property tax rates on buildings constructed under the (slum rehabilitation) scheme.

21 According to the provisions of the Maharashtra Ownership Flats Act of 1963, the builder/developer is legally required to convey the land and the building to the newly registered owner within four months of the society's formation or any legal body of the apartment purchasers. In the case of Sangharsh Nagar, Sumer conveyed its 45 acres of land (under phase I) to the Slum Rehabilitation Authority (the SRA) and the SRA conveyed the land to the various registered CHSs. The CHSs were responsible for their respective courtyards and each building had its own committee called the building committee (select members of which were part of the CHS managing committee) that was in charge of the rooftop, the elevator, the hallway, and other building-specific spaces. For all common areas not owned by the housing societies, Nivara helped form a federation of all registered CHSs. The federation, the Mahasangh, was registered in September 2012 and became the official entity responsible for common areas and facilities including the schools, the community hall, and any other common facilities that were part of the plan approved by the city's Municipal Corporation for the resettlement site.

22 Leela was born in Mumbai and her parents came from Uttar Pradesh. The MNS Party she referred to is Marathi for a regional party and translates as The Army for the Reconstruction of Maharashtra. As a variant of the Hindu nationalist party, the Shiv Sena (Army of Shiva), the MNS Party aggressively campaigns for its "sons of the soil" agenda and specially targets lower-class migrants from Bihar and Uttar Pradesh. The influx of political parties and their brokers is discussed in greater detail later in this section.

23 Members of some building clusters were able to afford gates—tall, ornamental wrought iron gates painted black and gold—to encircle their clusters. The same type of gates was put up around the borewells, previously used by women as a hangout space (Figure 4.1 and 4.2). As one woman I frequently encountered when entering the apartment building housing Nivara's office said, "Because the tank held water, the concrete made for a good, cool place to sit, wait to catch up with friends or better still to check out the collection of *sarees* that the walking salesmen brought with him each week!" All gates, other than a single, wicket gate attached to the main entrance for pedestrian traffic, were locked. Some clusters even hired a security guard to control cars, cabs, autorickshaws, salespeople, and emergency vehicles entering through the main gate. Women I spoke with had mixed feelings about the gates. On one hand, women believed they engendered a sense of safety, but on the other, they gave rowdies a designated area to loiter.

24 This was the case with Maske (referenced in Chapter 3), a beloved corporator who won the 2007 municipal elections in Shakuntala's home ward during the last few years she lived in the park. In Sangharsh Nagar, a local Member of the Legislative Assembly (MLA) and a former state textile minister (2009–2014), Mohammed Arif (Naseem) Khan of the Congress Party, allegedly pressured the SRA into handing over management of a school built on the site to a charitable trust he owned. According to plans submitted by the Sumer (and Nivara, the joint-developer and architect) and approved by the Municipal Corporation, a two-story school building was constructed in the southwestern

corner of Sangharsh Nagar. It was sanctioned by a special arrangement with the SRA in which all the area in the site's plan earmarked for preschool centers was combined and a new plan created and approved to build a school and a community hall in its place. Nivara thwarted Khan's attempts to gain control over the school's management by inviting the state's Chief Minister to the site and successfully demanding that the school be handed over to its legitimate administrator, the city's Municipal Corporation.

25 I adopt Nussbaum's (2000, p. 6) description of justice that holds that below a certain threshold level of capabilities, justice is sacrificed. At that stage, government is obliged to provide individuals with the means to live a dignified life. Spatial justice will be achieved when women are free to organize their built environment on their terms. If those terms aren't met, justice occurs when the government helps create such conditions. In my final chapter, I list the criteria I consider essential as the basis for a just resettlement and rehabilitation plan.

26 Vaijayanti, 35, a mother of two, relocated to Sangharsh Nagar in 2010. She worked as a domestic help in a gated housing complex near the resettlement site doing the same work as previously.

References

Afzulpurkar, D. K. (1995). *Report of the study group appointed by the government of Maharashtra for the rehabilitation of slum and hutment dwellers through reconstruction.* Programme for the Rehabilitation of Slum and Hutment Dwellers in Brihan Mumbai: Government of Maharashtra.

Archer, M. S. (2007). *Making our way through the world: Human reflexivity and social mobility.* New York: Cambridge University Press.

Aziz, F. A., Hussain, N., & Ujang, N. (2016). The implications of slum relocations in low-cost high-rises: An analysis through the infrastructure of everyday life. *Environmental-Behaviour Proceedings Journal*, 1(2), 33–42.

Bayat, A. (2010). *Life as politics: How ordinary people change in the Middle East.* Palo Alto, CA: Stanford University Press.

Balakrishnan, S., & Bharucha, N. (2002, December 10). Slum rehabilitation body is accused of illegal TDR release. *The Times of India.* Retrieved from https://timesofindia.indiatimes.com/city/mumbai/Slum-rehabilitation-body-is-accused-of-illegal-TDR-release/articleshow/30894043.cms.

Belenky, M. F., Clinchy, B. M., Goldberger, N. R., & Tarule, J. M. (1986). *Women's ways of knowing: The development of self, voice, and mind.* New York: Basic Books.

Bharucha, N. (2004). Slum TDR rates go into free fall. *The Times of India*, September 13. Retrieved from https://timesofindia.indiatimes.com/city/mumbai/Slum-TDR-rates-go-into-free-fall/articleshow/848713.cms.

Bus No: 498LTD. (2016). *go4mumbai.* Retrieved from http://go4mumbai.com/Mumbai_Bus_Route.php?busno=4981.

Chatterjee, P. (2004). *The politics of the governed: Reflections on popular politics in most of the world.* New York: Columbia University Press.

Frenzel, F. (2014). Can slum tourism reverse the plight of Johannesburg's marginalised communities? Favelas at LSE. Retrieved from http://eprints.lse.ac.uk/60633/1/Can%20slum%20tourism%20reverse%20the%20plight%20of%20Johannesburg%C3%94%C3%87%C3%96s%20marginalised%20communities_%20_%20Favelas%20at%20LSE.pdf.

Ghertner, D. A. (2010). Calculating without numbers: Aesthetic governmentality in Delhi's slums. *Economy and Society*, 39(2), 185–217.

Hazare loses case against slum authority. (2004). *The Times of India*, April 8. Retrieved from https://timesofindia.indiatimes.com/city/mumbai/Hazare-loses-case-against-slum-authority/articleshow/605595.cms?from=mdr.

Ickes, H. L. (1935). *Back to work: The story of PWA*. New York: The Macmillan Company.

Kimani, E., Zulu, E., & Undie, C. (2005). Health and livelihood implications of marginalization of slum dwellers in provision of water and sanitation services in Nairobi city. Poster presentation at the 4th International Conference on Urban Health, Toronto, Canada, October.

Laquian, A. A., & International Development Research Centre (Canada). (1983). *Basic housing: Policies for urban sites, services, and shelter in developing countries*. Ottawa, Canada: International Development Research Centre. Retrieved from http://hdl.handle.net/10625/8043.

The long road from the forest slums to the high rises of Chandivili. (2013). Nivara Hakk Slum Movements, Sanjay Gandhi National Park, Borivali. Retrieved from www.nivarahakk.com/slum-movement-national-park.php.

Nainan, N. (2008). Building boomers and fragmentation of space in Mumbai. *Economic and Political Weekly*, 43(21), 29–34.

Nussbaum, M. (2000). Women's capabilities and social justice. *Journal of Human Development*, 1(2), 219–247.

Slum Rehabilitation Authority, Housing and Special Assistance Department. (1997). *Guidelines for implementation of Slum Rehabilitation Schemes in Greater Mumbai*. Maharashtra, Mumbai: Author.

Smart, N. (1987). *Religion and the Western mind: Dreams, religion, and psychology*. Albany: State University of New York Press.

State may approve Azmi's slum plan. (2002). *The Times of India*, June 24. Retrieved from https://timesofindia.indiatimes.com/city/mumbai/State-may-approve-Azmis-slum-plan/articleshow/13903030.cms.

Yap, K. S. (1996). Low-income housing in a rapidly expanding urban economy: Bangkok 1985–1994. *Third World Planning Review*, 18(3), 307–323.

5 Buildings and Business, Love and Forgiveness

For the most part, everyday life at Sangharsh Nagar did not appear rosy. Even a fleeting glance at the words of women who recollected their first two to three years in Sangharsh Nagar reveals a residential development devoid of the ingredients they considered elemental for livability. Waterless taps, unclean air, limited access to public transportation or health-care facilities, scant room for recreation, lack of employment opportunities, and unsafe conditions all made their list of grievances. Taken together, they depicted the antithesis of livability. Both planners and scholars have argued that creating conditions for urban livability whether within the physical or the social environment requires a clear set of ideas regarding the actors who shape the city, their interests, and their ability to identify and satisfy heterogeneous interests. Authentic dialogue[1] is especially challenging when the opposing parties involved—the state and the slum dwellers, the NGOs and the state, NGOs and the builder lobby—have a history of conflict, power imbalances, and mutual suspicion. In the case of Sangharsh Nagar, the actor stakeholders were mediators of the site's livability who had thus far found it difficult to come together. The NGO Nivara struggled to convince the state (and its one-time ally, the builder Sumer) of the importance of design details and quality of construction for dignified and enduring habitation. After the city's real-estate boom crashed, Sumer became reluctant to build a project as costly as the NGO's original prototype. The community of eligible slum dwellers was rendered future-blind. Stated differently, they lacked the resources necessary to involve themselves in matters of choice, design, and management related to the relocation project. Politicians saw the lacunae in essential services at the resettlement site as an opportunity to gain access to a large voting constituency, a routine perfected in slums similarly wanting in everyday services and most acutely experienced during a slum's formative years. The state (including its multiple forms operating at the supra-local (ward), municipal, and state levels) had granted the slum dwellers the symbolic concession of a "free home", but, in the first two to three years, it largely rendered itself invisible in the day-to-day lives of those who relocated to Sangharsh Nagar. Without direct state involvement in the provision of such basic amenities as potable water, safe streets, schools, public transportation, and hospitals, the quality of life suffered.

The invisibility of the state reintroduced into the new state-sponsored environment the very injustices and inequalities of slum life that many of the site's residents had moved away from. While both the residents and observers like me can point to the many failings of the resettlement process and its mediators, I think highlighting imperfections is useful only to a point. I would notice how some 30 minutes into their focus-group discussions, the participating women would grow restless and some would become visibly exasperated with their fellow participants' defeatist comments and would implore each other to "stop complaining and start pulling yourselves up by your bootstraps".

Take the case of feisty 45-year-old group participant Champa, who listened for 40 minutes to 10 other women talk about their post-relocation misadventures, until she abruptly interjected[2]:

> Even God should not be blamed so much! We have gotten a good home. All of you just shut it and sit. Even if you were to die in hunger, no one, no one will come asking why you are sleeping on a hungry stomach. So, get ready to work. Do not say anything against your homes because they have given us a good house. Now the government has done so much for us, and hence we have gotten an all right home. To say something about the house is [incomplete]. Is there rain falling on your heads?

Champa's outburst kindled another hour-long discussion about what women were implementing to enhance living conditions for themselves, their families, and Sangharsh Nagar. While Champa did not participate in my other focus-group discussions, I heard similar sentiments in the 10 other discussions and 20 personal interviews I conducted at Sangharsh Nagar. They came in personal conversations with a participant who proactively walked me to her shop in Sangharsh Nagar's evening *bazaar*, with another woman who invited me to her monthly *bishi* (informal rotating savings and credit group) meeting (that I was unable to attend), from a third woman who demonstrated how she attached metal clasps on bracelets while she babysat for her four-year-old grandson, and from a fourth woman who told me how her husband's struggles to find work (as a self-employed furniture repairman) had "pushed" her out of the home to work as a cook in three other households (a grueling job but a welcome respite from the daily bickering and constant quarreling with her stay-at-home husband).

In this chapter, I share the various livelihood strategies I observed at the resettlement site depicting women not as passive, stereotypical "victims" of misery waiting to be rescued, but as agents actively making sense of and giving sense to their livelihood options. I present them as previously ignored agents who displayed the ability to both define problems and design solutions. Their definition and design of livelihood options occurred independently of the aims of the NGOs, government organizations, political parties, and for-profit builders with a presence in their resettlement site. Once again, I am not suggesting that the perspectives and activities of the women differed from those of the male residents at the resettlement site. My intent is to add their voices to the broader and otherwise gender-neutral conversation among scholars and practitioners about how best to design and develop slum resettlement and rehabilitation (R&R) policy and practice[3].

All Justified in the Name of Resilience?

Before sharing the assorted strategies women described to me over the course of my data collection, I think it is essential to acknowledge an unfortunate lack of uniformity in existing scholarship (and practice) in urban R&R. Scholarly works and policy proposals too often use the term *resilience* without adequate qualification. *Resilience* may be used to connote "a positive trajectory of functioning and adaptation after a disturbance"[4] (Norris et al., 2008, p. 130) or to imply indifference to the many losses and disturbances that residential evictions create. In bringing the voices of women into broader discussions on post-displacement resettlement, I am not suggesting that nothing is gained by contesting evictions or advocating for on-site resettlement. There is a lot to be said about their merits. As recounted in Chapters 2, 3, and 4, women deeply cherished their homes in the *zopadpattis*, the *chaalis*, and all their "vibrant matter". High levels of perceived tenure security defined their pre-demolition lives in the slum[5]. The perceived security came not only from the materials composing their homes and the built environment of their *chaalis* and *zopadpattis* but also from the many informal-sector livelihoods available within walking distance of the park. Their former lives in the park slums were also a repository of familiarity and belonging, of sentimental value where many had commenced their conjugal lives in the city, where responsibilities evolved to include motherhood, where some saw their status transformed from matrimony to detachment and for others was a place infused with life-long continuity within a community, from childhood into adulthood. Since the 1960s, urban scholars had warned that a policy of slum clearance, even when accompanied by relocation into ready-built public housing, would only increase overcrowding and exacerbate housing problems elsewhere in the city. Their appeals came amidst an era when multilateral donors and banks, particularly the World Bank, began investing in the shelter sector on the assumption that incrementally improving or upgrading slums had value.[6] Yet despite years of research and appeals for a more humane approach to slum dispersal, large-scale demolitions (and construction of public housing) are rampant approaches to slum resettlement in cities throughout the developing world. As Gilbert (2007, p. 710) commented bitterly, "How better to create cities without slums than by obliterating the eyesores?"

Besides being inequitable and "just plain wrong", wholesale slum clearance is often pursued by state and municipal housing authorities (and authorized and legitimized by judicial rulings) as the solution to "salvage" the city's ecology and bring "secure tenure" to the displaced. Such dislodgings become ever more ineffective when accompanied by a poorly conceived process of relocation and resettlement. Donors and planners regularly justify clearance, especially when slums are located in high-risk, environmentally dangerous areas.[7] Relocation and resettlement are also justified if internal factors (e.g. unity, leadership, community participation) and external factors (e.g. location of the new settlement, the compensation awarded) are accounted for (Viratkapan & Perera, 2006). Few, if any, such relocation and resettlement projects are successful in rebuilding the lives of those who are uprooted and relocated. Cities, like humans, are defined and refined through exchanges between imperfect actors. In the event of demolitions, the government must direct its policy toward the physical relocation and housing of the displaced, but most importantly in rebuilding post-displacement lives. Governments have yet to recognize that women "play an especially important role in defining and refining 'community management.' Because women are more directly concerned than men with the welfare of the household, and with 'community' issues … they are normally more aware than men of the needs of a housing project, and more committed to its success" (Wilson, 1993, p. 46). One means to achieve better, livable relocation outcomes is to systematically invite those directly affected into discussions on implementation.

Women who participated in my study identified their needs and deficits with an ease that rivaled the policy proposals drafted by professional planners or international lending institutions. Hearing them deliberate over their suggested solutions was extraordinarily liberating. I could picture them standing up in a meeting between the SRA and the private developer, the most improbable place to find a woman from the slums, and effortlessly articulating the ideas described in the following pages of this chapter. None of these proposals was official or academic, but all were clear and sprang from lived experience.

For clarity, I've organized the voices in this chapter into four categories of women: (a) those who harbored grievances, but were the most energized by the resettlement site's potential for upward social mobility; (b) women who had supported their households previously from within the confines of their homes, but had begun working outside the home since relocation; (c) those whose lives post-relocation closely resembled their previous routines for managing home and work; and (d) women who were calling on external agencies to live up to their pre-relocation promises to provide the conditions they believed necessary to pursue a livelihood they chose. Table 5.1

Table 5.1 Characteristics of the 120 women grouped by categories of how they made sense of post-resettlement livelihood options

How participants made sense of livelihood circumstances after resettlement	*Number of women*	*Marital status*	*Age group (in years)*	*Religion*	*Caste/ethnic grouping**	*Level of education (top three categories)*	*Source of livelihood in the slum versus the resettlement site (top three sources)*	*Avg. family members below 18*	*Avg. family members 18–25*	*Avg. family members over 25*	*Avg. family size*	*Avg. earners per family*	*Avg. female earners per family*
The young/not-so-young and the restless	33	45.45% never married; 27.27% married; 21.21% widowed; 6.06% divorced/separated	60.60% 18–25; 18.18% 42–49; 12.12% 34–41; 6.06% 50–57; 3.03% over 60	66.67% Hindu; 27.27% Buddhist; 3.03% Muslim; 3.03% Others	45.45% Dalit; 27.27% UC; 21.21% OBC; 3.03% Muslim	30.3% 6th–10th; 21.21% graduate and above; and, 21.21% higher secondary (i.e. 11th or 12th)	27.27 % still pursuing out-of-home employment; 21.21% stay unemployed and are 18–25; 21.21% were not employed and are currently employed out-of-home and are 18–25	1.42	1.93	2.21	5.57	2.45	1.3
"As a result of getting out, madam, I have learned a whole lot"	19	65.15% married; 26.31% widowed; 10.52% divorced/separated	31.57% 34–41; 26.31% 42–49; 26.31% 50–57; 5.26% 18–25; 5.26% 26–33; 5.26% 58–65	52.63% Hindu; 21.05% Muslim; 21.05% Buddhist; 5.26% Others	31.57% Dalit; 26.31% UC; 21.05% OBC; 21.05% Muslim	42.1% 6th-10th; 36.84% no education; and 15.78% below primary (i.e. 1st–4th)	47.36 % transitioned from not being employed to out-of-home employment; 15.78% from home-based self-employment to employment-out of-home; 10.52% from subcontracted work at home to out-of-home employment; 10.52% were self-employed home-based workers and are out-of-home employees	1.78	1	2.1	4.89	2.05	1
Been there, done that, can do it again	22	90.9% married; 4.54% never married; 4.54% divorced/separated	40.9% 42–49; 36.3% 34–41; 9.09% 26–33; 4.54% 18–25; 4.54% 50–57; 4.54% Unknown	77.27% Hindu; 9.09% Buddhist; 4.54% Muslim; 4.54% Christian; 4.54% Jain	36.36% UC; 27.27% Dalit; 22.72% OBC; 4.54% Muslim; 4.54% Christian; 4.54% Other	40.9% 6th–10th; 36.36% no education; 9.09% below primary	31.81% were and are out-of-home workers; 22.72% were and are also subcontracted home-based workers; 18.18% were and are also self-employed out-of-home workers	2.04	1.4	2.5	5.95	2.45	1.18

How participants made sense of livelihood circumstances after resettlement	*Number of women*	*Marital status*	*Age group (in years)*	*Religion*	*Caste/ethnic grouping**	*Level of education (top three categories)*	*Source of livelihood in the slum versus the resettlement site (top three sources)*	*Avg. family members below 18*	*Avg. family members 18–25*	*Avg. family members over 25*	*Avg. family size*	*Avg. earners per family*	*Avg. female earners per family*
"I'll wait until conditions are right, but can you help?"	46	73.91% married; 26.08% widowed	43.47% 34–41; 21.73% 50–57; 13.04% 42–49; 13.04% 58–65; 4.34% 26–33; 2.17% Over 66; 2.17% Unknown	67.39% Hindu; 19.56% Buddhist; 10.86% Muslim; 2.17% Christian	34.78% Dalit; 34.78% UC; 21.7% OBC; 8.69% Muslim	47.82% no education; 30.43% 6th–10th; and,15.21% below primary	54.34% were and are non-earning members; 15.21% were employed and are not currently employed; 10.86% pursued home-based sub-contracted work and are not employed	1.36	1.15	2.36	4.89	1.82	0.39

summarizes the key characteristics of each of the aforementioned categories of participating women.

The Young/Not-So-Young and the Restless

The words of the participating women recounted in this section resembled those of positive psychologists who hold that "negative emotions help us respond to threats, avoid risks, and appropriately mark losses, while positive emotions help us take advantage of everything life has to offer" (Cohn & Frederickson, 2009, p. 21). Young unmarried women and women accustomed to stepping out of the domestic domain to earn a living belonged to this young-/not-so-young-and-restless category. Young adult women participating in the various focus-group discussions and three of the 20 face-to-face interviews that I conducted, were focused on sampling the rewards of the future in the present. They had the highest average level of education among the women in this research and ranged from a fourth-grade education to post-graduate degrees. Their responses to my questions about satisfaction with life post-relocation offered valuable insights into how a positive approach resolved negative sentiments or was maintained over the long run. Their ways of thinking were helping them look beyond the everyday nuisance of catcalling rowdies loitering in and around the site to envision a way out of the mediocrity of their former lives in the slum, as well as the daily downers of their current lives in Sangharsh Nagar. Shared here are the words of young adult women, ages 18–25, expressed in two of my 11 different focus-group discussions. One discussion I cite is an exchange involving Anupama, Roshni, and Vidya[8] who were in a group comprising seven other participants. The conversation commenced with complaints about life at Sangharsh Nagar (in comparison to lives in their previous homes):

ANUPAMA: All age groups of girls are teased. Small kids also engage in it. They will push you, and will say that they did not do it. They will blame you for doing it. They will question you in return.

ROSHNI: The big ones [older boys] teach the small ones. That is how it happens. And those kids are learning.

VIDYA: What we as girls need is that there should be an organization that brings all our talents out.

ROSHNI: Yes.

ANUPAMA: Miss, what happens is that someone is fond of dancing. Now to dance here, there is dance here during the Ganapati festival. When we dance, the boys whistle from behind. They say 'what an item'. They talk like this.

AUTHOR: Really? Like what kind of talents are you referring to?

VIDYA: I can dance. I have come first and second in *surya namaskar* [the yoga pose, salutation to the sun] when I was in the seventh standard [grade]. That I have to keep hidden because there is no one like that here. I cannot go out and do it. I don't come to know what is happening and where. I can move forward, but I cannot get support. [I need someone to ask me:] Will you do? I'll say I can and that is the type of support that one must get.

ROSHNI: If you proceed to do it, then parents are the first to tell you …

VIDYA: First to tell you not to.

AUTHOR: It wasn't this way there. Wasn't it this way there?

ANUPAMA: There, nothing would happen. Here, those that are talented are forced to keep it suppressed.

In another discussion Ruchi, Meghana, and Jyoti[9] shared their hopes with five other participants.

RUCHI: Theirs [parents] is the support you need. Yes, if parents give it, then the kids can move forward because the parents are behind us. If we fall, it is the parents that …

AUTHOR: But not everyone's parents are this way, right? There are many parents that are supportive.

THREE OF THE PARTICIPANTS (SHAKUNTALADEVI, VAIJAYANTI, AND JYOTI): No, no [not everyone's parents are this way], we let our daughters do what they want to, but they need to tell us the truth [about what they are up to and with whom].

TARA: They support but in my home, my parents support, but here it is not that way.

JYOTI: It is because of the environment here that they do not support.

MEGHANA: They see the situation and the parents too are afraid. Fearing, what if something were to happen to their children?

RUCHI: First of all, the mentality must change.

They wanted some yet-to-be-identified agency to take the lead in educating parents about the advantages of granting them the freedom to step out of their homes to learn new skills and crafts or simply meet with friends. In another focus-group discussion with nine other women, Amrapali and Leela (introduced in Chapters 2 and 3 respectively) mentioned this when they talked about how to handle local rowdies hanging around the site:

AMRAPALI: They [parents] have to be made to understand. Girls too, their parents too. If the thinking is right, then the person in front of you can do nothing.

LEELA: The girls stay indoors and think that if they step out, then the boys outside will be there at this time. The class is at these hours. How do I go when boys are watching me? The boys will recognize us. They have to think differently. We are of a higher quality now. We have to think well. We have to think that what we are doing is good. We should not listen to what the person in front of us is thinking. That is the thinking that needs to come to everyone.

AMRAPALI: And some parents are such that they see other girls chatting with boys, they see them coming and going with boys, become friendly with them and they don't want their daughters to do the same thing. That is why they keep their daughters under control.

But in spite of their complaints about over-protective parents, neighbors or annoying local *tapori*s (rowdies in the so-called *Bombaiyya* Hindi), these young women were more concerned with actualizing self-identities as upwardly mobile working, urban "professionals" (see Amrapali's comments in Chapter 4). They wanted external support to persuade parents that allowing them greater freedom of movement would lead to more opportunities in the city's labor market where they could help the family deal with another frequent complaint of high-rise living, namely more cash inflow to help pay the monthly maintenance dues. As seen in the extract below, they wanted progressive agencies like Nivara to extend invitations to other nongovernmental agencies to provide free skills-training classes within the site. Some of these like jewelry making, embroidery, beautician courses, photojournalism, and English language training were in progress over my two-to-three-week site visits. They were held in the room where I conducted my focus-group discussions. Sunita[10], Leela, and Dhruti noted what they observed to be key changes in the extent of opportunities currently available in and around Sangharsh Nagar:

SUNITA: Okay, after coming here, there is lot of benefit, lot of benefits with education. Education is very close here. While there, we did not know what the world had. What I mean is, what the level of studies is. Meaning, we did not know anything about the number of courses that exist (Figure 5.1). After coming here, we have come to know that there is a standard to this. We now have the knowledge of what can happen in the future with our education.

AUTHOR: Because there are several organizations that come here? Because agencies did not come there?

LEELA, DHRUTI: No, they wouldn't come.

DHRUTI: There was nothing. After coming here, we have come to realize that we can do something.

AUTHOR: How do you know this, Sunita? You hardly lived there [in the slum].

SUNITA: I have made friends [after relocating here]. They tell me about the changes they see and my husband tells me, no? [Her family relocated to Sangharsh Nagar just 15 days after her arrival in Mumbai's park slum post-marriage. Her in-laws and husband had lived in the park for over two decades.]

LEELA: Like Nivara people, other organizations [recruiting participants for training] go to each sector [cluster] and ask if we want to learn this and that. Nivara should call many more to come.

Yet, attendance in these classes at Sangharsh Nagar was poor, prompting further discussion on how classes could appease both students and their nervous parents.

AMRAPALI: If girls have to step out and if their parents, their in-laws, do not permit [it], then they should be made to understand nicely. They have to be made to understand that if they want to do it, they should be allowed to. That they should not be told not to. This is our class, this is our institution—we want to have them stand on their own two feet. We will give them good training and they can go out. Parents have to first understand that yes, their daughter can do something. That she is old enough and can help with household expenses.

DHRUTI: They can stand on their own two feet and can work, they can earn, help out with the bills. In the future, they won't need anyone. That is the thing.

LEELA: Do such programs work, Madam? You must know this, Madam, won't you? [Her question was directed to me and I admitted to my lack of knowledge about the utility of programs that target parents or in-laws.]

AMPRAPALI: Of course, it will. Madam, next time you do a project, you must study what happens [if such programs were to be implemented].

The intent behind these pleas for outside intervention was not merely to cajole parents and in-laws but also to urge agencies to help carve spaces for extracurricular activities where women, young girls, and even boys could safely meet and socialize for vocational training and play. Women in another discussion group envisioned these as gender-segregated spaces:

RUKMINIDEVI[11]: The boys have their groups, but if they had a place to play, they may not feel the need to loiter. Can you imagine how good it would be if it [the resettlement site] is made safe for everyone at all times?

VIDYA: And to increase our confidence. I mean, now in college, all the students that are there, they need to have confidence, self-confidence. That is very important. Now, the way things are now, this thing is very important. For that reason, like there is Nivara, like that there should be another agency [to build self-esteem among women]. We should enjoy being out.

ANUPAMA: Who are you so concerned about? The boys that tease you? They are useless. Just do not look or say anything. This has never

Figure 5.1 A ground-floor apartment repurposed to run private tuition classes

happened to me because I don't turn around to look. That is what I have to do.

AUTHOR: Has anyone ever gone to the police [with complaints about harassment from boys]?

VIDYA: Police? As soon as they [the police] hear the name of Sangharsh Nagar, the police folks do not take the case [file a case]. There is so much of discrimination here [against residents of Sangharsh Nagar]. There is already a police station, but it is so full [of complaints from Sangharsh Nagar residents]. In one year, in two to three months, and the complaints went up. Who will they take? There are too many people here. Which complaint will they file [and which will they ignore]?

AUTHOR: So what are you suggesting?

ANUPAMA: See, why do we have self-defense? Karate, taekwondo. If anyone, just anyone, attacks any one of us, then only if we keep ourselves safe can we keep others safe. One just has to try such a thing. You have to. If you cannot be verbally assertive, then you must learn self-defense.

VIDYA: Who knows when this might [prove to] be useful? They [boys] will push you, and will say that they did not do it. They will blame you for doing it; they will question you in return. We need a ladies police *chowky* [a checkpoint staffed by female police officers] here, right here in Sangharsh Nagar.

Comments from Rukminidevi, Vidya, and Anupama brought vigorous nods of agreement from other participants. It was an eerie taste of the public uproar that erupted exactly two weeks after this discussion over a savage sexual assault in New Delhi. On December 16 2012, a 23-year-old female medical student and a male companion returning from an evening movie in India's capital city discovered that the unmarked private bus they were riding on with five other passengers had veered off-route. When the student's friend began shouting about the detour, the five other male passengers began to thrash and gag him until he was unconscious. They then took turns savagely beating and raping the woman over the next two hours. This all unfolded while the bus meandered through the city streets. After the attack, the pair was thrown into the street where the bus driver unsuccessfully tried to run them over. The woman later died from internal injuries caused by the beating and rape. The savagery of the attack in a supposedly safe and well-policed urban setting generated unprecedented and clamorous protests throughout India and demands for speedy justice for the victim and greater legal and political commitment to the problem of sexual assault against women.

The young adult participants in this study were not demanding legal and political attention but they were seeking community-based solutions. They wanted more support from their parents and did not want their parents' fears of the (un)known rowdy standing on the street corner to stifle their pursuit of vocational training or meet outside with friends. Comments from young adults like Leela and Amrapali point to a second type of desired change. They suggested that programs to increase knowledge and change attitudes among parents and in-laws needed to include evaluation of their impact on changing outcomes for the intended beneficiaries of such programs, namely the employability and self-esteem of the women. As noted by Morrison, Ellsberg, and Bott (2007), many interventions developed to reduce the risk of gender-based violence in developing countries have focused on changes in knowledge and attitudes but stop short of measuring behavioral outcomes. Although absent any lived experience of post-intervention outcomes, young women participants expressed confidence that their self-esteem would increase if they were provided with safe, gender-segregated physical spaces to mingle among themselves. Another suggestion was to provide them with self-defense training (see Anupama's comment about karate, taekwondo cited above). They felt that creating segregated spaces and programs for such purposes would improve their employability and self-esteem. They lent such efforts the potential to promote assertiveness and boundary setting, enhance self-efficacy in responding to threatening assault situations, and reduce feelings of self-blame.

Notwithstanding the daily stresses of parental control, vexing rowdies, and unsafe corners within Sangharsh Nagar, young unmarried adult women positively appraised their lives after relocation, including their joy in acquiring new skills. Joining them in this positive appraisal were women in the 34–49-years age range who expressed relief over not needing to trek up and down (the hills and subsequently their apartment buildings) to fetch water, stand in line to use the *chaali* toilet, or worry about the safety of their kids as they stepped out to pursue jobs (quite unlike the over-protective parents described by the young unmarried adult women). Sumitra, who in Chapter 4 had complained about the challenges in the first year after relocation, later on in the same discussion group, expressed a sense of great relief in the years since:

SUMITRA: Now, it is comfortable. There is light, there is water, a bathroom. More than us, for our children, a lot of good has happened.

Others in focus-group discussions also expressed similar sentiments. Kausalya had migrated more than 40 years ago from Osmanabad, a district in the mid-western portion of Maharashtra, and lived in a second-floor apartment unit in Sangharsh Nagar with her husband, their two sons, and a daughter-in-law. Kausalya had contributed to her household's income during her days in the Damu Nagar slum of the park when the entire family of Kausalya, her husband and their two sons, would head out to work as casual laborers in construction sites across the city. Joining her in this segment of the focus-group discussion were Lakshmidevi (introduced in more detail in a following section of the chapter) as well as Champa (introduced earlier in this chapter) and Beena.[12]

KAUSALYA: Life has changed. It is okay. Meaning, we are happy at home. Meaning, we eat a dry, simple bread.

LAKSHMIDEVI: We get peace.

KAUSALYA: Peace.

LAKSHMIDEVI: Once we finished cooking, then there was the tension of getting water. In the hills, we had to get up and get water.

AUTHOR: Was the water free or did you pay for it?

BEENA: That water was free. There would be fights there. We had to get water from that turn [a crossroads near her *chaali* in the park]. Children would be very scared. There were fights, a big crowd there. We had to get water from that turn. The forest folks would tear down our houses and go. We had to tie our homes with mats and blankets and that is how we stayed. We are more healthy here! All ladies have built their bodies. Over there, the tension with water would not make that happen.

LAKSHMIDEVI: She said the right thing.

CHAMPA: The body is made here. All day we would get water and here [that is not the case] so the bodies are made.

"As a Result of Getting Out, Madam, I Have Learned a Whole Lot"

If some positively appraised the site for its opportunities for better education, better livelihoods, and relief from daily chores, then a second category of participants perceived relocation as a transition into a life of new burdens that exerted pressure to help pay for higher, new expenses. For these women, the new experience of stepping out of the domestic domain to earn a living was motivated by the need to identify new financial sources. They devised coping tactics from venturing into self-employment (e.g. operating grocery stores, grinding grain from the window openings of their ground-floor homes, setting up shop in the unauthorized evening *bazaar* on the fringe or inner roads of Sangharsh Nagar) and seeking work outside the home (e.g. on the crammed factory floors for poorly paid, informal jobs) to finding a loan.

As described in Chapter 4's "Prestige Is Up, But So Are Expenses", section, living expenses rose substantially with residents' move to apartment housing, and sometimes more distant jobs to help support their new lifestyle were scarce. For some women (e.g. the young, those taking classes) Sangharsh Nagar represented more employment opportunities, and for others (e.g. those not taking classes, those used to the type of jobs they'd taken on in the slum), it represented the opposite. Yet the paucity of employment opportunities commensurate with ones skills was a burden that many women were overcoming. Take the case of Alpana, 35, who had moved in after living in the Kranti Nagar slum of the park for nearly two decades with her husband and their two teenage children. In the slum, Alpana had worked from home stitching surgical facemasks, an informal enterprise that she said her suspicious husband (a truck driver for a city-based company) had encouraged her to pursue. The home-based, piece-work enterprise brought in about INR 5,000–6,000 a month. When the move left Alpana and those like her without their previous outlets for sub-contracted home-work, she and her husband started a *petty-shop* in the *bazaar* adjoining the resettlement site. Alpana now managed the shop on her own, selling fresh flowers, fruit, incense sticks, vermillion, camphor, cotton wicks, books, and other items used in Hindu rituals and festivities (Figure 5.2). However, within a month of launching their new enterprise, altercations between the couple hit a new low:

AUTHOR: When did you move into your own home in 2007?

ALPANA: Yes, into 17AB [in building number 17]. Our own. The house is good, it is made well [she decorated it well].

AUTHOR: Then, can I ask you what happened?

ALPANA: He [her husband] would beat less over there [in the Kranti Nagar slum]. We came here and he started beating more. Then, it was [a lot of] fights. If someone incited him [then] he would listen to [believe] their story [about what I was up to]. They call such a person *shanki* [someone who is prone to be suspicious].

AUTHOR: Understood.

ALPANA: He started to doubt [me]. Now that I have put a shop and am sitting on the road, then he has problems with me talking to a man, even to a woman. I stitch blouses [for *sarees*] with my sewing machine now. Anyone who comes, even if it is a woman who comes to get some piece of cloth tailored, he suspects that the woman is teaching me something. I mean, his mind; he has always been this way. 'Then why did you [he] take me outside? Why did you [he] set up a shop [to have me work in]? Why did you [he] teach me to stitch?'

AUTHOR: He taught you all this?

ALPANA: He taught me. He put up the shop, helped pull electricity from a transmission line nearby to light the bulb in my shop and taught me how to close the shop [by night]. He bought me the sewing machine [in the slum]. He taught me a lot. He has a lot of brainpower to make money, but he does not have the brains to respect a woman. That is the problem.

AUTHOR: What caused him to suspect you so much?

ALPANA: He had this sickness from the start. He would hit me, he would hit my legs. Yes. You know a rolling pin, no? A rolling pin. He fractured this bone [with it]. This entire hand, this, all of it was [incomplete]. So, my mother too came and my mother said wait a few days and see what happens. If you stay with him, then he will kill you or such. Then a case was filed.[13]

When I first met and interviewed her in December 2012, the police case against her husband was due soon for a court hearing and Alpana and her daughter Aarti were renting an apartment unit on the seventh floor

Figure 5.2 Alpana's petty-shop in the evening bazaar

of another building in the resettlement site. Aarti, 15, was completing high school and occasionally helped her mom run the shop in the *bazaar*. But without any financial support from her husband, making ends meet was a perpetual challenge. Their 225-square-foot apartment unit cost INR 3,500 in rent[14] and Aarti's school-related expenses and the dreaded monthly maintenance fees and other household expenses sent Alpana helter-skelter in search of finances. Earnings from their tiny shop were good, during the *Diwali* (Hindu festival of lights) season, bringing up to INR 5,000 a day. At all other times of the year, Alpana commonly took home just INR 200–250 a day. With her only other income coming from occasional tailoring of *saree* blouses, Alpana confessed that she received substantial financial and emotional help from her friend Madhavi.

Madhavi, 36, also participated in a focus-group discussion for this study. Originally from Aurangabad, she had migrated to Mumbai in 1997 to join her husband and had lived in the same *chaali* in Kranti Nagar slum as Alpana. Her name came up in many casual conversations I had with the women who described her as kind and helpful. Intrigued, I headed to her ground-floor unit at Sangharsh Nagar. Within minutes of our meeting, Madhavi told me I no longer needed to walk the site in search of recruits; she could convene some for me. She got on her cell phone and soon a dozen women had assembled in her living room eagerly offering to take part in my research.

By all accounts, Madhavi was relatively well off. Her husband had begun work as a chauffeur within a week of the family's relocating. In their apartment, each room was painted a different color, the floors were covered in ceramic tiles and a brick wall separated the living room from a tiny study room constructed for the use of their two sons, ages 15 and 11. On the day I first met her, her boys had just returned from school, and, in faltering English, they invited me into their little room to see their brand new laptop. Her financial means had enabled Madhavi to start a rotating savings-and-credit group among women who lived in her cluster of apartment buildings. Groups like hers, called *fund* or *bishi*, were common in the slum. They reemerged with renewed rigor after relocation led by women with authority or business acumen who mobilized members from their own caste and ethnic affiliation. All the women in Madhavi's group were Maharashtrians and all of them, save Alpana, identified themselves as *Jai Bhim*[15]. In my conversation with Alpana later that month, she told me how grateful she was for all that the *fund* had done for her:

ALPANA: These folks are there so it feels a little good here. Or else, it sometimes feels like there is no use in living. I have a daughter. Everyone [in the group] says that I should get her educated.

AUTHOR: Have they helped you financially?

ALPANA: She [Madhavi] has supported me so much. She took me to the hospital [when my husband beat me and I fractured my foot]. Gave me so much support.

AUTHOR: That is great. How have they helped you otherwise?

ALPANA: I am going to now buy goods worth 10,000 rupees and store it [at home]. From that if he [her husband] were to take it away and go, then what am I going to do? How am I going to repay my debt?

AUTHOR: So you have accumulated debts?

ALPANA: After coming here, I have debts of at least 60,000 to 70,000 rupees.

AUTHOR: How come?

ALPANA: For the court case, my daughter's education, my hospital visits, what else do I do?

AUTHOR: Who did you take the loans from?

ALPANA: Now, once I do business, I must return it to them at 5 percent interest.

AUTHOR: From the company, from Kurla? [Kurla is a suburb of Mumbai and is home to the company where Alpana purchased the goods at wholesale prices to sell at her shop in the *bazaar*.] The Kurla folks give you a loan?

ALPANA: No, the people here.

AUTHOR: Who all?

ALPANA: I mean, just like that, I started contributing to a *fund*. There is a *fund* in [building] number 15. In that, you have to give [and then take] 5,000 rupees at 5 percent interest. So for 5,000 rupees, 500 rupees, I mean

> 250 rupees, is gone. I have to pay the interest and once I earn, then I shall repay. This way I take a loan, buy the supplies and return it to them. In that, if I make 100 rupees a day, then the rent for the room is gone. Over here, if I do some tailoring, then I am able to buy groceries.

These informal groups played a critical role in both the financial and social lives of women at Sangharsh Nagar. The way they operated, every member would contribute a predetermined sum, which varied from INR 10 to INR 500 per month, depending on each group's financial means. The size of the *fund* (also called *bishi*) varied, ranging from 15 or 20 to as many as 100 women, and whose members were all age 35–55. They were made up exclusively of women from the state of Maharashtra and were never found among non-Maharashtrian Hindus, Muslims, or other minorities. To my knowledge, this practice, though common in other states in India, had not yet taken hold among women (originally) from other states living in Sangharsh Nagar. Membership within these groups was nearly always determined by one woman or by her group of close friends. These were invariably savvy businesswomen or women whose spouses or children had well-paying jobs. Several types of these rotating savings-and-credit associations operated at Sangharsh Nagar. In Alpana's group of 40 women, each member deposited INR 150 per month in cash to a common fund (hence the term *fund*) or kitty. The total collected would then be allocated to one member or sometimes more than one if the designated recipient did not want the whole amount. The *fund* was allocated to a different member every month until all members of the group had received it. Each participant held the position of both debtor and creditor. At Sangharsh Nagar, *funds* were distributed by lottery, seniority, negotiation, consensus, brown-nosing, or at the discretion of the organizer. Alpana said her group drew lots or *chits* to select the recipient. Once Alpana received the kitty, she had to pay the predetermined sum (i.e. loan plus interest) in monthly installments.

Members of groups with higher contributions than Alpana's *bishi* admitted that their non-financial transactions were equally important. Members of this group spent time gossiping about goings-on in their building, planning the next *haldi-kumkum* celebration [turmeric-vermillion, a Hindu ritual where women pray for the long life of their husbands], group outings or just chitchatting late into the night. These groups and especially their events like the *haldi-kumkum* were deeply political sites. After an hour-long ritual of *haldi-kumkum* that select members of another *bishi*[16] operating in Sangharsh Nagar recollected, the wife of corporator[17] delivered a speech commending the *bishi* for its commitment to the party and the cluster's welfare. As with the Shiv Sena Party, women workers of the MNS occupied an important but structurally subordinate position in the party's hierarchy (Gottlieb, 2002). Party members were segregated by gender, but this offered the women valuable private spaces to "formulate their own modes of solidarity in ways that sometimes have the potential to threaten the overall male-dominated right itself by contesting male power" (Bacchetta & Power, 2002, p. 5). At Sangharsh Nagar, the development of *funds* and *bishis* and the interactions among women within these spaces carried tremendous potential for building social and political capital. In effect, these *funds* and *bishis* provided women with training grounds for civic involvement and open discussion, and were forums for community mobilization.

But spaces for social and political engagement were not the norm. Excluded from such groupings were the Muslims, residents originally from UP, the *Biharis* (from the state of Bihar) and the other non-Maharashtrian women who called Sangharsh Nagar home. Except for small talk about each other's spouses and trips to the evening *bazaar* and the ration shop, they lacked the outlets of the *fund/bishi* women to share their thoughts. But the move to Sangharsh Nagar had brought other forms of pride and empowerment to some, spurring them into employment they wouldn't have considered otherwise. This situation proved true for Shaista, a 35-year-old mother of eight children, age six to 20. She was a Muslim (of the Sheikh community of Uttar Pradesh [U.P.]) who had migrated to Mumbai in 1995 after losing her first-born:

> My father-in-law brought me here. I was very unwell, so he wanted me to live with them. [Her husband's family had migrated to Mumbai 10 years earlier.] They squatted on land in Gautam Nagar. We lived there for 15 years. Now, I have to work. The light bill, the maintenance costs. How can a man do it all alone? I never thought how difficult it is to earn until I started working two jobs. Yesterday he [her husband] brought home 100 rupees. My daughter went with the money to buy veggies and some other groceries and that is it, it was done. In one day, all gone.

Her husband was self-employed, peddling little bottles of perfume called *itr* from a leather bag through the streets of the city's business district of Churchgate, and occasionally planting himself on street corners. On good days, he earned about INR 100–200, not enough to meet the family's needs. That led Shaista to gather her courage and do something she had never considered before, outside domestic work. She swept, mopped, dusted, cleaned toilets, and hand-washed clothes for two nearby homes, earning INR 4,000 per month. Work as a domestic helper was highly sought among the women of Sangharsh Nagar despite the poor pay, unstable tenure and lack of safety or health provisions. But the proximity to home and the short, four-hour workday appealed to Shaista:

SHAISTA: This area is not good. The children are getting spoilt, so I have to pick them up and be here when they get back [from school]. Do you know how many [other families] have left [Sangharsh Nagar] because of that [the poor atmosphere for rearing children]?

AUTHOR: Yes, others have told me similar things. But your husband is okay with you heading out to work, no?

SHAISTA: People tell me that I do not look like a mother of so many children. A man who roams in the sun [her husband] will look older. I take my children to school. I now realize how difficult it is to work. He does not object to my going. He thought I would be distracted and I told him to come and see me work. I have taken my children to my workplace. They should know what their mother and father do to bring them up. They came back home and told him that mother does this and that and that the people are real nice. This is important.

Shaista was thankful for discovering the "good people who gave her good money" for the work she did and talked about the presence of discreet civility among residents from different states living in her apartment building at the resettlement site:

> Over there [in the slum], most of my neighbors were Sunni Muslims from UP, but here we are all from different places. I only speak Hindi, read the Quran and know no Marathi, so they [the active womenfolk in the *funds* and *bishis* that operated in her cluster and other adjoining buildings] do not need or ask for me, but I do not really need them either. They are happy in their homes and I am happy in mine.

The residential enclaves composed of Sunni, Shia, and *dawoodi bohra* Muslims from states like U.P. or Bihar that existed in the slum may have dissipated with relocation, but divisions between Muslims and non-Muslims and among different ethnicities and sects within the city's heterogeneous Muslim community had not. Although Shaista did not express any problems related to these divisions at the resettlement site, we know from existing research that such exclusion has adverse social, psychological, and political consequences. The future peace of Sangharsh Nagar and the health and vitality of community life hinges in large part on the level of integration among the site's minorities, female, and other residents.

This challenge of integration also surfaced when women discussed the likelihood of forming a settlement-wide savings-and-credit association, a task that Reema, Nivara's only full-time female staff member, was responsible to create. Reema joined this discussion group to serve as a Marathi-to-Hindi translator because one group participant spoke a dialect of Marathi that I had found difficult to comprehend.

AUTHOR: Are women [across the resettlement site] speaking to one another?

REEMA: I have set up two savings [and credit] groups.

SHARADA: I go with her [with Reema around the site] telling women to join but they don't.

KAJAL: No, no. There are several [such groups]. They all save by themselves [in their own groups]. She has it [a group] in building 12, mine is in building 10, hers is in building 13, also hers is in building 13.

AUTHOR: So everyone won't come together to make a savings group for all of Sangharsh Nagar?

REEMA: Exactly. I've tried but it isn't happening.

SUMITRA: For the whole Sangharsh Nagar? [indecipherable chatter among participating women] Who is going to give [as in manage] the account? There is one [group] for a cluster. Now, take for instance building 12. Take her for instance. My *bishi* is here, hers is in 13, and hers is in 11. If you speak of a cluster, even if one person comes from each cluster, even then it would not work.

AUTHOR: It wouldn't work?

SUMITRA: No. [more indecipherable chatter among participants] We make it with those we're comfortable with. That's why it works.

KAJAL: You [speaking to Reema] shouldn't be upset. If they don't come, it is because they don't need it. Think of other things. If we get together, get some kind of work, then women, all women will come. Slowly but surely they will come. We are all hungry for money, and for money, we need work. Get work and see how they'll start listening to you.

I bring up the implications of this discussion in the concluding section of this chapter, but suffice it to state here that settlement-wide solidarity of the type that Nivara envisioned for the resettlement site was a challenging goal. For the foreseeable future, women like Shaista who were part of no such savings-and-credit group expressed their satisfaction with the discreet civility prevailing among the site's diverse residents.

Been There, Done That, Can Do It Again

If Alpana and Shaista felt compelled to work and even began relishing their radically different routine of stepping out of their homes to earn a livelihood, other participants were very used to managing household chores while working outside. A majority of such women were upper-class Hindu women in the age range of 34–49. Forty-five-year-old Bhagyashree started assembling switches for a contractor within a few years of migrating from the village of Devihasol in Maharashtra's Ratnagiri district some 20 years ago. She had lived with her husband and two sons in the same home in the park slum until relocating to Sangharsh Nagar in 2008. When I interviewed her in December 2012, Bhagyashree sat in the corridor just outside her fifth-floor apartment unit assembling accessories for a standard push-button light switch. She reminisced about the circumstances that made stepping out of her building/home an option she had never considered:

> He [her husband] works at a private hospital. He is responsible for turning on the water-pump and for that he has to keep three separate shifts in a day. He comes home for lunch and dinner, so I have to be here to cook, no? The money was never enough, so I took up this job of light button switch stuff from home. The *seth* [the employer subcontracting Bhagyashree and some dozen other women in Sangharsh Nagar] is a nice man and he followed us to Sangharsh Nagar.

Her *seth* operated out of Dahisar, a suburb about 30 miles north of Bhagyashree's former home in the park and six more miles from Sangharsh Nagar. In the park, he had subcontracted about 20 women to assemble switches, and, for all practical purposes, their relocation should have ended the relationship. The park, after all, still hosted plenty of migrants, new and long settled, who could take on the work. However, Bhagyashree and some dozen other women who had relocated consented to continue working for him for a significantly reduced piece-rate wage. Their earnings dropped more than half when the *seth* subtracted the cost of transporting the raw and finished materials to and from Sangharsh Nagar from their pay. Those accustomed to home-based work thus either suffered a drastic pay cut or began sourcing raw materials from contractors still operating from the park. Hamsika, who was introduced in Chapter 4, was one of the women who traveled back to her former slum to fetch dough to make *papad*s (dry flatbread made of lentils) only to hear from another focus-group member that a truck from a different *papad* manufacturer was supplying dough directly to Sangharsh Nagar:

HAMSIKA: All the residents have come here. In Kandivali, they [the unnamed *papad* company] would prepare the dough and give it by the kilo and then women had to make the *papad* and had to deliver them there. Their truck used to come there. Here, we do not know anything [any company doing that].

AMBIKA[18]: Let me tell you that a truck has started coming near building 11. I see some women get the dough from them and two days later, they come to pick it up.

HAMSIKA: Yes? Whatever you may say, I miss drying *papad* in the sun during the summer months. The terrace is locked.[19] You remember, right? When you came to my house [for her intake interview], I was using a kerosene stove inside the house to dry the *papad*. It takes about eight to 10 hours to dry it, to dry it enough for giving back to the *seth*.

AMBIKA: It would be good to get more space.

ZOHRA[20]: We have the space, the community hall [a topic addressed in the next section]. We just have to get it. Why can a floor not be just for women to do what they are already doing at home? I can teach them to tailor blouses [worn with *sarees*].

Some women accustomed to informal home-based employment had begun to rekindle the interest of leading employment contractors, but for most this was a pipe dream. Sangharsh Nagar did adjoin a road (Khairani Road) filled on both sides with small- and medium-size informal enterprises (enterprises known to employ workers without paying employment benefits or social security). However, most employers wanted workers physically present on their shop floor. For example, an informal maker of seals for a well-known pickle manufacturer wanted its laborers to sit along an assembly line to insert a piece of aluminum foil inside metal lids, pour the prepared pickle sourced from another contracted enterprise, and then vacuum-seal the glass jars. This work was done mostly by hand with the workers squatting on the floor.

Gomati, a participant who appeared in Chapters 3 and 4, did similar work for a small-scale garment factory. For more than eight hours a day, she sat on the shop floor cutting loose threads from denim jeans, which were then shipped to another city-based enterprise for tailoring. She had migrated to Mumbai from Uttar Pradesh in 1987. In a focus-group discussion of six women, she recollected the first day she left home to pursue her job at Khairani Road:

GOMATI: Then I started going to the company and my husband got angry and told me not to go. I then asked him how else we would manage. We cannot pay the fees for our children; there is no food at home. How will it work out? What am I to do? I have to help a little. I go. I now go at 9:30 and come back by 6 or 7 in the evening.

AUTHOR: From 9:30 until 7?

GOMATI: Until 7, but I come back [earlier sometimes]. Because I keep sitting, I am not able to get up. I am not able to get up. I have given birth to my children. I have to do something. What am I to do? Even if it is difficult, it takes half an hour [to walk to work].

SHARADA: That is how it is in companies.

SUMITRA: Is it thread cutting?

GOMATI: Yes. Because there is difficulty, I do it. The children are hungry; at least I am not stealing. I am working hard to bring a few rupees home to pay the fees for the children. Two members have to earn. One person earns and four folks eat. How can that work? I have five kids and they all eat, but there is no one to work. There is sickness all the time.

AUTHOR: This is not so easy, is it?

GOMATI: No, madam, just think how much trouble we have gone through. We get out and where are the children? What have they eaten? I cook and leave. I come back and they [incomplete sentence]. I have stepped out of the house in great desperation, despite all the challenges I have.

SHARADA: You [referring to me, the author] can give us a job, no?

AUTHOR: I cannot give you a job.

GOMATI: You cannot do anything? It is important to do it.

AUTHOR: Why?
GOMATI: So that we don't have to go out. That we shall get it right here.
SUMITRA: We are the ones who need to fight for our conveniences.
GOMATI: If there is unity, only then will you fight, no? You [to me] cannot fight on your own. No, no, if you go somewhere, you know, 10 folks will listen to you. If I speak by myself, then they will think I am wrong.

Women like Gomati and Shaista, who by working outside the home were challenging familial and societal norms within their religious or ethnic communities, wanted employment opportunities closer to home, preferably within Sangharsh Nagar. Other women, like Hamsika and Bhagyashree, who were already pursuing home-based subcontracted employment, shared their concerns about home-based work, such as the size of their apartments, the cost of raw materials, and access to spaces like the terrace to sun-dry their *papad*. But they were full of suggestions on how to meet these challenges. Besides asking me to do an undefined "something" to bring employment opportunities to Sangharsh Nagar, they hoped that Nivara, Sumer, and the state would designate space for women to freely and legally pursue existing self-employment and organize other new opportunities. I discuss this in detail in the next section.

As in the park slums, residents had already taken matters into their own hands at Sangharsh Nagar. From late afternoon until 10 or 11 p.m., the unauthorized roadside *bazaar* bustled on the site's western periphery, providing an invaluable source of livelihood for some residents. Butchers selling fresh-cut chicken sat cheek by jowl with the barber who worked with a chair, a mirror placed atop a rickety metal table, a bucket of water, blades, scissors, cream, and a towel thrown over his shoulder. On a paved street off the main thoroughfare, 60-year-old Shakuntala (introduced in Chapter 3) squatted on a mat displaying plasticware she bought from a wholesale shop in Kurla, a suburb eight miles away. She'd store her wares at home and peddle them from 4:30 to 7:30 p.m. Her third-floor apartment was in a newly occupied building with an empty elevator shaft just over a wall from her roadside business. Unlike other businesses in the main thoroughfare that stole electricity from a transmission line, she relied on the meager light that filtered in from the lightbulbs that lit the courtyards of adjoining apartment clusters. But illumination was the least of her problems:

SHAKUNTALA: See what happened in the evening [last evening]. I sit in front of my building, no? A lady from 4 [building number 4] came and said, 'No, no! I have kept [this spot] for the past two years. This belongs to me'. I did not say anything.
AUTHOR: What does she sell?
SHAKUNTALA: She does not sell anything. She has merely reserved that place, just like that.
AUTHOR: So you have to pay her a rent?

SHAKUNTALA: Not now, if I reserve a place then I do not have to pay a rent. If I take up someone else's space then they will say, give, give me money. I said, 'This is my first day, so why should I fight with anyone?' I do not like that. I told her 'If tomorrow you want to do business here, then you do and I will sit in another place'. What else do I do?

Shakuntala did just enough to resolve the conflict. For half a year, the woman from building 4 claimed the spot was hers, periodically threatening Shakuntala to leave. Finally, on a summer afternoon in 2013 when I was visiting Sangharsh Nagar, Shakuntala gleefully reported that the threats had ended after she complained to the office of the newly elected local municipal corporator, Tayade. She described how she stood in line outside the office when a young, friendly-looking aide assured that she could occupy the spot. That ended the nuisance. She rejoiced over this costless victory and credited her good fortune to a tactic she'd used previously in the slum: confidently seek help from the local ward office (described previously in Chapter 3).

But setting up shop in the *bazaar* came to most others for a hefty price. With space at a premium, even the tiniest two-by-three-foot space commanded as much as INR 1,000–3,000 per month in rent from its de facto owner. Street hawkers in Mumbai and other cities in India were long known to make periodic payments to state authorities, usually low-level municipal workers and police. However, because the roads in Sangharsh Nagar were yet to be recognized by the Municipal Corporation, such under-the-table payments were exchanged between original and newer squatters. This was a cost Vasudha and her family, who had relocated from the park's Damu Nagar slum in late 2012, found difficult to afford. Vasudha came to Mumbai as a young bride in 2007 after marrying within her own upper-caste Lingayat community. The birth of her first child in November 2011 came one year before her father-in-law had received an apartment in the newest Sangharsh Nagar building. Her joy was visible in the apartment's freshly painted walls, tiled kitchen floor, sunmica-covered kitchen cabinets and the new toys and deflating balloons scattered about. I visited their apartment less than a week after they'd relocated in 2012, a witness to what Vasudha described as a "double joy and celebration: a son and a home! We could not have asked for more. But we need work here", she added. From a mat on the living room floor, I directed questions to Vasudha[21] but also got back responses from her father- and mother-in-law who were there:

VASUDHA'S MOTHER-IN-LAW: My son has gone there [back to the slum] now to his shop [a wheeled cart on the side of the road where he sold finely ground spices].

AUTHOR: Where exactly?

VASUDHA: That Apoli road by Damu Nagar, right in front of the police station.

MOTHER-IN-LAW: I would put up the shop at 5:00 [p.m.] and would return home at 9:45 [p.m.].

AUTHOR: How much did you earn?

MOTHER-IN-LAW: 400, 500 rupees, that is all we would get.

VASUDHA: When there were a lot of people there, then it was that way but now it has gone down.

FATHER-IN-LAW: We [he and his wife] once had a shop at the bottom [of the hill]. We bought a room for [INR] 55,000, tore it down and then put in a *lakh* [INR 100,000] to build a shop by the road. The shop had everything, everything you need for a home, rice, spices, lentils, soap. Over there now, the number of people is coming down day by day. They are removing the folks from there, no? He [his son, Vasudha's husband] did business for 200 [rupees] yesterday and returned.

AUTHOR: Did you help out at the store?

VASUDHA: No, I would go to a company to make imitation jewelry. Over there, many women worked. There is a lot of work; even now, there is a lot of work. Here there is nothing.

AUTHOR: And how about putting up a shop [here]?

VASUDHA: What are you saying? Do you know how bad it is here?

FATHER-IN-LAW: We folks do not have a spot here. Nothing. We are new here. I am sitting here at home being useless. See, so much of the things are sitting just like that [motioning toward the many jars of spices and bars of soap on their living room shelf].

FATHER-IN-LAW: We are looking for a place now. We are taking money from here and there and we are looking now. Now it is up to God, it is the will of God. For a place by the road, they are asking for 1,000 rupees a month.

AUTHOR: Who are they?

FATHER-IN-LAW: They have squatted over there because they came earlier.

AUTHOR: Did you ask?

VASUDHA: Yes. They came earlier, fought and squatted there, no. That is why they are asking for it.

By December 2014 (during another of my multiple visits to Mumbai), Vasudha's husband had stopped traveling to the park to sell ground spices and was selling his remaining stock from home. The family had given up all hope of squatting in the *bazaar* because, Vasudha said, they couldn't afford the INR 20,000–25,000 it would cost to purchase a spot. The couple now had a second son. To make ends meet, her husband had recently started doing temporary housekeeping for a major multinational company. His mother was working in a garment factory on Khairani Road and his father had contracted home-based work packaging *masalas* for a well-known national brand of spice mixes. Vasudha planned to stay home until her youngest son started school and then look for work at the garment factory where her mother-in-law was employed:

I have been there [to a factory], done that [working long hours] and I will do it again! I won't work as a housemaid like all the other women here are.

Many of these difficulties would have been answered by the layout Nivara had originally proposed. According to Nivara staff, plans for construction of a multi-storied marketplace had been submitted to the SRA and had been stalled before reaching the city's Municipal Corporation for approval.[22] In the meantime, those doing or wanting to do work from home sought greater control over the use of the site's community hall. Shakuntala explained how gaining access to at least one floor would mean that she "would not have to endure the city's crazy rains and [could] do business in peace every day". Women waited for amenities like the hall to open up. This waiting strategy is the subject of the next and final section on options the participants devised for their continuing livelihood.

"I'll Wait Until Conditions Are Right, but Can You Help?"

Forty-six of the 120 women (38 percent) who participated in this research described themselves as "housebound housewives", women who, as of 2012, were not pursuing paid work whether inside or outside their homes. A key reason that emerged to explain why they did not work for money was a lack of support from others in the family (mostly sons, sons-in-law, and grandsons) or from other women. Lakshmidevi said her husband "brought" her to the city from Mangrauni, a village in Bihar's Madhubani district, about 14 years ago. He worked as a priest, performing religious ceremonies, and her two teenage sons, 18 and 14, were construction laborers. Lakshmidevi, 40, had never done paid work, but in the course of our intake conversation noted that she was now interested in earning to help meet what she referred to as the "super" high expenses of life at Sangharsh Nagar. Until then, she considered it her "duty to run the house within the income that comes in". Madhavi, who ran the *fund/bishi* and Kausalya had similar philosophies. Kausalya had migrated more than 40 years ago from Osmanabad in Maharashtra and lived in a second-floor apartment with her husband, two sons, and daughter-in-law. The three discussed their status and roles within—and outside—their homes:

LAKSHMIDEVI: Whatever a man earns, that is the amount with which you should run your home because we do not have an employment or business.

AUTHOR: You desire to contribute by earning as well?

LAKSHMIDEVI: Yes, we can. If we get, we will. It is not like that. But we do not get work for the skills we had; that is why.

MADHAVI: I ran a machine [in the slum making surgical masks], no? You know that. The other thing is that I am not educated. I cannot go outside. It will be good only if I get at home, right? I can take care of the children as well.

LAKSHMIDEVI: If we get work, then why will we not work? The one who is not educated cannot work.

AUTHOR: There is no work for the uneducated?

KAUSALYA: God did not give it all, does not give to an uneducated one. A woman who is not literate, there is no work for her. They are blind even though they are sighted.

[Focus-group participants laugh.]

As they continued talking, three of the women suggested that I conduct literacy classes. I endorsed their idea, but said the teacher should be someone who lives in the city permanently. Kausalya and Madhavi replied that all they needed was a few other women who would accompany them to an adult literacy class. The women's comments about their illiteracy were laced with regrets that they had not learned to read and write earlier in their lives. They indicated that the help they needed now was support for finding options relevant to their current circumstances, as women with minimal education found it difficult to step far from home to earn a living:

KAUSALYA: When I was nine years old … I got married when I was nine. At that age, one could not get to read and write earlier. My father had TB [tuberculosis], what I mean is that my father had a lot of coughing, you see. My father died and my mother was left with tiny-tiny children. What was she to do? She got us married hurriedly. I have been working hard since I was nine years old. I did not get to read and write. Nothing, not one word do I know. If you told me to go there, I cannot even read the number on the bus. Someone has to tell me that this is the number of the bus, only then I see where it goes. My man did not teach me, he does not read. Both are uneducated. The kids could have. One studied until the 5th [grade] and another up to the 8th.

AUTHOR: No, do they not teach you?

KAUSALYA: They don't teach me. They go do their own work, where will they teach me? They too have to go and do construction work. They go in the morning and come by the evening at 10. Where will they teach their parents to read and write?

CHAMPA[23]: You see, we don't have that much knowledge in our brains. Now I am so old, I am 45 years old, my children have been taught until the 10th but my children do not have time for me. It is not like they can spend at least an hour with me, saying, come on, mom, let me teach you A, B, C, D, one, two three, ka, kaa, ki, kii, those are the first words of Marathi. My husband has studied up to the 12th. … He has never said to me that, come, I shall teach you two alphabets. Now, I too do not have that much of time. I too was busy with my youthfulness and I did not study. I had a lot of fun.

[Other participants in this 11-member focus group laugh.]

CHAMPA: This is our life, isn't it right? Whose husband is not educated? Tell me. Everyone is at least a little educated, the children are educated but we are [not]. Laugh, you can all laugh a lot. Everyone feels that way, but, because of our parents, our lives got ruined.

KAUSALYA: Over here, just 10 women; if 10 women go [to a literacy class], then I will go too.

CHAMPA: Now that we are here, I feel it. I feel that I should, but I know it's too late.

If some perceived their lack of education to be a deterrent to employment in the relatively more upscale vicinity of Sangharsh Nagar, others like Deepali (introduced in Chapter 3) felt pressure from the family to stay home. Deepali had provided for her family of three daughters by doing home-based subcontracted work in the slum, but was told to stay put now because she had done enough:

> My son-in-law and daughters won't let me earn now. They say I have done enough and it is now time to take care of the grandson.

The women I talked with had many suggestions on how to tackle their literacy and poor employment options. Focus-group participant Zohra shared relative satisfaction with her life, but expressed enthusiasm to try new ventures to other women of her focus group:

ZOHRA: We fall, we rise, we study, we work hard, that is how life is moving. Yes, we are managing the lives of our respective homes. We are managing our respective kids, we are doing something or the other. Man and wife are the wheels of the vehicle of life. Our children are sitting in that vehicle, we have to drive life's vehicle.

AUTHOR: Okay, so what do you think should happen to keep the vehicle running?

ZOHRA: I have been thinking that for several days that I work, but how? If there is a women's coalition made up of at least a few smart women, like my daughter [who accompanied her to the discussion], then we should get many [sewing] machines.

Fellow focus-group member Ganga was skeptical of Zohra's notions. She and Zohra could not have had more different life histories. Ganga had migrated to Mumbai in 1996, about four years after marrying Pradeep, 40, who now sold life insurance. She belonged to the Yadav community, traditionally cow-herders from Uttar Pradesh. Women in her caste group rarely worked outside the home. She had lived in the Gautam Nagar slum and had raised two sons, now 18 and 15 years old. Asked in my intake interview if she'd like to contribute to her household's income in the future, she had tentatively replied, "I want to work, but will do so only if I do not have to step out of the house". When I queried Zohra about her idea for starting a women's work enterprise, Ganga spoke up:

AUTHOR: So have you done anything about it?
GANGA: No, we won't. That much? We do not have that much capacity.
ZOHRA: So if she [the author] does not, then I will. If a woman were to be like me, she will break that norm and do it.
GANGA: Then it can happen?
ZOHRA: It [the cost of living at Sangharsh Nagar] has become a challenge. I should do something, I should do something to earn. I wanted to earn all of my life, earn. I still feel that I should earn. I shall do some hard work and earn. That I must do, my tailoring. Everything here [in the coming years] will be a challenge; things will keep rising. If you [the author] take the lead, then we shall go forward and get a large factory to come here.
GANGA: And for that we [would] need start-up funds, we [would] need money. You move forward and we will come with you.
AUTHOR: But I, sadly, do not live here nor can I be here for the long term.

My reluctance to lead their efforts brought forth other suggestions, including opening a workshop where Zohra and others would train girls and women how to do tailoring:

ZOHRA: I know how to stitch. There is a machine in every home and where they sell maxis, we must get orders from that factory. Where is it, in Bombay?
AUTHOR: Maxi?
ZOHRA: We should start work on nighties [sleepwear worn by women across India].
GANGA: Nighties.
AUTHOR: And keep sleeping?
[Participants laugh.]
ZOHRA: We can keep learning and sending it to America. The folks in America wear nighties, don't they?
GANGA: The folks in America [wear] just pants and jeans.
ZOHRA: All women, children, elders, all can wear loose, very loose nighties.
GANGA: You want to start a new fashion in the US? Wear nighties? [It will work] only here, for here they wear it and go to the vegetable market, to the sister's house. Going here and going there.
[Participants laugh again.]

Another suggestion was to encourage the *Mahasangh* (the grand federation of Sangharsh Nagar's cooperative housing societies) to set aside a floor of the community hall or a portion of a floor as a workspace for women. Divya and her husband Saif, who were introduced in Chapter 3, were subcontracted tailors making shirts for a small-time designer in the city. With their move to Sangharsh Nagar, they had downsized from 20 tailors to just the two of them operating five sewing machines (Figure 5.3).

DIVYA: There used to be 20 machines and there was a cutting table that hung this way. And everyone used to live there too. [After the demolitions, their workshop doubled as both work space and home.]

AUTHOR: Who does 'everyone' include?

DIVYA: I mean two children and two of us. All four of us. We have lived, lived through some very difficult days.

SAIF: Even now we are going through difficulties.

DIVYA: Difficulty means that over there we had 20 machines and now we have five.

AUTHOR: The work there was good? I mean, in the place that you had taken on rent?

DIVYA: The work was close by, no? The amount that is spent on transportation today got saved, no?

SAIF: The workers were also available.

AUTHOR: Where did you get the workers from? Your own village folks?

SAIF AND DIVYA: No, no.

DIVYA: The ones who lived there would come and work.

SAIF: It was next to the [railway] station, no? They would come and will be looking [for work].

DIVYA: It was an industrial-type area.

AUTHOR: Would you say that your work life after relocation has changed?

DIVYA: It has changed a lot. We kept five machines and sold the rest.

SAIF: The tensions have been removed [of not having a secure space]. Educating the children is our sole focus now and not [to] grow our business. That is what we have thought; that we are done [with our business]. Only if the raw materials come can we move forward, no? We need money.

DIVYA: Over here, the rental charges [for a space to place more sewing machines] are too high.

AUTHOR: You inquired?

DIVYA: Yes, we inquired in Khairani Road [the road adjoining Sangharsh Nagar that is home to many small and medium-size enterprises], you know. When we inquired, we found it to be 10,000, 8,000 rupees [monthly rent] with 100,000 rupees in deposit and that too for one year.

SAIF: In this [business] we know a lot of stuff [the ins and outs of the business] so we can do a lot, but the main issue is over money.

AUTHOR: Wasn't the biggest issue space?

SAIF: Space. The very biggest is space.

DIVYA: If we have space, then money will come too.

AUTHOR: And how would that happen? If there is no [affordable] space in Khairani Road, then where else [would you go for space]?

DIVYA: The community hall. Madam [Shabana, the president of Nivara] said we could use it. There has been talk that we can take space in the community hall and start our work. Yes, we will start our work but that [space], they will not hand us the space. They will want us to clear out the space if they hold an event. We need a permanent spot.

AUTHOR: You mean the federation will not let you use the space permanently for your purposes?

DIVYA: Yes, they want to make money now.

AUTHOR: So what would you use the space for? For conducting tailoring classes?

DIVYA: I have thought of how we [she and her friends] shall buy *sarees* at wholesale prices, some matching ornaments and we shall make blouses to fit and petticoats [worn under a *saree*]. Just one room, if they just gave us one room, we can do it all. Men, women, everyone will get employment. Just some permanent space and start-up money is needed, and that can take care of it all. No company, no contractor, just us as our own bosses.

AUTHOR: That sounds possible.

DIVYA: We [the same group of friends who would like to launch a business selling *sarees* and blouses, all of whom are Nivara-loyalists] started two savings groups. Two groups are working now. The plan was that if Madam [Shabana] does not support us, then we will bring the two savings [and credit] groups together. In that [group] we put 100 rupees

Figure 5.3 Saif and Divya in their third-floor apartment in Sangharsh Nagar

each month. The way we have [a] fixed deposit, no? The bank will give us a loan and, using the loan, we will rent a room.

AUTHOR: Hmm.

DIVYA: Nivara promised to give us space for business. They promised us a marketplace too. But now the market is gone, we don't know whether the market will be made or not made. We are willing to pay for the space, you know. We can pay for it. We don't want anything for free. Only money speaks, we know that. We'll rent a room in my building if the hall thing [allocation of space in the community hall] doesn't happen.

Divya was eager to use the community hall space where she and her husband could start a small business selling clothes that would employ others within Sangharsh Nagar. The four-story hall was constructed according to Nivara's plans and was sanctioned by the Slum Rehabilitation Authority. During the period when I was collecting data, the hall was being managed by a federation of registered cooperative housing societies of resettled residents called the Sangharsh Nagar *Mahasangh.* Once registered as a cooperative society in September 2012, the federation elected nine people to represent the cooperative housing societies and designated 13 others as ordinary members. A majority of these were people considered loyal to Nivara, leaving residents to hope that the hall would be made available to community members, particularly for vocational training and to host small-scale employment enterprises requiring more space. In my visits to Sangharsh Nagar in December 2014 and 2016, I noted that the hall was fairly busy hosting weddings, political-party meetings, and other events whose rent helped support maintenance of the four-story premises.

Conclusions: Women Making Sense of and Giving Sense to Likely Alternatives

Gioia and Chittipeddi (1991) first established the interrelated concepts of sense-making and sense-giving, now widely used in strategic change literature. Top-level organizational managers, they noted, create meanings around an intended change and negotiate with (i.e. give sense to) other organizational members to implement the change. Scholars like Dutton et al. (1997) have argued that at the early stages of an intended strategic change process, the meaning surrounding organizational change is rarely internal. Instead, meaning is shared with and given to others not by top- but by mid-level managers who are in close association with a key external stakeholder, namely the organization's clientele. As those closest to the clients (residents of Sangharsh Nagar), mid-level managers (Nivara's Sangharsh Nagar staff and its loyalists) are the primary agents, creating and giving meaning to change. This chapter examines a similar process of change. But unlike prevalent literature, it identifies the primary agents as the women who are simultaneously making and giving sense to an alternate vision of the resettlement site. Documented in this chapter are the dynamics of sense-making and -giving in the words and actions of women who escape the attention of government, business, and nongovernmental actors with a stake in the project's future.

Whenever women made assertions such as "This must happen", "This should happen", "If only they could … ", or "Even if they did not … ", they were engaging in sense-giving. Such sense-giving was an attempt to persuade others and gain support for an alternate vision for Sangharsh Nagar among the other women participating in their discussion groups and from me as facilitator and interviewer. This sense-giving typically occurred at the end of the discussion when someone would raise the question, "Now what?" "Now what is it that you [the author] can do for us?" or "What else should we do?" Their questions concerned direct action, combining the questioners' depictions of their emerging vision for the resettlement site with the necessity of enlisting internal and external stakeholders to act on their suggestions. Many of the women suggested that I share the audio- and video-recordings of the discussions with others in the resettlement site and with the external stakeholders—NGOs, the state, private developers, and national and international donors—who could act on their behalf. The suggestions symbolized an emerging desire for change and called for the full and continuing engagement of the women affected in the full R&R process of planning, design, monitoring, and evaluation.

For unmarried women, the way forward included some yet-to-be-identified entity in the resettlement site taking the lead to formally petition the government to establish a police checkpoint in the resettlement site. They also envisioned that an agency like Nivara could advocate for the allocation of a gender-segregated space for recreation and skills-training purposes, and visualized that a similar entity could work to convince parents that skill-building workshops could lead to financial gains. As they persuaded each other of the need for safe spaces for recreation, the women recognized that they were not the only group denied such spaces. They attributed the uncontrolled rowdiness among young male residents and the perceived fear it engendered to be at least partly related to the absence of sanctioned spaces like playgrounds and gardens in the site. Their request for segregation reinforces existing patriarchal norms, encouraging the women to remove themselves from public spaces and assigning responsibility for handling the harassment chiefly in the women themselves. Unmarried adult women found practical virtue in segregation as protection and regarded it as a crucial component in winning greater independence from parental control. They never denied the need for gender awareness and consciousness-building programs among boys and girls and women and men their age, but deduced that the target of interventions needed to be parents. If parents believed the resettlement site to be a safe host of practical skill training opportunities that would enhance their daughters' employment potential, then they were more likely to encourage them to step outside the confines of home.

Those who had emerged from their homes to pursue outside employment for the very first time struggled to make sense of their changed routines. They justified the change as a necessary move to help meet the higher costs of living at the site. They tried to recruit me to negotiate for jobs they could pursue within their homes or at least within the boundaries of the Sangharsh Nagar resettlement site. They were convinced that contractors would not voluntarily seek out residents on-site when they could easily find workers among the new and needy migrants to the city who continued to swell areas like the park peripheries that was their former home. But within the site, participants identified the need for a designated space to increase their home-based productivity, a solution especially attractive to those with physically or socially restricted mobility. Women pursuing home-based informal jobs had begun to identify measures that could improve the scale of production and the terms of their employment. Embedded in comments about lowered piece rate wages since relocation and the limited space in which to pursue home-based work were suggestions about how well-known agencies like Nivara or outsiders like me could work to attract lead contractors directly to Sangharsh Nagar. They envisioned doing such work in spaces like the community hall. This arrangement would additionally facilitate the women's ability to negotiate higher piece rates than they could working for individual contractors.

Still, contracted work, whether pursued in the slum or in legally tenured housing, is undoubtedly exploitative. It offers poor compensation and no overtime bonuses, holiday or sick pay, maternity leave, insurance, pension or other government benefits. It is unaffiliated with labor organizations and impinges on residents' living space. Women aspiring to and pursuing such work did not challenge and change the "conventional mores and values regarding femininity" (Fernandez, 2011, p. 236). In fact, as Radhakrishnan and Solari (2015, p. 796) argue in their global analysis, the eagerness many Sangharsh Nagar women displayed to pursue home-based, contracted work defies the "multifaceted notion of women's empowerment" advocated by myriad NGOs, feminists, and economists. This includes political participation, collective action, and control over one's body, in addition to economic self-sufficiency. The scope of experiences and reflections of the women recorded in this research argue that universal, neoliberal notions of empowerment may not be suitable for settings such as Sangharsh Nagar where female economic empowerment takes more traditional and limited forms. That does not exempt home-based workers from deserving support or improved working conditions. Carr, Chen, and Tate (2000, p. 137) advocate the need to document the number, contribution, and the working conditions of home-based workers, and help them bargain and gain access to labor and product markets, both local and global. In addition, they call to increase the visibility and voice of home-based workers and women workers in the informal sector and policy initiatives that target improvement of the work environment of home-based women workers.

There is no shortage of women willing to take new business risks within or outside their 225-square-foot homes in Sangharsh Nagar. A sizeable number of women also stand eager to join the labor market and begin contributing to the financial welfare of their households. The risks that women are taking, often bolstered by new familial or social support, and the pride they display in their efforts—running grocery stores from their ground-floor windows, grinding grain from their extended verandas, hawking goods in the roads within and around the resettlement site—suggest several alternatives for organizations dedicated to undertaking successful R&R. The prevalence of informal savings-and-credit associations that women carried over from their experiences in the slum, points to the resource pool already existing within the resettlement site. The talents of women who had organized themselves into informal *bishis* could be utilized to attract members into more structured, formal savings groups. Their financial resources could be coordinated and carefully brought into the formal banking sector. Creation of a settlement-wide, formal savings-and-credit association that Nivara envisioned for the site could provide a better foundation for challenging the inequalities that the informal savings and credit associations (formed exclusively among Maharashtrian women and that too in select apartment buildings or clusters) were perpetuating. Vonderlack and Schreiner (2002) note that poor women across the world take part in informal savings groups where they benefit from low transaction costs and external support to develop financial discipline. They suggest that formal savings mechanisms might add attractive features such as safety of deposit, interest on savings, timely access to funds, and loan and depositor anonymity to the already-recognized benefits of informal savings groups. But achieving such settlement-wide solidarity, some women discussed, stood a greater chance of success if a more urgent point of entry, namely bringing jobs to the resettlement site was considered.

The attitudes expressed by those housebound wives who lack experience outside the home suggest that confidence-building training might be as important as the development of the occupational skills training desired by the young, never-married participants. NGOs offering programs to encourage women's enterprises might want to invite the daughters, spouses or experienced businesswomen to take part to boost the confidence and the eventual outcomes of the targeted group.

It seems common sense to assume that R&R efforts able to incorporate existing assets that emerge naturally from the ways of life and forms of livelihood of the targeted residents would offer the soundest foundation for organizing, developing and regulating a resettlement process that will satisfy both residents and those charged with developing, orchestrating, and maintaining it. Yet, not only does the identification of assets demand a pro-active commitment, it also requires continuing monitoring and policy intervention. Policies broad and flexible enough to identify and accommodate needs and to seek solutions from the bottom-up can extend from the regulation of street hawking and changes to building facades to the development of more formal institutions and skills building that expand internal resources beyond current parochial caste boundaries. Interventions that recognize and utilize the site's natural assets and changing needs while staying mindful of the whole R&R project are integral to future success.

Notes

1 Drawing on the works of organization scholars like Argyris and Schön (1978) and Mazutis and Slawinski (2008, p. 438), I define *authentic dialogue* to comprise dialogue that displays characteristics of self-awareness, balance, congruence, and transparency. Such dialogue facilitates learning at and between multiple levels of an organization. I apply this to the context of managing the resettlement of park dwellers, a process that had the potential to be "authentic".

2 When I met Champa, she was renting a seventh-floor apartment in Sangharsh Nagar where she hoped to buy an apartment. Her landlord was a one-time resident of the park's Kranti Nagar slum who lived in a home he had built in the Nalasopara suburb of Mumbai and rented his residences in the slum and in Sangharsh Nagar. As discussed in Chapter 4, this scenario was common among migrants who had done well for themselves. Before relocating to Sangharsh Nagar in 2009, Champa lived in another slum resettlement site called Shivshahi Prakalp. Her family was evicted from their home in the *Jari Mari* slum adjoining Mumbai's international airport and resettled in a 225-square-foot apartment in Shivshahi Prakalp. This apartment was part of a large resettlement site of 33 apartment buildings located an hour's walk from Kranti Nagar. Champa befriended a woman in the Kranti Nagar slum and over the years grew chummy with many other women residing in her friend's *chaali.* Hearing of her bitter squabbles with her husband, her Kranti Nagar friends convinced Champa to move to Sangharsh Nagar. She had never lived in the park slum but insisted on accompanying two of her friends whom I'd recruited for my focus-group discussion held in December 2012. Not expecting an onlooker, I welcomed Champa on the condition that she not participate in the discussion, a condition she apparently found impossible to keep.

3 This chapter's content draws on Ramanath (2016).

4 Emphasis in the original.

5 According to Roseman and Smith's (2001) relational appraisal theory, thinking is the precursor to feeling. Thus, changing feelings requires an adjustment in thinking. Urban scholars employ the same theory when they argue that people perceive their tenure secure if they think eviction is unlikely (De Souza, 2001; Payne, 2001; Varley, 1987; Turner, 1976). This perception includes both thinking and feeling states of mind (Van Gelder, 2007; Gelder & Luciaono, 2015) and is supported here in the women's narratives on how they invested in improvements to their homes in the slum even without formal title to their homes. In the years preceding the High Court's order to clear encroachments in

the park, several of the participants admitted to perceiving (i.e. both thinking and feeling) it as safe and worth the risk to invest their resources in housing (and neighborhood) improvements. Such risk-taking, as shown in Chapter 2, was more likely if a tenant had the financial wherewithal, access to networks and squatted in a location conducive to organizing a livable space. But after the High Court's ruling in 1995 and the introduction of possible eviction, slum dwellers' perception of security changed. The women testified that this perception of insecurity persisted despite attempts of NGOs, the state and political parties to quell fears and negotiate housing alternatives on their behalf. Fear of eviction was most acutely perceived by those classified as ineligible for alternate accommodation and was also felt by those eligible for sponsored resettlement but without the means to pay the INR 7,000 required to prevent demolition. But these were by no means the only two groups who experienced a fear of homelessness. As evidenced in narrations (Chapter 4) of residents' haphazard responses once demolitions commenced, some eligible residents risked staying put amidst the rubble of their former *chaalis* and *zopadpattis,* others rushed to other slums across Mumbai or back to the villages/towns they'd migrated from, or even abandoned their "sanctioned" slum home to commence life in newly built, brick and mortar homes in a far-off suburb. I recall these reactions to emphasize that investments in housing improvements and occupation of homes were driven more by the slum dwellers' perception of security of tenure than by possession of a legal title. This perceived security was reinforced by easier access to multiple options for livelihood and the collective efforts of slum residents to gain and improve access to basic amenities like water, electricity and sanitation, addressed in Chapter 2.

6 In the 1970s, the World Bank (and later the UN-Habitat) entered the urban housing sector in developing countries. Former World Bank President Robert McNamara (1968–1981) launched its shelter lending portfolio in 1973 on the premise that if cities did not deal more constructively with poverty, then "poverty may begin to deal more destructively with cities" (World Bank Group Archives, 2018). The Bank's shelter sector lending from the 1970s to the 1980s was deeply influenced by the works of such architects as John Turner (a Brit whose idea of self-improvement was informed by his work in the squatter settlements of Peru) and planners like Charles Abrams (a U.S.-based planner who held that demolitions of slums without replacement only exacerbated crowding and inflated housing costs). Their "aided self-help" paradigm inspired the Bank and several other multilateral donors to adopt "slum upgrading" as an approach to tackle poverty in Lima, Burkina Faso, and Mumbai among other cities where populations were soaring as were the costs of affordable housing. Upgrading slums in their original locations rather than removing (or neglecting) them became the more constructive approach to tackle poverty. Slum dwellers were considered capable of improving their own livelihoods (and eventually owning land) if government took the lead by providing basic amenities like water and sanitation. After discussions between the Bank and the state government of Maharashtra, this approach to housing was put to the test in Mumbai, among other cities. The World Bank's Bombay Urban Development Project (BUDP) of 1985–1994 fell flat despite its significantly more enlightened philosophy than previous slum clearance policies. The program depended on community consent and participation and the leasing of existing slum land to community groups of slum dwellers at favorable rates, and loans for environmental and house improvements. But the tedious procedures involved in getting the land under different types of ownership—national, state, municipal and private—approved and cleared for upgrade work turned into a huge stumbling block (Desai, 1996; O'Hare, Abbot, & Barke, 1998, p. 279). This

(and other programs like the sites and services approach also funded by the Bank) declined in significance in 1991 when the state government began heavily promoting a market-driven approach to slum redevelopment and, subsequently, slum rehabilitation (discussed in Chapter 4).

7 Slums located on and near unstable hillslopes (Khalifa, 2011; Schuster & Highland 2001; Alexander 2005), on floodplains (Rashid, Hunt, & Haider, 2007), and close to airport runways (Zhang, 2017) are all cases in point. Lands contiguous to urban infrastructure services like rail tracks are also identified as vulnerable to clearing operations because they endanger lives and reduce train speeds, thus increasing commute times (Bradlow, 2010; Nair & Kumar, 2005).

8 When interviewed in 2012, Anupama was 20 years old and was designing jewelry for a diamond-setting company located in Mumbai's export processing zone. Her mother was the only full-time female staff member of Nivara's office in Sangharsh Nagar, her father worked as a part-time security guard, and her 17-year-old sister was in college. Outside work, Anupama regularly attended classes on website development and computer-aided design that were run out of ground-floor units within Sangharsh Nagar by enterprising residents or by private firms who had purchased/leased the apartment units from their original owners. She was born in the Satara district of southern Maharashtra and came to live in the park's Appapada slum soon afterwards.

Roshni, 20, was born in a village next to Varanasi in Uttar Pradesh and started life in Mumbai in 1994. Her family's migration to Mumbai started with her grandfather's arrival several years earlier where he rented a home in the Damu Nagar slum and passed on his lease to her father. Two years after Roshni was born, her mother and the three children joined their father who was working as an autorickshaw driver in Mumbai. Roshni got married young and in an uncharacteristic arrangement, her husband supported her decision to finish high school (12th grade) at her mother's home to free her to complete state-board education exams. Roshni partook in every no-cost training class offered in Nivara's offices, including sewing, beautician, and henna-application classes.

Vidya, the third voice in this conversation, was also not born in Mumbai. She was one year old when her mother brought her to the city, to the Ravanpada slum of the park. Ten members of her household now lived in one 225-square-foot apartment unit in Sangharsh Nagar. Her father worked a forest guard in the park and her two brothers, whose respective families lived in the apartment, were temporary laborers for a courier company. Vidya had completed 12th grade and was eager to earn an advanced degree in fashion design.

In terms of caste affiliations, Anupama identified herself as part of the *Maratha* (also called *Maratha-Kunbi*) community. Roshni was of the *Teli* caste from Uttar Pradesh and Vidya was with the *Jai Bhim*. These various caste groupings are explained later in this chapter.

9 I introduced Ruchi and Vaijayanti in Chapter 4. Meghana was 23 years old and was in her first year of college pursuing a three-year bachelor's degree in banking and finance. She belonged to the Sambha caste (designated a Scheduled Caste in the Indian Constitution) and lived together with her two brothers, a sister-in-law, and her parents in a sixth-floor apartment unit. Her family had relocated from the Kranti Nagar slum of the park in early 2007. I first met Meghana when she was completing beautician training at Nivara's office space in Sangharsh Nagar.

Tara had a bachelor's degree in accounting and belonged to the Maratha (also called *Maratha-Kunbi*) community. She lived with her parents and two siblings and never failed to sign up for the many courses that Nivara hosted. Tara had a certificate in tally accounting and basic computer programming.

She said her family was relatively well off. Prior to relocating to Sangharsh Nagar, they had all lived in a house the family owned in the suburb of Nalasopara. When they were allotted a unit in Sangharsh Nagar, Tara's father decided to move them back to the city for its better quality schools for her younger siblings, better job opportunities for his work as a tailor, and for her mother's employment as a cook in a college cafeteria.

Jyoti was born in Mumbai and had a 5-year-old son. For reasons I did not probe, Jyoti lived with her parents, brother, sister, and her sister's husband. She had dropped out of school before completing 10th grade and worked, like her mother, as a domestic help in a gated, upscale housing community nearby. Before coming to Sangharsh Nagar, this family of seven (her son was not yet born) spent 10 years, after their home in the Kandivali slum was demolished, in a rental apartment near the park. She belonged to the *Jai Bhim* community.

Shakuntaladevi, 50, was born and brought up in Mumbai and lived in the Appapada slum for well over three decades. She'd relocated to Sangharsh Nagar in 2007 with her family comprising two sons, ages 28 and 22, a 24-year-old daughter, and nine other members, including her husband, two daughters-in-law, and three grandchildren, all living in one apartment.

10 Sunita had migrated to the city five years earlier from Maharashtra's Latur district. She lived a mere 15 days in the slum before she and her new family (her husband and his parents) relocated to their fourth-floor apartment unit in Sangharsh Nagar in 2007. She now also had a son, age 4, and a 9-month-old daughter. To help make ends meet, she had recently started work as a part-time community health worker for a private hospital.

11 Rukminidevi was a participant in this group that consisted of Anupama, Vidya, and seven other women. She had migrated to Mumbai from the Janephal village of Buldhana district in the north-central region of Maharashtra, and did so soon after her marriage at the age of 16. She lived all of her years before relocation in the Kranti Nagar slum of the park. Now 50 years old, Rukminidevi was one among six other members in her household comprising her husband, a 22-year-old son and another 30-year-old son and his wife, and their 3-year-old son. During my intake conversation with her, Rukminidevi was concerned that her 22-year-old son was far too lazy to get a job and might go astray like the many other boys she came across while walking in and around Sangharsh Nagar. To provide for household income, she had started work as a domestic help, her first paid job.

12 Beena hailed from Nagra, a village in the Ballia district in eastern Uttar Pradesh. She had migrated to the park's Damu Nagar slum three or four years after her marriage, in 1997.

13 As of December 2016, Alpana moved out of her rental unit and rejoined her husband who lived in their allotted unit in Sangharsh Nagar. Her rationale against filing for divorce highlighted the issue of the property title brought up in Chapters 3 and 4. Alpana was worried that her husband would remarry and that she would find it incredibly hard to assert her equal rights to the apartment unit.

14 At Sangharsh Nagar, the first three floors rented out for INR 4,000 per month and the rent for floors four to eight was INR 3,500. The INR 500 difference, Alpana and others explained, was because homes on lower floors allowed residents to remodel their homes to run a grain-grinding mill, run an English-training class or run a grocery store from their windows. The potential to conduct business from within one's home made these homes far more attractive than those on upper floors.

15 Madhavi identified herself as *Jai Bhim*, as did all but Alpana in the group of 40 women she led. *Jai Bhim* are followers of the late political thinker and activist,

Dr. Bhimrao Ramji Ambedkar (1891–1956). Ambedkar, the most significant leader of the *dalit* movement, was the chief architect of the Indian Constitution, India's first law minister (1947–1951) and a much-revered convert to Buddhism. *Dalit* was a term he first used in 1928 in his journal, Outcaste India (*Bahishkrit Bharat*), to characterize the experiences of deprivation, marginalization and stigmatization suffered by India's outcasts (Omvedt, 1994). Over time, the term has come to refer to a non-Hindu, a political minority and a member of the country's most marginalized socioeconomic groups. The Indian Constitution has coined its own phrase, the Scheduled Caste (SC), to refer to this same category of people, a phrase first adopted in 1935 when the British listed the lowest-ranked Hindu castes in a schedule appended to the Government of India Act for the provision of employment and educational assistance. Ambedkar was a *dalit* from the *Mahars* or untouchable community, required to perform menial work and avoid polluting contact with the upper castes. Alpana was the only member in the group who identified herself as a *Teli*. Traditionally oil pressers, the *Telis* are part of a more recent administrative listing of the Indian Constitution called the Other Backward Castes (OBC). They are neither upper caste nor listed in the schedules (scheduled caste and scheduled tribe) of the Indian Constitution. Madhavi, the group's founder-leader, invited Alpana to join the group at a time when she was in desperate need of support.

16 The 100 women in another group I became familiar with were all part of the *Maratha-Kunbi* community. Although designated in the Constitution as the Other Backward Caste (OBC), some *Maratha-Kunbis* identified themselves as an upper-caste group. They all lived in a cluster of 18 apartment buildings registered as a single cooperative housing society led by a tight-knit coterie of four friends who lived in the same building. The president was recruited by the Maharashtra Navnirman Sena (described in Chapter 4) to serve as the political party's ally in the cluster. As part of its recruitment tactics, the MNS offered her seed money to start a fund for women in the cluster. The group began its lending activities in 2011. Without knowing the details of her *bishi*, I had recruited this woman to join a focus-group discussion. She said her *bishi* had grown into a monthly social event that she eagerly looked forward to and she invited me to meet the rest of her fund's executive leadership. On my visit, I found a boisterous assembly of 15 women who showed me pictures from a temple tour they'd taken in a van hired with their saved money. I was told that their regular monthly meetings would typically begin at 10 p.m. and run as late as 1 or 2 a.m. They would meet by a temple in their cluster, a small place of worship constructed under the aegis of their cluster's cooperative housing society. It was a space they considered safe and least likely to attract the prying eyes of men. "Besides", said the group's president, "even if they did stare or eavesdrop, do you think we'd let them? We'd shoo them away so loud that they'd pee in their pants". The meeting started with each woman depositing her INR 500 dues. Those who didn't contribute were fined INR 25. The money collected was loaned to women most in need based on a decision of the leadership team (the president, vice-president, a secretary, and a treasurer). Rarely was all the money loaned out. A large portion of the surplus was saved for the yearly Ganapati festival, the *haldi-kumkum* and for outings like the recent temple tour. Borrowers were charged 2 percent interest a month and they typically used the money for such expenses as school admission fees, medicine, or payment toward a deposit for an apartment rental unit. These women had enjoyed no such grouping in the slum, but gleefully reported that financial dealings typically would take up about an hour of the meeting. They spent the rest of the time teasing each other, snacking, and exchanging dirty jokes.

This OBC group's affiliation with the MNS Party has an interesting historical precedent. During the 1980s, many OBCs obtained education in the numerous colleges and educational institutions that had mushroomed in small towns and villages across Maharashtra. As Hansen (1996) observed, despite this education, young OBC men struggled to enter the political-administrative sector tightly held in Maharashtra by the Congress Party. That monopoly began weakening in the late 1980s and finally collapsed in 1995 when the alliance between two right-wing political parties, the Shiv Sena and the Bharatiya Janata Party (BJP), won the state elections for the first time. For the period preceding and following their victory, many young OBCs were recruited by Shiv Sena-BJP (Palshikar, Deshpande & Birmal, 2009). As described in Chapter 4, MNS is a breakaway group from the Shiv Sena that, like its parent party, depends on OBCs as its core caste group.

17 Tayade, as noted in Chapter 4, won the 2012 corporator elections when he defeated the BJP contender by a substantial margin.

18 Ambika had migrated to Mumbai nearly four decades earlier from the Parbhani district of northeastern Maharashtra to join her husband who had recently purchased a plot of land in the park's Damu Nagar slum. Ambika could barely fight back tears when she talked about her husband's death from heart disease and diabetes a month before our first conversation in August 2012. Ambika, about 50, worked as a domestic helper in an upscale apartment complex nearby and shared her home with four sons (age 24–30), two daughters-in-law, and two grandchildren.

19 The presidents of the respective cooperative housing societies held the keys to the terraces, the use of which for drying *papads* or spices, although restricted, depended on the strictness of each society's regulations and control.

20 A lifelong resident of Mumbai, Zohra lived with her two daughters, a son-in-law, his mother, and four grandchildren. She was one of the oldest participants of this research. She came to the focus group with her daughter, a university student whom she considered far smarter and hence ideal to take part in a discussion held "by this teacher from the U.S.". Through her 60 years, Zohra had held several positions, including vending garlic and coconuts and even selling nightgowns on the street side. Her longest job was work for a Muslim family who had migrated to Saudi Arabia and later Dubai. She worked for them for more than two decades before returning to Mumbai 10 or 12 years later for surgery to repair a herniated disk.

21 For the first part of this interview, Vasudha squatted in the hallway of her apartment building making tea on a kerosene stove outside her apartment. They hadn't yet bought a gas cylinder, partly to avoid ruining the newly painted walls with soot from cooking! Sharing my mat was her one-year-old son, who slept through much of the interview.

22 Besides the marketplace, the plan included numerous other amenities like streetlights, a fire station, a police *chowky* (checkpoint), playgrounds, a cremation ground and a cemetery, two hospitals, and places of worship.

23 Champa is the uninvited focus group bystander whose words were shared in this chapter's introduction.

References

Alexander, D. (2005). Vulnerability to landslides. In T. Glade, M. Anderson, & M. J. Crozier (Eds), *Landslide hazard and risk* (pp. 175–198). Hoboken, NJ: John Wiley & Sons.

Argyris, C., & Schön, D. (1978). *Organizational learning: A theory of action perspective.* Reading, MA: Addison-Wesley.

Bacchetta, P., & Power, M. (2002). *Right-wing women: From conservatives to extremists around the world.* Abingdon: Routledge.

Bradlow, B. (2010). *Towards a pro-poor "agenda for change": Opportunities and experiences of slum policy and practice in Sierra Leone.* London: Y Care International.

Carr, M., Chen, M. A., & Tate, J. (2000). Globalization and home-based workers. *Feminist Economics*, 6(3), 123–142.

Cohn, M. A., & Frederickson, B. L. (2009). Positive emotions. *Oxford Handbook of Positive Psychology*, 2, 13–24.

De Souza, F. A. (2001). Perceived security of land tenure in Recife, Brazil. *Habitat International*, 25(2), 175–190.

Desai, V. (1996). Access to power and participation. *Third World Planning Review*, 18, 217–242.

Dutton, J. E., Ashford, S. J., O'Neill, R. M., Hayes, E., & Wierba, E. E. (1997). Reading the wind: How middle managers assess the context for selling issues to top managers. *Strategic Management Journal*, 407–423.

Fernandez-Kelly, M. P. (2011). Maquiladoras: The view from the inside. In N. Visvanathan, L. Duggan, L. Nisonoff, & N. Wiegersma (Eds), *The women, gender, and development reader* (pp. 225–236). London: Zed Books.

Gilbert, A. (2007). The return of the slum: Does language matter? *International Journal of Urban and Regional Research*, 31(4), 697–713.

Gioia, D. A., & Chittipeddi, K. (1991). Sensemaking and sensegiving in strategic change initiation. *Strategic Management Journal*, 12(6), 433–448.

Gottlieb, J. V. (2002). Female "fanatics": Women's sphere in the British union of fascists. In P. Bacchetta & M. Power (Eds), *Right-wing women: From conservatives to extremists around the world.* New York: Routledge.

Hansen, T. B. (1996). The vernacularisation of Hindutva: The BJP and Shiv Sena in rural Maharashtra. *Contributions to Indian Sociology*, 30(2), 177–214.

Khalifa, M. A. (2011). Redefining slums in Egypt: Unplanned versus unsafe areas. *Habitat International*, 35(1), 40–49.

Mazutis, D., & Slawinski, N. (2008). Leading organizational learning through authentic dialogue. *Management Learning*, 39(4), 437–456.

Morrison, A., Ellsberg, M., & Bott, S. (2007). Addressing gender-based violence: A critical review of interventions. *The World Bank Research Observer*, 22(1), 25–51.

Nair, P., & Kumar, D. (2005). Mumbai urban transport project: Development and challenges. *The ICFAI Journal of Infrastructure*, March, 34–42.

Norris, F. H., Stevens, S. P., Pfefferbaum, B., Wyche, K. F., & Pfefferbaum, R. L. (2008). Community resilience as a metaphor, theory, set of capacities, and strategy for disaster readiness. *American Journal of Community Psychology*, 41 (1–2), 127–150.

O'Hare, G., Abbott, D., & Barke, M. (1998). A review of slum housing policies in Mumbai. *Cities*, 15(4), 269–283.

Omvedt, G. (1994). *Dalits and the democratic revolution: Dr. Ambedkar and the dalit movement in Colonial India.* New Delhi: SAGE.

Palshikar, S., Deshpande, R., & Birmal, N. (2009). Maharashtra polls: Continuity amidst social volatility. *Economic and Political Weekly*, 42–47.

Payne, G. (2001). Urban land tenure policy options: Titles or rights? *Habitat International*, 25(3), 415–429.

Radhakrishnan, S., & Solari, C. (2015). Empowered women, failed patriarchs: Neoliberalism and global gender anxieties. *Sociology Compass*, 9(9), 784–802.

Ramanath, R. (2016). Defying NGO-ization? Lessons in livelihood resilience observed among involuntarily displaced women in Mumbai, India. *World Development*, 84, 1–17.

Rashid, H., Hunt, L. M., & Haider, W. (2007). Urban flood problems in Dhaka, Bangladesh: Slum residents' choices for relocation to flood-free areas. *Environmental Management*, 40(1), 95–104.

Roseman, I. J., & Smith, C. A. (2001). Appraisal theory. In K. R. Scherer, A. Schorr, & T. Johnstone (Eds.), *Appraisal processes in emotion: Theory, methods, research* (pp. 3–19). Oxford: Oxford University Press.

Schuster, R. L., & Highland, L. (2001). *Socioeconomic and environmental impacts of landslides in the western hemisphere* (Report No. 01–0267). Retrieved from https://pubs.usgs.gov/of/2001/ofr-01-0276/.

Turner, John F. C. (1976). *Housing by people: Towards autonomy in building environments*. New York: Pantheon Books.

Van Gelder, J. L. (2007). Feeling and thinking: Quantifying the relationship between perceived tenure security and housing improvement in an informal neighbourhood in Buenos Aires. *Habitat International*, 31(2), 219–231.

Van Gelder, J. L., & Luciano, E. C. (2015). Tenure security as a predictor of housing investment in low-income settlements: Testing a tripartite model. *Environment and Planning A*, 47(2), 485–500.

Varley, A. (1987). The relationship between tenure legalization and housing improvements: Evidence from Mexico City. *Development and Change*, 18(3), 463–481.

Viratkapan, V., & Perera, R. (2006). Slum relocation projects in Bangkok: What has contributed to their success or failure? *Habitat International*, 30(1), 157–174.

Vonderlack, R. M. & Schreiner, M. (2002). Women, microfinance, and savings: Lessons and proposals. *Development in Practice*, 12(5), 602–612.

Wilson, E. (1993). The sphinx in the city: Urban life, the control of disorder, and women. In M. Miles, T. Hall, & I. Borden (Eds), *The city cultures reader* (pp. 79–85). London: Psychology Press.

World Bank Group Archives. (2018). President McNamara Nairobi speech 1973. Retrieved from www.worldbank.org/en/about/archives/president-mcnamara-nairobi-speech-1973.

Zhang, Y. (2017). The credibility of slums: Informal housing and urban governance in India. *Land Use Policy*. doi:10.1016/j.landusepol.2017.05.029.

6 The Depth of Place

Sometimes I lived in a house made of sacks, sometimes of plastic sheets. Sometimes we used to make our homes of sack-cloths, the same cloths that are used for grains. Then, we used to make a house made of mats. Then slowly, slowly, we made a house made of tin sheets. Five kids together. At that time, there was one earner and seven mouths to feed. So that is how we used to live there and kept living there. After that, when to get this building, Shabana Madam started a long battle and asked us to give 7,000 rupees and you will get a house. Only our heart knows how we managed to collect that 7,000 rupees. We were hungry, thirsty and after filing 7,000 rupees we got this house. There was some peace there, but after coming here, there was some peace, but I have such a big family and yet we got just one room. For such a big family, to live in one room is a big problem.

A widowed mother of two daughters and two sons

In the *chaali* [an association of slum dwellers formed to qualify for basic infrastructure such as a municipal water connection], the neighbors from nearby would come and chat outside and the time would pass in the afternoons. Those that don't have work, they could stay at home and now what's happening in the buildings is that you either go to work or you mostly shut your door and keep watching your television. That is how it is. So that is why it feels that one must directly move from here and head back into the *chaali* [in the slum].

A young college student who grew up in a slum

I have made these switch buttons for 20 years. If I do not do it, then what will I do? My husband does not like it if I were to do any business outside. He tells me not to do anything on the road. Women should not.

A *Maratha* woman working in 2012 as a subcontracted, informal laborer for a manufacturer of standard push-button light switches

The other thing is that I am not educated. I cannot go outside. It will be good only if I get [work] at home, right? I can take care of the children as well.

A woman who'd led a slum *bishi* (informal rotating savings-and-credit group) of some 50 women and had stitched surgical masks for a living

But what is the point of making a garden? Boys and girls will sit there and make love! They are not going to let the older folks sit. It is good that there is no garden here.

A shop owner in Sangharsh Nagar's evening *bazaar* who shared a third-floor apartment with her husband, two children, her mother-in-law, and her brother-in-law's family of four

It is not enough to have a discussion; there needs to be unity amongst the women. In the big buildings they get water for 24 hours, they have bedroom, kitchen, they have conveniences after conveniences. We have been picked up from the slum and put in a slum. What is the convenience? Given a home, we will die in the house and no one will come to check on us. What do we do with this house? We do not like it at all.

A 40-year-old lifelong resident of Bombay who continued to work as a domestic helper, now for new households

The public will be mobilized only when you do something that the political leaders have not been able to. The politicians come and someone is sick or someone has a marriage and the politician hands them 1,000 or 2,000 or 10,000 [INR] and the public begins to take his side. They don't get anything from there [as in from Nivara]. Nivara does not give money.

A well-known Nivara loyalist who stitched shirts for a small-time designer in the city

We spent 20 years there. Over there, at least those we knew were there. We were familiar with everyone. We could borrow from everyone. 100 rupees, 200 rupees, we would get from someone or the other and manage. Whoever it was. For children. Be it [from] an Aunty, a brother, an older sister-in-law, a boss. Everyone, we could borrow from everyone.

A 60-year-old resident who had migrated to Mumbai from Uttar Pradesh in the early 1980s and made subcontracted jewelry from home

A lot of them have sold. They sell it. To Nalasopara [they've sold their unit in Sangharsh Nagar and moved to Nalasopara, a suburb about 60 kilometers north of Sangharsh Nagar]. They have a home, another home. The one who is more secure [financially] goes to the village. The ones who have another home have also sold and gone.

The Nivara loyalist who worked at home with her husband as subcontracted tailors stitching shirts on the five sewing machines they owned

The same place—whether slum or resettlement site and the myriad spaces contained within a place—holds different meanings for different women, meanings that change in response to new needs or circumstances. Without understanding the significance places represent for different residents, policymakers and implementers will (a) find it difficult to describe why some consider a place special and (b) not know how to plan and design new places and/or repair existing ones towards greater functionality and livability for all its residents.

Tuan (1971) and Relph (1973) were the first to emphasize the range and totality of experiences through which we come to know and make places. Place to them is a vital component of one's identity and responding to the need to build place-identity relations, according to Relph (1976, p. 45), "is not merely the recognition of differences and of sameness between places—but also the much more fundamental act of identifying sameness in difference". He described this attribute of identity as the "'spirit of place,' 'the sense of place,' or 'the genius of place'—all terms which refer to character or personality" (1976, p. 48). Tuan (1977) similarly urged a humanistic interpretation of place, one that highlights experience and that describes rather than definitely concludes. Following their precepts, this book seeks to document the spirit of place locating it within the "aspirations, needs and functional rhythms" of women before and after resettlement (Tuan, 1977, p. 178). The book's exclusive focus on women makes no claim to the uniqueness of female experiences, but singles them out for attention to correct the under appreciation of their role in making and maintaining a place such that it "bears the essence of the notion of home" (Bachelard, 1971, p. 5). To achieve depth in how housing is received by its residents, it argues that all R&R processes must incorporate experiences occurring at the crossroads of gender and such prerelocation factors as sociodemographic characteristics (including the size and location of the former residence, nature and location of employment, age, years settled in the particular slum, family size, household income, marital status, ethnicity/religion, and level of education), time spent awaiting relocation, and the strength of ties with other residents and external agencies. My conversations with 120 women over the course of my trips to Sangharsh Nagar where they had all resettled made their present lives visible. Their words–shared in conversation with other women or in individual conversations with me–evoked comparisons with the slum that had been their home (Chapter 2), portrayed how various saviors presented themselves as guarantors of their right to housing (Chapter 3), described their chaotic transition to a residential life laden with promises of improved city-zenship (Chapter 4), and presented the adjustments they were making to navigate their new residential lives (Chapter 5). Such sense-making and giving has no finite end for it will be redefined continually as the women construct and/or maintain their identity as residents within an ever-changing metropolis. However, through the stories they shared, particularly their visions for the future of the resettlement site the women identified several concrete components as critical in maintaining and building the "spirt of place". This spirit was more than the topography and appearance of their permanent new homes. It was the economic and social functions that occurred within and outside those homes and their inhabitants' past and present circumstances. It was more than a simple sum of these parts; it was their most current reality.

Tracing Boundaries of Home Through Networks and Differences

"What begins as an undifferentiated space becomes place as we get to know it better and endow it with value" (Tuan, 1977, p. 6). Place-making unfolds over time. From the same cookie-cutter space of their 225-square-foot, three-room apartment units in a cookie-cutter apartment building in Mumbai's Sangharsh Nagar, arose places that matter. A majority of the women who participated in this study had migrated to the brisk city life of Mumbai from small, sleepy towns and villages near and far and had settled with their young families in the buffer zone of Sanjay Gandhi National Park situated right in the center of the city's ballooning sprawl. Their first roof in the city was often a tiny, makeshift dwelling they built themselves, a structure within a growing series of slum settlements that, despite repeated acts of state-led demolitions, still shelter several thousand new and old migrants to Mumbai. The rough and undulating topography of the park became home to migrants because of its proximity to industrial precincts made up of small- and medium-scale manufacturers, as well as ancillary operations of large production companies. Their park homes signified their inhabitants' first forays into a relatively affordable and secure urban life. The many ways in which they adapted to slum living and converted the space into place form the backbone of my analysis. As in other slums across urban India, networks of 30 to 40 migrant households formed to obtain basic amenities such as water, electricity, and sanitation. Residents pooled their financial resources to purchase electricity through an informal service provider who illegally tapped into an overhead electrical line or a distribution feeder using cables. Over time, residences in the park's lower elevations organized themselves into *chaali*s to qualify as collectives entitled to municipal water connections and toilets. The formation of groups among proximate homes was a prevalent means to create more habitable accommodations. Through these associations, networks like the *bishis* (the informal rotating savings-and-credit associations), youth *mandals*, and *mahila mandals* (women's groups) emerged and thrived across numerous settlements of the park. As illustrated in Chapters 2 through 4, these networks were equally significant sources of safety and security, political engagement, and maneuvering for advantage.

When amenities commonly found in the park's lower-elevation slums were absent in those on higher gradients or when the quality of such services was poor, women recollected with fondness how they travelled in groups to satisfy their daily needs. Collectively heading to the relative privacy of the park's wilderness to relieve themselves, fetching water from a nearby well or standpost, going downhill to visit the evening *bazaar*, going to a friend's home to do schoolwork under a working bulb, or visiting a neighbor whose front door stayed open all day were all experiences that made ordinary, even embarrassing, chores something to look forward to. These activities were an instinctive locus enabling interactions and conversation to convey news about an impending demolition, organize resistance, and weigh the trustworthiness of a promise made by Vidya Chavan or a Nivara. It took hearing about a trusted neighbor who had walked to the Forest Department and paid the requested INR 7,000 for protection from demolition for another eligible household to do the same. Similarly, seeing a woman stitch surgical masks from her home or make *papads* from dough delivered to the slum by a company truck prompted others to seek out similar forms of livelihood. This is not to say that those from U.P. and Bihar, many of whom were the city's more recent migrants, and the Maharashtrians, all got along or that the Hindus and Muslims or lower and upper castes lived more peaceably amidst each other in the park than they did at the resettlement site. However, the configuration of space with its shared amenities and familiarity with each other's habits and circumstances—and where they were all eking out a living in a metropolis that has historically struggled to accept them—had created a sense of place.

In their brand new high-rise homes with indoor toilets and unfamiliar surroundings at Sangharsh Nagar, women craved the place-making experiences they had known in the slum, including, above all, interactions with other women. Although Nivara initially intended to control which household should go where, the eventual disbursement did not follow any predetermined plan. The long wait between the first court-mandated demolitions in 1997 and the inauguration of the resettlement site in 2007 had hampered more deliberative apartment assignments. As seen in Chapter 3, that long wait created frictions that could not be/were not predicted or accommodated in the resettlement process. During that period, some allottees had surreptitiously sold their homeownership rights to others, others rented out their assigned unit while they lived elsewhere, and still others were untraceable. The new residents ranged from unshakable NGO loyalists to others who barely knew the NGO before they secured an apartment.

Given the random assignment of units, the importance of designated space for regular interactions of residents is imperative. The challenge for Sangharsh Nagar and any resettlement site is not simply to create physical space but also to reframe these place-based interactions into a truly "participatory space" (Eversole, 2010). Take the case of women who had formed friendly groups for saving and credit operations to help meet the higher costs of living. Unaided, these associations are unlikely to morph or expand beyond their restrictive, informal, ethnic, regional, or political origins into broader, more formal, and better-secured savings-and-credit groups. Transforming these already well-accepted and functional informal savings-and-credit *bishis* with government-chartered associations can mean greater profitability and less economic uncertainty to members. Bringing their monthly savings and withdrawals into the folds of a banking environment offers users greater security, returns, more timely access to funds, and loan and depositor anonymity.

Women are yet to wholeheartedly endorse the creation of a space for a formal, settlement-wide savings-and-credit group. Chapter 5 recounts how Nivara enabled the formation of two such savings-and-credit groups, both of which had attracted only women that residents considered to be Nivara loyalists. Nivara even used the opportunity of this research project to express frustration over how to expand membership. A comment from Nivara's only female staff member in charge of mobilizing the women of Sangharsh Nagar to form a settlement-wide savings-and-credit coalition brought immediate responses from at least three other women in the group I was meeting with. They suggested that greater participation depended on work. They urged Nivara to concentrate on bringing semi-skilled jobs right to Sangharsh Nagar:

KAJAL: If we get together, get some kind of work, then women, all women will come. Slowly but surely they [women] will come. We are all hungry for money and for money, we need work.

This was one of numerous examples of how women envisioned the site developing from spaces to place. Procuring a cooking gas connection for the whole settlement, inviting a lead contractor directly to the site and devoting the community hall to a space for contractual work, and training of residents all emerged as suggestions in both individual and group conversations. To build livable places, residential plans need not include open doors, water standposts, common toilets or open spaces for hygiene, and recreation needs or any other "vibrant matter" that women knew in the park slums. When women are allowed room to reshape and expand the terms of their own empowerment and the use of their environment, then newer types of spaces emerge, spaces that seek to recreate the spirit of place through relationships they crave. Sangharsh Nagar may never achieve the type of solidarity that provides stability and power to all women in one unified space (such as through one activity or one committee). Creatively envisioning a path forward in solidarity with some others is an idea worth exploring.

Building Social Mobility and Safety Through Benevolent Segregation

For all of the participating women, the move to state-subsidized high-rise living represented a move into the urban middle-class establishment. Barring women's preoccupations about the lack of space and livelihood options to support apartment living, legal tenure and, perhaps more significantly, the site's location in an upscale residential area had given them an immediate boost in social standing. Although the young unmarried women I spoke to expressed the most nostalgia for the amusements and diversions of slum life, they were also the most visibly enthusiastic about the possibilities they envisioned in their new residential environment. They had stories by the dozen about their frustrations with street harassment from boys, the lack of safe spaces for recreation, and the heightened surveillance, and control from parents and in-laws who failed to recognize the potential that relocation held for their precious daughters' future.

They expressed surprise at the number of for-profit and nongovernmental agencies that had set up shop in ground-floor quarters of the buildings. Apartment owners rented out a portion of their homes to these agencies to run a variety of enterprises, such as classes in speaking English, computer programming, or after-school math and science tutoring to prepare students for the dreaded 10th- and 12th-grade exams. Agencies like Nivara hosted training courses provided by other NGOs in its own office space or in the tiny room across from its office in building number 13. These classes, usually exclusively attended and taught by women, represented a pathway toward joining the modern urban female demographic of middle-class young women who worked in the formal manufacturing and service sectors, accumulated capital and controlled their lives. These Mumbai-born daughters of migrants identified themselves far more with this social and economic demographic than with their parents or in-laws. Leela and Shailja articulated the constraints to their mobility and self-improvement (see Chapters 5 and 4 respectively, for more of their thinking and feeling):

LEELA: The girls [in Sangharsh Nagar] stay indoors and think that if they step out, then the boys outside will be there at this time. The class is at these hours. How do I go when boys are watching me? The boys will recognize us. They have to think differently. We are of a higher quality now. We have to think well. We have to think that what we are doing is good. We should not listen to what the person in front of us is thinking. That is the thinking that needs to come to everyone.

SHAILJA: When we go out, that is when we can talk. When we get together, when we go walking together, only then [can we talk to one another]. My own friend who lives right by me, I don't talk to her as much because we cannot do this and that in the building. When we come here [classes at Nivara's office], that is when we talk. Despite living close to one another, we cannot talk.

The familiarity they had known with fellow residents in the *chaalis* or *zopadpattis* may therefore have robbed young adult women of the sense of daily camaraderie that they enjoyed with their immediate neighbors in the slum, but short-term courses, especially those that were women-only courses, offered them a safe and free space essential for the fun they sought. Such gender-exclusive spaces and activities might be labelled regressive, indicative of a lack of self-esteem and confidence in coping with real-world boys and men. Feminists and others[1] have also criticized such arrangements for excluding men and boys who also may benefit from co-participation.

Livelihood options in and around Sangharsh Nagar were wanting for both genders. However, these short-term classes of two or four weeks were hardly long enough to provide room for remedial relationship building. Some women had expressed that they were far from the only ones in need of space to grow, learn, and have unrestricted fun. As one of them said, "The boys have their groups, but if they had a place to play, they may not feel the need to loiter. Can you imagine how good it would be if it [the resettlement site] is made safe for everyone at all times?"

Echoing the sentiments of scholars like Cockburn (1983, 1991), the participating women suggested that setting aside sanctioned spaces like playgrounds and gardens and segregated vocational training classes, although helpful, were short-term remedies for their safety and advancement. They viewed longer-term benefits involving gender equality as even more beneficial. That included addressing the intense social control they felt from overprotective parents, in-laws and even prying neighbors. They sought help "nicely" convincing parents and in-laws that sending girls and women out of the domestic domain for skills-based training could help relieve the family's higher cost of apartment living, a concern widely shared. Perhaps, as one participant stated, if parents had more evidence that the resettlement site was a safe place to send their daughters outside their buildings *and* that doing so could help increase cash inflow, then they'd have more freedom and the classes too wouldn't suffer from poor enrolments. More transformative change would also require improved self-esteem and confidence. To that end, self-defense classes for girls and women were cited along with the addition of a police station or checkpoint staffed by women and located within rather than outside the dense and crowded resettlement site.

A deeper sense of belonging to a place following relocation is defined not merely by social networks but is also related to the perception of safety and freedom from harm and social control. Women's feelings of increased vulnerability may be related to not knowing others in the 150-plus occupied apartment buildings that constituted Sangharsh Nagar. Comments from the young adult women as well as mothers, sisters, grandmothers, and mother-in-laws indicated that the site's spatial configuration with few open spaces for gender-segregated leisure-time activities and the absence of policing to help monitor undesirable male behaviour, left them feeling less free to move about the site and express themselves as they had before. This restriction on fundamental movement kept the women from feeling that the space belonged as much to them as to the site's male residents.

Restoring and Improving Livelihoods

Leaving the domestic domain in both the slum and the resettlement site was an economic necessity for many of the women. However, following relocation to Sangharsh Nagar, finding and keeping work became ever more urgent as the new residents ran up against new monthly expenses.

Slum life had expenses too but, as it was made clear throughout the book, the relocated residents were ill prepared for the full financial implications of cooperative homeownership in Sangharsh Nagar. Bills for shared pump water, housing maintenance, electricity, cable TV, and cooking gas cylinders were household obligations not fully explored prior to the move. Coping with new bills was especially hard with the smaller variety of informal-sector jobs available or considered suitable at the new location.

This does not mean that a new category of informal workers will not emerge and multiply in Sangharsh Nagar. However, the *Mahasangh* (i.e. the federation of housing societies governing the use of common areas and facilities in the site, like the community hall, roads, and electricity lines that serve all the residents but not administered by any particular cooperative housing society) must be more generous with how it lets tenants utilize the space in and around Sangharsh Nagar. After all, businesses, not its laborers themselves, prefer informal employment relationships that allow them to avoid regulation and taxes. A majority of urban workforce (of women and men) in developing countries work in the informal sector (Tsoutouras, 2014). Bhowmik (2001) estimates that over 65% of the Mumbai's workforce is in the informal economy. These enterprises range from large to small-scale businesses employing several hundred workers to single-person operators working from homes with no basic infrastructure to support greater productivity. The informal businesses and the chains of subcontracted relationships they utilize hire workers on a casual or semi-permanent basis with no contracts, little job security, no job ladder, and little room for labor-management negotiations. The chains of production can be so long that most workers do not know the identity of the lead firm which has set the terms and conditions of their employment.

Although these informal modes of production can be undoubtedly exploitative to the women doing these jobs, they represent sites of autonomy, productivity, and entrepreneurship (Castells & Portes, 1989), a duality worth embracing. Take the case of Alpana, recently separated from her abusive husband, who found stepping out into the evening *bazaar* to run her little business genuinely liberating. It signified her ability to freely interact with others and absent a couple's joint ownership of Sangharsh Nagar apartments, separated women like Alpana felt that doing informal work was the only surefire means to support themselves and their child's education. For Divya and her husband, who collectively managed a tiny workshop of subcontracted tailors making shirts, the move to Sangharsh Nagar had meant downsizing from 20 tailors to just the two of them operating five sewing machines from their apartment home. To improve earnings, she along with her female friends living in the site were lobbying the *Mahasangh* to open up the community hall space to start their own tailoring business employing others in Sangharsh Nagar. "Just one room", said Divya. "If they just gave us one room, we can do it all. Men, women, everyone will get employment".

Echoing Roy's (2005) central argument, informality is a mode and method of production that, like the origins and growth of a slum settlement, is encouraged and endorsed by the state. It is the poor's response to the state's inability to satisfy their needs. The way to improve conditions for both making a living and sustaining slum resettlement sites is to "decrease the costs of working informally and to increase the benefits of working formally" (Chen, 2007, p. 11). Most of the suggestions the women forwarded in the course of their discussions and interviews followed these lines. I briefly revisit them here.

The first suggestion for improvement addresses the situation of tenants with limited psychological mobility, in other words, the perception of ones capacity to make transitions into a new vocation or continuing the same vocation in a new location. Psychological mobility's impact on women's livelihood options depended on virtually every single demographic characteristic including age, level of education, marital status, caste, class, and religion, and the number of earning members in her household. For instance, older women who had spent over two decades in the slum doing more visible forms of informal work as domestic helpers in middle-class homes (versus the invisible informal workers who toil in backstreet sweatshops and inside their own homes) believed that they were less desirable employees in the more upscale residential housing around Sangharsh Nagar. The common perception was that the gated, high-rise communities with lush gardens, elevators, gyms, and swimming pools housed "big people", many only speaking English, who preferred helpers not only as cleaners and cooks but also as nannies who could read to their children and fetch groceries from fancy stores. Women who called themselves "housebound housewives" and who had not done paid work outside their own homes previously shared similar sentiments about their new residential environment. Kausalya from Maharashtra's Osmanabad district said that "a woman who is not literate, there is no work for her. They are blind even though they are sighted". The perception was that literacy was a key component of the labor market in the new location and that the more educated residents, especially younger women, were better positioned to get these jobs. This, however, did not directly translate into requests for adult literacy classes, but it did invite requests for help in business development from their more educated daughters who had acquired business-related skills. Zohra, for instance, said to the other women assembled in the room, "I have been thinking that for several days that I work, but how? If there is a women's coalition made up of at least a few smart women, like my daughter, then we should get many [sewing] machines". Anupama, a young unmarried 18-year-old, said young girls and women like her needed space (i.e. room) in which to build confidence.

If women perceived literacy as a limitation in getting jobs close to Sangharsh Nagar, some also saw a conflict between work and their familial responsibilities as well as their societal obligations dictated by caste and kinship norms. Their role in the family influenced their spatial mobility since household work, particularly childcare, limited their choices regarding work location. It is therefore no surprise that many participants, especially those who had never before worked outside the home, wanted jobs right within their homes and within Sangharsh Nagar. This inability to leave for long periods of time (often expressed with guilt at the cost it exacted on one's familial roles) not only created ambivalence about life at Sangharsh Nagar but also limited women's access to employment markets. Women like Madhavi who had done home-based work while in the park slum were eager to secure jobs but only if it was work that could be done from within the four walls of their home. "I cannot go outside", she said. "It will be good only if I get at home, right? I can take care of the children as well". Women who were balancing roles as wage earners with their roles as mothers might compromise by selling goods from home (for instance, making shirts for a retailer or hawking goods purchased from a wholesaler). For them, the space available at the resettlement site limited their productive capacity. It elicited the suggestion that more permanent space like a floor within the community hall or in the proposed multi-story marketplace be allocated for their use. It would offer room for training and production and would make the goods produced more accessible to a wider base of customers beyond the residents in their own apartment buildings.

A third and final suggestion was to improve the conditions of home-based informal labor. Women noted that Sangharsh Nagar was unlikely to attract the amount of intermediary contractors like they'd seen in the park slums. To compensate for the higher costs of transporting raw materials to the site, existing contractors were offering workers reduced piece-rate wages. The women suggested that firms be brought directly to the site where women could negotiate better piece rates while also fulfilling their roles within the home. In the Indian context, female seclusion norms often influence choices of work location, making home-based work a popular income option. Participating women had identified the specific changes in the informal-jobs sector they desired at the resettlement site, namely supportive measures to improve the scale of production and the terms of their employment.

The years following displacement were turbulent times filled with doubts, hopes, disappointments, and ambitions, which if not captured may fade from individual and collective memory. The words and observed actions of the women I spoke with made it amply clear that Sangharsh Nagar was still "becoming". To borrow Sztompka's (1991) conceptualization, "social becoming" is a process that captures the middle ground of activities taking place between the availability of resources and the ability of those who need resources to (re)build lives. The changes in the housing conditions of women displaced from slums had generated a variety of adaptations. Typically, women are described as the most vulnerable "victims" of such disruptions. Rarely is their agency, as those who actively make sense of and give sense to creating more livable conditions, portrayed. In answering questions about place-making–such as the key challenges they had faced since displacement, relocation, and resettlement; their aspirations for life since relocating; and how, if at all, they shared these aspirations with others–women detailed the multiple ways in which they were speaking up, envisioning, and/or acting outside of and sometimes against state- and NGO-supported solutions. As it becomes a place, Sangharsh Nagar will continue to reflect the ongoing interplay between structure (i.e. the rules and resources of organizations and groups) and agency (the adaptive strategies of residents, in particular, its female residents). I turn now to some final thoughts on how future planning of slum resettlement can bring together the availability of resources and women's agency (Sztompka, 1991).

Women Actively Making a Place

International housing policy has a long and checkered history as a guide for clearing slums and resettling slum dwellers. Beginning with government-led slum demolitions and the infrequent relocation of displaced residents into new but poorly built public housing in the 1950s, slum clearing and improving became a preoccupation in the 1970s and 1980s. By the 1990s, calls had intensified for reducing government monopoly in the public-housing process worldwide. Unlike previous government-centered top-down approaches to the process, the "enabling" framework advocated in the 1990s encouraged multiple players to partake. Within this process, NGOs received particular attention. They were assumed to enjoy a comparative advantage over governments and for-profit players in nurturing community participation and delivering housing more efficiently. This resettlement strategy, according to Cernea (1995), prescribed several action steps for mitigating a key concern in all types of resettlement, namely the prevention of pauperization and the reorganization of livelihoods.

Although the current, more inclusive resettlement environment has enabled NGOs and for-profit developers to serve ostensibly as bridges between slum dwellers and resettlement projects, in reality this type of "governing beyond the 'state'" has not translated into a "governing from below" and wider participation in the resettlement process (Zérah, 2009). We know from existing research that NGOs have functioned more as contracted agents of the state than representatives of the poor. They are well known to be "strapped for resources, their agendas driven by foundations and donors" (Roy, 2005, p. 154). Some observers have gone so far as to accuse NGOs of lacking direct links or accountability to the affected constituencies they're purported to serve (Batliwala, 2002). They criticize them for managing resettlement processes on "a short-term basis, and for demographically and epidemiologically circumscribed projects" (Geissler et al., 2013, p. 534).

For-profit developers have been involved in slum resettlement more on the strength of local real-estate forces than in the interest of slum dwellers (Bardhan et al., 2015; Kumar, 2005). In essence, analyses of slum resettlement initiatives treat organizations and groups—including NGOs, donors, government agencies, and private firms—as instruments of change with scant attention given to resettlement processes that may already be in motion.

The slum housing left behind may have had serious flaws, such as inadequate basic services, unsanitary conditions, insecure tenancy, and flimsy structures erected in dangerous locations. Yet, it also had advantages over the small, cookie-cutter, legally tenured apartments they moved into at Sangharsh Nagar. In their narratives, women noted that they had been near employment centers that offered plentiful opportunities for home-based employment activities. Slums permitted diverse types of tenancy, including ownership and renting, and provided a variety of housing structures—from single-story homes to those of two or three stories, with a shop on the first floor and living quarters above—to meet a family's multiple needs. The slum's physical layout also accommodated stronger social ties evidenced in such activities and behaviors as communal sharing of amenities, mutual financial support, and regular exchanges with neighbors. Resettlement plans rarely account for these assets. In the case of Mumbai's Sangharsh Nagar, acquiring rights to a piece of real estate in a big-ticket city was a dream come true for many. Shakuntala, for instance, felt so grateful that she could never bring herself to complain about living in a building with a non-working elevator, a kitchen without a faucet, and a site with no guaranteed place to conduct business:

SHAKUNTALA: You know, I don't know them [the NGO that many believed was chiefly responsible for "giving" them their status as legal homeowners], they don't know me. I don't want them to think I am ungrateful. I am happy, very happy here. We should take whatever we get. What is our right? They'll say to me, 'We gave you an apartment and now you are complaining?' It is not nice to hear such things.

AUTHOR: Have they said such things to you?

SHAKUNTALA: No, no, not such things, but I just can't ask. I used to go to the corporator in Mulund. That Maske [Vishwanath Shankar Maske, a local corporator who won the T Ward's municipal elections in 2007].

AUTHOR: Why would you go to him?

SHAKUNTALA: If I had to do some work with my ration card [for a food subsidy], I would go. I have shaken hands with him. Something to do with the house, I would go for that. If I had a need for papers, I would go for that. Here too I do the same with Tayade [the corporator for the L Ward representing Sangharsh Nagar]. I went to him about a place in the market.

Her description of maneuvering her way through state and non-state actors may appear trivial and relatively routine, but it offers critical takeaways for planners and policymakers.

First, Shakuntala's self-consciousness in sharing grievances underlines her lingering feeling of being a part of the city's "expendable poor" (Kumar, 2005), feelings that do not disappear with the demolition of slum housing. That psychological transformation entails conscious efforts built into the design and development of resettlement sites. Deficiencies in R&R—like Shakuntala's non-working amenities or difficulty finding a secure place to earn a living—may never find expression until they reach an individual and/or collective crisis point. While housing providers cannot be expected to anticipate every personal need, it is possible to provide conditions that encourage "vibrant matter" to develop and where tenants are made to feel at home. This requires the type of pre-relocation "discovery" that recognizes the value of the physical and sociocultural contexts of tenants' previous behavior and experiences. A review of my conversation with Shakuntala (and others detailed in Chapter 2) reveals the contours of her daily challenge to procure drinking water. It may have been "fun" for younger girls, but for older women and especially those doing paid work (whether home-based or not), it was an unwelcome, "tension-filled" chore. Recollections of these experiences and their place in their narrators' life histories offer clear and important indications of what elements of lives in the slum were valued and what has emerged as disenchantments of life after relocation. The future livability of the resettlement site hinges on utilizing the "push" of women's stories–in other words, the part of their stories that highlight the core elements missing from their homes in Sangharsh Nagar–to both "pull" in new and build on the existing financial, technical and other resources needed for collective action.

Second, building livable resettlement sites must position migrant women as central to the design and development, and acknowledge their understanding of home as a place that they *must* make. In making homes, women have come to accept state and non-state agencies as highly fragmented, imperfect actors who struggle to coordinate internally and among themselves. For instance, the perceived largesse of an NGO like Nivara—that fought to give displaced slum dwellers a tangible product (i.e. a legal home)—is well regarded but not without simultaneous awareness of the NGO's limitations in seeing them through the remainder of the resettlement process. That Shakuntala mobilized a local elected official (admittedly at no cost to her) to help secure a place to sell plasticware in the site's evening *bazaar* was a carryover of a tried and tested method perfected during her days in the slum. Ingratiating oneself with local officials was necessary to stay in business and resurfaced in the resettlement site when promised amenities such as a marketplace, were never met.

But not everyone is a Shakuntala who will devise solutions independently. Many women expressed reservations in stepping out and many felt pushed into earning a living, a new role for which they felt ill prepared.

Interconnected issues related to age, family size, household income, marital status, ethnicity/religion, and level of education were among the factors influencing women's disparate capacities, but each had a suggestion for how best to organize the future for themselves and those like them. Of interest to those responsible for design and development is that each story holds a vision for the future of the place that women wish to call home. For architects and planners, NGOs and government agencies, this requires facilitating a meeting of the minds—a meeting between their own knowledge and practices and the knowledge, institutions, and practices that women consider valuable to place-making. Forging such a meeting point would require engaging in informal, ethnographic interactions in which the multiple realities of life in the slum, at the resettlement site, and all the years in the interim, can emerge.

Note

1 See Polletta (1999) and Leathwood (2004) for a review of literature on women-only spaces.

References

Bachelard, G. (1971). *The poetics of reverie: Childhood, language, and the cosmos.* (D. Russell, Trans.) Boston, MA: Beacon Press.

Bardhan, R., Sarkar, S., Jana, A., & Velaga, N. R. (2015). Mumbai slums since independence: Evaluating the policy outcomes. *Habitat International*, 50, 1–11.

Batliwala, S. (2002). Grassroots movements as transnational actors: Implications for global civil society. *Voluntas: International Journal of Voluntary and Nonprofit Organizations*, 13(4), 393–409.

Bhowmik, S. K. (2001). Hawkers and the urban informal sector: A study of street vending in seven cities. Retrieved from www.wiego.org/sites/default/files/publications/files/Bhowmik-Hawkers-URBAN-INFORMAL-SECTOR.pdf.

Castells, M., & Portes, A. (1989). World underneath: The origins, dynamics, and effects of the informal economy. In A. Portes, M. Castells, & L. A. Benton (Eds.), *The informal economy: Studies in advanced and less developed countries* (pp. 11–37). Baltimore, MD: John Hopkins University Press.

Cernea, M. M. (1995). Understanding and preventing impoverishment from displacement: Reflections on the state of knowledge. *Journal of Refugee Studies*, 8 (3), 245–264.

Chen, M. A. (2007). *Rethinking the informal economy: Linkages with the formal economy and the formal regulatory environment* (DESA Working Paper No. 46). Retrieved from www.un.org/esa/desa/papers/2007/wp46_2007.pdf.

Cockburn, C. (1983, November 16). Caught in the wheels. *Marxism Today.* Retrieved from http://banmarchive.org.uk/collections/mt/pdf/83_11_16.pdf.

Cockburn, C. (1991). *In the way of women: Men's resistance to sex equality in organizations* (Vol. 18). Ithaca, NY: Cornell University Press.

Eversole, R. (2010). Remaking participation: Challenges for community development practice. *Community Development Journal*, 47(1), 29–41.

Geissler, P. W., Kelly, A. H., Manton, J., Prince, R. J., Tousignant, N. (2013). Introduction: Sustaining the life of the polis. *Africa*, 83(4), 531–538.

Kumar, A. (2005). Mumbai's expendable poor. *Economic and Political Weekly*, 40 (6), 506–510.

Leathwood, C. (2004). Doing difference in different times: Theory, politics, and women-only spaces in education. *Women's Studies International Forum*, 27(5–6), 447–458.

Polletta, F. (1999). "Free spaces" in collective action. *Theory and Society*, 28(1), 1–38.

Relph, E. C. (1973). *The phenomenon of place: An investigation of the experience and identity of places* (Doctoral dissertation). University of Toronto, Canada.

Relph, E. (1976). *Place and placeness*. London: Pion.

Roy, A. (2005). Urban informality: Toward an epistemology of planning. *Journal of the American Planning Association*, 71(2), 147–158.

Sztompka, P. (1991). *Society in action: The theory of social becoming*. Chicago, IL: University of Chicago Press.

Tsoutouras, D. (2014, April 9). Study finds urban informal workers are integral to city economies but unsupported by city policies and practices. Inclusive Cities. Retrieved from www.wiego.org/sites/wiego.org/files/Informal-Economy-Monitoring-Study-Press-Release.pdf.

Tuan, Y. F. (1971). Geography, phenomenology, and the study of human nature. *The Canadian Geographer*, 15(3), 181–192.

Tuan, Y. F. (1977). *Space and place: The perspective of experience*. Minneapolis: University of Minnesota Press.

Zérah, M. H. (2009). Participatory governance in urban management and the shifting geometry of power in Mumbai. *Development and Change*, 40(5), 853–877.

Index

Note: Page numbers in **bold** denote references to Tables.